Andrew Brown 2005

# PRAF…

- Enquiries reach the Comp. … …man propers (Mass and Office) for the Saints in the C… …glish versions of some masses (NOT Offices) may be sought … …t finalised and authorized versions in either language are 'unlikely … …ation of the Missal is published in English (perhaps in five years' time).' (An… …urce: 'two years'.) Nor are official translations of new Propers available.
- PLEASE WRITE TO THE COMPILER with comments, questions, suggestions. He hopes to be able to continue to supply materials mentioned on various pages of the ORDO: but PLEASE say what you need and don't just say 'send everything'. Because of the exigencies resulting from early retirement he must insist on a stamped and addressed envelope and IN ADDITION *at least* one loose FIRST CLASS STAMP. Clergy who desire several items and who have discretionary funds . . .

Fr John Hunwicke SSC
Lewdown Rectory
Devon EX20 4DN

- Some recently beatified Blesseds may seem more relevant than many of the older names in the Calendar. See February 8, September 5, October 11. These are not authorized for use in the Universal Church, although Mother Teresa is in the Calendar of the Ebbsfleet Apostolic District. Commons would need to be used.

# ORDER
## FOR THE
# EUCHARIST

AND FOR

MORNING AND EVENING PRAYER

IN THE

CHURCH OF ENGLAND

**2004–2005**

CALENDAR AND

LECTIONARY

Common Worship • BCP

Scottish, Welsh, Irish

National Calendars

Surviving Material From

*Lent* • *Holy Week* • *Easter* and

*The Promise of His Glory*

together with an

ORDO MISSAE CELEBRANDAE

ET DIVINI OFFICII PERSOLVENDI

IN ECCLESIA ANGLICANA

PRO ANNO LITURGICO

2004–2005

☐ Roman provisions are given clearly distinguished for optional use ☐

Faith House
7 Tufton Street
London SW1P 3QN

Tufton Books is a publishing imprint of the Church Union

First published in 2004



ISBN 1–83511–580–0

ACKNOWLEDGMENTS

The *Revised Common Lectionary* is © the Consultation on Common Texts, 1992 and is reproduced with permission. *The Christian Year: Calendar, Lectionary and Collects* (1997), which includes the Church of England's adapted form of the Revised Common Lectionary (published as the Principal Service Lectionary), the Second and Third Service Lectionaries and the *Common Worship* Calendar, and the Weekday Lectionary are © The Archbishops' Council 2002.

The Calendar and Lectionaries in *The Alternative Service Book 1980* are © The Archbishops' Council 1999; the Daily Eucharistic Lectionary derives, with adaptions, from the *Ordo Lectionum Missae* of the Roman Catholic Church.

The Lectionary authorised by the Convocations in 1961 and the Lectionaries from *Lent, Holy Week and Easter* (1986) and *The Promise of His Glory* are copyright © The Archbishops' Council 1999.

Material from these Lectionaries and Calendars is reproduced with permission.

Typeset by Rowland Phototypesetting Ltd, Bury St Edmunds, Suffolk
Printed in Great Britain by St Edmundsbury Press Ltd, Bury St Edmunds, Suffolk

# HOW TO USE THIS ORDO

## FOR EXAMPLE

| The Liturgical Colour ↓ | | | Matins and Evensong readings CW ↓ ↓ ↓ | | Matins and Evensong readings (1922/1961) for use with BCP ↓ ↓ ↓ |
|---|---|---|---|---|---|
| *MONDAY* | | | *Feria (☐ S Jane Frances de Chantal Rel)* | | |
| **12** | P (or W) | MP | Ps: 99, 100 (or 95), 101 | Isa 44:24–end | Isa 17 |
| | | | | I Thess 4:13 – 5:11 | Mk 4:21–end |
| | | Mass | *of Advent 2; no Gl or Cr; Pref of Advent (1) (or of the Saint)* | | |
| | | | *Isa 35; Ps: 85:7–end; Lk 5:17–26* | | |
| | | EP | | Isa 6 | Isa 18 |
| | | | Ps: 102 | Mt 15:21–28 | Rev 12 |

Monday is an ordinary weekday, or 'Feria'.
MP: Two lines in Roman type give Psalms and readings for Matins. EP: ditto.
Mass: Lines of italic give directions for the Eucharist; the second of these lines gives the Roman readings ('The Weekday Lectionary') which are permitted by CW. These form a continuous course of readings, and so are suitable where mass is said (almost) daily. Where mass is not said so often, the mass of last Sunday is more suitable.

Instead, the minister has the discretion to observe the (Colour, Hymns, Collect of the) 'Optional Memorial' of S Jane. ☐ shows that the Saint is 'unAnglican'; in fact, S Jane is from the Roman Kalendar.

| | | | | | |
|---|---|---|---|---|---|
| *TUESDAY* | | | *S Lucy, V & M (Ember Day)* | | |
| **13** | R | MP | Ps: 105:1–22 | Isa 45:15–end | Isa 21:1–12 |
| | | | | II Thess 1 | Mk 5:21–end |
| | | Mass | *of the Saint (**Charles Simeon**)* | | |
| | | | *Isa 40:25–end; Ps: 103:8–13; Mt 11:28–end* | | |
| | | EP | | Isa 8:16 – 9:7 | Isa 22:1–14 |
| | | | Ps: 105:23–end | Mt 16:1–12 | Rev 14 |

Tuesday is a 'Memorial for General Use', and so S Lucy (Colour, Hymns, Collect) displaces, compulsorily, the Feria. The readings given for mass, however, are still the weekday ones, since those saying mass often will probably take advantage of the permission to keep this continuous course of readings as unbroken as possible by using them even on memorials. If preferred, readings for the appropriate class of Saint can be used, and are more suitable where mass is not said daily. The 'Weekday Missal', in its more recent Editions, suggests appropriate readings for most Saints; and so does CW. See Introduction, pages xxvi and following. V & M: abbreviations inside front cover.
(***Charles Simeon***) in the Mass line: see Introduction paragraph 3.

# ORDER FORM

# ORDER FOR THE EUCHARIST 2005–2006

*to be published June 2005*

## ORDER NOW TO RESERVE YOUR COPY

*Please supply ...................... copy(ies) (1–3) at £8.75 each (inc. U.K. postage)*

**Discount to Parishes for 4 or more copies**

*Please supply ...................... copy(ies) (4 or more) at £8.25 each (inc. U.K. postage)*

**SPECIAL OFFER:** ONE copy of *Order For The Eucharist 2005*, and ONE copy of *Church Book and Desk Diary 2005* at the Special Combined Offer Price of £20.00 ☐

I wish to pay by: CHEQUE for £. ................ payable to **SCM-Canterbury Press Ltd**

or by VISA, DELTA, MASTERCARD, or SWITCH

No ....................................................... Expiry ............./............. Switch only:
Issue no .....................
Signature .................................................................... Valid from ......../........

*Name* **Rev/Mr/Mrs/Miss/Ms** ............................................. *(Please PRINT details clearly)*

*Delivery Address*

..............................................................................................................................

..............................................................................................................................

..............................................................................................................................

*Post Code* ......................................... *Telephone No.* ...................................................

*To order, this form must be returned with your payment, to:*

CANTERBURY PRESS NORWICH, ST MARY'S WORKS, ST MARY'S PLAIN, NORWICH, NORFOLK NR3 3BH Tel: 01603 612914 Fax: 01603 624483
e-mail: orders@ scm-canterburypress.co.uk website: www.scm-canterburypress.co.uk

*To order other books in our Publishing Group ask for the following catalogues:* (✓)

CANTERBURY PRESS NORWICH ☐
SCM PRESS ☐
RELIGIOUS & MORAL EDUCATION PRESS (RMEP) ☐

# CONTENTS


Abbreviations — Inside front cover
How to use this ORDO — v
Order Form for next year — vii

INTRODUCTION — xi–xxxvi
Calendar — xi–xv
Transferences — xii
Colours — xiii
Self Denial — xiv
Biblical Translations — xiv
Mass — xv–xxi
Law of Public Worship — xv
Penitential Rite — xvi
Gloria, Collects, Readings — xvi–xvii
Creed — xvii
Prefaces — xvii
Eucharistic Prayers — xvii–xix
Communion and postcommunion — xix
Conclusion — xix
Embers, Rogations, Votives, Ritual Masses — xix–xxi
Divine Office — xxii–xxiv
Hymns and Psalms — xxii–xxiv
Readings — xxiv
Canticles and Ritual — xxiv
Resources — xxv–xxvi
Appendix 1: Particular days — xxvii–xxviii
Appendix 2: Local days — xxix–xxx
Appendix 3: Commons — xxx–xxxi
Appendix 4: 'Lesser Festivals' and 'Commemorations' — xxxii–xxxiv
Advent and December — xxxv–xxxvi

DECEMBER 2004–NOVEMBER 2005 — 1–68
DECEMBER 2005–DECEMBER 2006 — 69–70

# INTRODUCTION

1 **THE purpose** of this ORDO is to provide for the recitation of Morning and Evening Prayer and the celebration of the Holy Communion in accordance with modern forms authorised (e.g. CW) or encouraged (e.g. LHWE, PHG) in the Provinces of Canterbury and York. These forms are *arranged* and *interpreted* in the spirit of what has become generally customary in Western Christendom since the Second Vatican Council.

Much of this material is taken from *Roman* sources. Other Roman material, not authorised by General Synod, is given clearly distinguished for use by those who desire it. The use of this material is covered by Canon B.5.1.

Those who prefer forms of Liturgy based on the *Book of Common Prayer* will find a Lectionary designed for use with the BCP printed in the far right hand column of each page.

# Calendar

2 □ Indicates observances for which there is no Anglican Synodical authority.

✠ Sundays and Holy Days of Obligation ('Principal Feast'; 'Principal Holy Day' CW).

**SOLEMNITY**: A major 'Red Letter' day or 'Festival' (CW).

**Festum**: A lesser 'Red Letter' day; 'Feast' (Roman); 'Festival' (CW).

*Memorial*: A 'Black Letter Day' to be generally kept; a 'Lesser Festival' (CW).

*Feria*: An ordinary weekday.

*Feria* (. . . . . .): An ordinary weekday (with Optional alternative Memorials).

This ORDO gives a majority of Saints as Optional Memorials (CW says they '*may*' be used). Rome prefers not to compel 'serious incursion on the weekday cycle' and desires 'to expand the number of celebrations while reducing the extent of obligation, i.e. to maximise choice and flexibility'; and CW urges the minister to 'remember the need not to lose the spirit of the season, especially of Advent and Lent, by too many celebrations that detract from its character'.

(*Memorials for Optional Use*) are from CW, or ASB, or Rome, or 1662, or 1928; or the New Roman Calendar for England.

Local, and other commemorations may be added, especially Dedication and Patronal Festivals (see Appendix 2). Those authorised by the Diocesan are *Optional* (Canon B.6.5).

Scottish, Welsh, and Irish Solemnities, Festa, and Memorials for *General* Use are included. (Memorials in the Scottish Calendar of 1991 marked '5' or '6' are *Optional.* Memorials in the Welsh Calendar of 1993 marked 'iv' or 'v' are *Optional.* This Order does not print them. Nor is the new Church of Ireland list of Diocesan Saints given.)

Rome and CW allow, on a 'green' Feria, the observance, for a good reason, of *any* Saint listed for that day on an authorised list.

3 **COMMEMORATIONS.** This ORDO follows a CW suggestion by including, in the line starting '*Mass*', names of uncanonised people who appear in CW as 'lesser festivals', urging that those who are unhappy to observe them liturgically may nevertheless

incorporate them into the Intercession. The present Pope particularly urges 'local Churches' 'to ensure that the memory of those who have suffered martyrdom should be safeguarded' and calls this 'the most convincing form of Ecumenism'.

## 4 ✠ DAYS OF EUCHARISTIC OBLIGATION

| CANTERBURY & YORK | | ORDO | ROMAN []= not in England |
|---|---|---|---|
| Every Sunday | Byz | ✠ | Every Sunday |
| | | | [January 1] |
| January 6* | Byz | ✠ | January 6* |
| February 2* | Byz | (✠) | |
| March 25 | Byz | (✠) | |
| | | | [March 19] |
| [Ash Wednesday] | | (✠) | |
| [Maundy Thursday] | | (✠) | |
| Ascension | Byz | ✠ | Ascension* |
| | | ✠ | Corpus Christi* |
| | Byz | ✠ | June 29 |
| | Byz | ✠ | August 15 |
| November 1* | | ✠ | November 1 |
| | | | [December 8] |
| December 25 | Byz | ✠ | December 25 |

*'Byz'* indicates days which, being among the Twelve Great Festivals of the Byzantine Rites, may be said to have Ecumenical Status. (Byz adds June 24; Aug 6 and 29; Sept 8 and 14; Nov 21)

*EAD* includes on its list June 29 and August 15, but allows them on the nearest Sunday, as it does the Ascension and Corpus Christi. It omits March 25.

**CW* envisages Jan 6, Feb 2, Nov 1 being transferred to a Sunday: see Paragraph 5(C). Parish Priests decide.

**R:* envisages Jan 6, Ascension, Corpus Christi being transferred to a Sunday: see Paragraph 5(C). Local hierarchies decide.

**R:* envisages Holy Days of Obligation falling on a Saturday or Monday being transferred to a Sunday: see Paragraph 5(B). Local hierarchies decide.

*In the Church of England* (Canons B6, B14, and C26) Mass is to be celebrated in every Parish Church and (except on Ash Wednesday and Maundy Thursday) every Bishop Priest and Deacon is to celebrate or to be present at Mass.

Good Friday (Canon B.6.4) is "ever to be observed . . . by attendance at Divine Worship."

CW added February 2 to the list of Principal Festivals, but, since CW is optional, it is unclear how far this creates obligations under Canon.

*The Roman Catholic Church,* less clericalist than Anglicanism, expects the participation of *all* God's Holy People.

## 5 TRANSFER? OMIT?

(A) *External Solemnity.*

When a Solemnity, or a Festum *of Our Lord*, falls in the week after a Sunday in Ordinary Time ('Green'), the Roman Rite allows all the masses and the entire office (including 1 EP) of the Day on the Sunday, *the Holy Day itself also* being celebrated on its proper day.

*Transference*

(B) Holy Days of Obligation, among English R.C.s, are transferred to the adjacent Sunday when they fall on Saturday or Monday.

(C) A 'Principal Feast' (CW) or 'Solemnity' (R:) supersedes an ordinary ('Green') Sunday 'per annum'. But other 'Festivals' (CW) or 'Feasts' (R:) falling on such a Sunday are, according to R:, omitted that year. According to CW, they must be observed: this may be on the Sunday or the first available day thereafter: see (D) below.

(1) *Epiphany* in the Roman Church is celebrated on the Sunday between January 2 and 8 in places where it is *not* 'of obligation'. According to CW, the Epiphany *is* of obligation and may be transferred to a Sunday between January 2 and 5 'for pastoral reasons'.

(2) *Presentation*, according to CW, may be celebrated *either* on February 2 *or* on the Sunday falling between January 28 and February 3. (According to R:, it could have an External Solemnity on the Sunday *before* but is *still* celebrated on February 2.)

(3) *Ascension*, In the Roman Church, is celebrated on the Sunday after the appropriate Thursday in places where it is *not* of obligation. There is no General Synod encouragement for this, but EAD permits it.

(4) *Corpus Christi*, in the Roman Church, is celebrated on the Sunday after the appropriate Thursday in places where it is *not* of obligation. There is no C of E encouragement for this, but Lectionary note 6 would cover it and EAD permits it.

(5) *All Saints*, according to CW, is celebrated on *either* November 1 *or* the Sunday between October 31 and November 6 *or* both. (According to R:, it could have an External Solemnity on the Sunday *before* but is *still* celebrated on November 1. R: also allows local hierarchies to transfer the day.)

(D) *Call it a Votive?* Anglican custom 1928–1980 made a Festum which fell on a 'Green' Sunday supersede that Sunday: CW (C above) allows either observance on the Sunday or transference. Roman rubrics dislike displacing the Sunday because they emphasise the priority of Sunday as the weekly memorial of the Lord's Resurrection. But the older Anglican custom can be harmonised with Roman regulations by regarding the mass of the Festum as a (First Class) Votive 'by command or permission of the Ordinary because of pastoral usefulness' (and *Liturgy of the Hours* permits votive offices). In EAD Ss John Baptist and Peter and Paul; the Assumption; All Saints; the Sacred Heart; Titles; and Dedications; 'may be observed on the nearest Sunday'. But this would not eliminate the observance on the proper day.

6 **EVES.** CW and recent Vatican reforms prefer the Liturgical Day to last from midnight to midnight. However, modern Western usage preserves the ancient custom of considering *Sunday* to begin on the evening of Saturday. So the Collect of each Sunday is used on the Saturday evening before it, and the practice is spreading of celebrating a Sunday mass on the Saturday evening: attendance at this fulfils obligations of Sunday worship. [Do NOT use the CW 'extended preface' for ordinary Sundays at Vigil Masses.]

*Solemnities* also have a First Evening Prayer. Here, again, obligations of worship can be fulfilled the previous evening. The Roman Missal provides 'Vigil Masses' for Christmas, Pentecost, S John Baptist, SS Peter and Paul, and the Assumption. These masses are said with *Gloria, Creed*, and the colour of the Solemnity, either before or after the First Evening Prayer. The collect of a Vigil Mass is also used at the First Evening Prayer.

*Festa* do not have a First Evening Prayer. But in years when a Festum displaces a Sunday office, or places where a Festum becomes a Solemnity because it is a Patronal Festival, it acquires a First Evening Prayer.

7 **COLOURS.** The capital letter under the day indicates the colour of the Office. This applies throughout the day, unless another colour appears for Mass and Evening Prayer. The colours suggested in the ORDO are 'traditional', (CW; CW itself suggests, without

being 'mandatory', the use of white up to the Presentation; of red between All Saints and Advent; of red on the Monday, Tuesday, and Wednesday of Holy Week.)

On very solemn days one can use 'festival', or more 'noble' vestments, even if they are not of the colour of the day.

In some churches a 'Lent array' of unbleached linen is used as an alternative to purple during Lent.

Votive Masses may be celebrated in the colour which best suits the character of the chosen Mass, but it is permitted to use instead the colour of the day or season.

Ember and Rogation Masses are said in the seasonal colour. Purple or Black is used at Requiems. In America, Rome allows White.

8 **SELF DENIAL etc.**

| | **A** | **B** | **C** |
|---|---|---|---|
| Roman Canons 1250–1253 | PENANCE | ABSTINENCE | FASTING |
| | Fridays<br>Lent | Ash Wednesday<br>Fridays EXCEPT Solemnities | Ash Wednesday<br>Good Friday |
| Canterbury & York (CW) | DISCIPLINE AND SELF DENIAL | | |
| | Fridays EXCEPT Solemnities and Festivals outside Lent; and EXCEPT during Eastertide.<br>Weekdays in Lent | | |

'A' and 'C' are not legally defined in the Universal Canon Law.
Local Episcopates may regulate 'B' and 'C' in detail, substituting charitable works or pious exercises, in whole or in part, for both Abstinence and Fasting.
*Abstinence* is abstaining from meat. (English Roman Catholics are allowed to substitute some other form of abstinence, or perform some act of piety or charity.) Abstinence binds those above 14 years.
*Fasting* is defined for English Roman Catholics as 'the amount of food we eat is considerably reduced.' It binds those who are more than eighteen until the beginning of their sixtieth year. It is *recommended* also on Easter Eve up to the Vigil.

9 **'EPIPHANY SEASON'.** The main CW innovation is the suggestion of an Epiphany season modelled on Eastertide: starting on Epiphany and ending on the Presentation. *Arguments in favour* include: it cheers up January and helps to rescue Epiphany and Presentation from oblivion. *Arguments against*: it introduces a new divergence from Roman and Orthodox practice (despite the 1968 pre-ARCIC agreement that we would 'not undertake any significant changes in the seasons') and it mars the (primitive and ecumenical) uniqueness of Easter, the Lord's 50-day-long Great Day of Festival.

If one wishes to follow this CW suggestion, one stays in white vestments and uses Epiphany Office Hymns and an Epiphany Preface until the Presentation; one calls the Sundays 'of' (not 'after') Epiphany; one treats the Presentation as a Solemnity (with 1 EP; Creed at Mass) and as a Day of Obligation. Saturday votives of the Immaculate Heart of Mary (see p. 39) will be particularly appropriate.

**Epiphany Hymns: MP 40 (NEH 48) EP 38 (NEH 46).**

9A **BIBLICAL TRANSLATIONS** The Vatican now insists on faithfulness to the inspired originals in matters such as grammatical genders and the preservation of as many as possible of the layers of meaning in the original texts, even when these may not be politically correct. 'For example, where the New Testament or the Church's tradition have interpreted certain texts of the Old Testament in a Christological fashion, special care should be observed in the translation of these texts so that a Christological meaning is not precluded . . . the word "man" in English should as a rule translate "adam" and "anthropos", since there is no one synonym which effectively conveys the play between the individual, the collectivity and the unity of the human family so important, for example, to expression of Christian doctrine and anthropology.' Among modern translations, such faithfulness can be secured by use of the RSV but NOT the NRSV. Psalter: See Para 29.

# Mass

10 **THE LEGALITY OF 'VARIATIONS'.** LHWE and PHG provided forms for 'occasions for which no provision is made' in BCP or ASB. (Such forms of service can be legal if authorised by the Convocations [Canon B:4:1] Archbishop [B:4:2] Ordinary [B:4:3] or Minister having the cure of souls [B:5:2].) *But* LHWE and PHG *also* provided *many* 'variations' in areas where ASB *did* already make *full* and *compulsory* provision; these 'variations' were 'commended by the House of Bishops'; the only legal basis for which can be the words in Canon B:5: 'the minister who is to conduct the service may in his discretion make and use variations which are not of substantial importance'.

Most of the useful material in LHWE and PHG has been superseded by the recently authorised materials. But LHWE and PHG established useful precedents concerning what is a 'variation not of substantial importance' within 'the discretion of the minister who is to conduct the service.' This formula – according to the House of Bishops in 1984 and 1990 – includes **unauthorised Greetings; unauthorised Confessions; unauthorised Collects; unauthorised Readings; unauthorised Prefaces; unauthorised Invitations to Communion.** The fact that some of this material was *subsequently* incorporated in and thus authorised by CW does not change the fact that it was totally unauthorised when the Bishops said it came under the umbrella of Canon B:5:1. So unless the Bishops were wrong in 1984 and 1990, it remains true that Canon B:5:1 still covers the use, at the discretion of the Minister who is to conduct the service, of **unauthorised Greetings; unauthorised Confessions; unauthorised Collects; unauthorised Readings; unauthorised Prefaces; and unauthorised Invitations to Communion. But his discretion is not confined to these areas: see Para 19 below.**

It is to be noted that the Bishops, either collectively or individually, have *no* canonical right to order, *or even allow, any* 'variations' to authorised services. The only right to 'make and use' such 'variations' is that of the 'minister who is to conduct the service' by virtue of Canon B.5.1.. The use of this canon by the Bishops in promoting LHWE and PHG was a creative use of canon law to loosen the straightjacket which otherwise surrounds the law of public worship. And they are still at it: see Para 18 below. But what is sauce for geese . . .

Dix (*Shape* pp. 587–9 and 716–7) wisely sets concepts of 'Liturgical Authority' against their historical background.

11 **CW 'SEASONAL PROVISIONS':** Sentences before the Confession and the Peace; Alleluia before the Gospel; and Proper Prefaces, of different lengths, for some but not all Eucharistic Prayers, appear ('*may* be used') all to be optional. CW does not itself provide, but invites the use of, Entrance and Communion Sentences.

12 **CONFESSION AND KYRIES:** both may be combined into the form of Penitential Rite now popular among Roman Catholics. The sentences prefixed * in the version given below may be varied according to the season. (CW gives three examples, and there are more in PHG and R:.)

*The priest invites the people to call to mind their sins, and a pause for silent reflection follows.*

*Minister:* *You raise the dead to life in the Spirit:
Lord, have mercy.
*People:* **Lord, have mercy.**
*Minister:* *You bring pardon and peace to the sinner:
Christ, have mercy.
*People:* **Christ, have mercy.**
*Minister:* *You bring light to those in darkness:
Lord, have mercy.
*People:* **Lord, have mercy.**

*Priest:* May almighty God have mercy on us,
forgive us our sins,
and bring us to everlasting life.
*All:* Amen.

**PHG also reminds us of the Asperges** (the people are sprinkled with holy water to recall them to their Baptismal commitment; this rite also replaces both the Confession and Kyries and is particularly suitable in Easter Time), giving on p. 249 an abbreviated version of the Roman texts, and on p. 229 versions of the traditional anthems. Or one could 'mine' the materials at CW pp. 48–9.

13 **GLORIA IN EXCELSIS** is used on Sundays outside Advent and Lent; Solemnities; Festa; and during Christmas week and Easter week; but not on weekdays and memorials. *Gloria* may be used at special more solemn celebrations.

14 **COLLECTS.** No more than one Collect is ever said at Mass. On Ferias CW orders the collect of the previous Sunday to be used; the Roman usage permits, during the 'green' seasons, any 'green' Sunday Collect to be selected.

On the Sundays between Trinity and All Saints, the Collect to accompany CW readings *will differ from year to year.* While the *readings* come from the 'Sunday of the Year', described by CW as 'Proper number x', the *Collects* are 'after Trinity'.

This new series of CW collects includes a number of the BCP collects from the ancient Roman Sacramentaries, given for use on the same Sunday as in BCP, and very lightly modernised in language (the BCP originals may be used). This welcome development will still leave us using fewer such collects than does the current Roman Rite (they are currently improving their translations). Dix (SL p. 367) describes these collects as 'both ancient and beautiful . . . lovely things, grave, melodious and thoughtful, and compact with evangelical doctrine – characteristic products of the liturgical genius of Rome in the fifth and sixth centuries. Cranmer's reputation as a writer of English prose largely rests on his translations . . . and rightly so, for they are among the very best translations ever made . . .'. There is nothing to stop a celebrant using the original, or lightly modernised, versions of those remaining BCP After Trinity collects which CW ignores.

For each weekday in Advent, Christmas, Lent and Easter, Rome provides a separate and seasonally appropriate collect (printed with the readings in the Weekday Missal).

Collects end thus (CW improves on R:):

*Longer Ending* (for the Collect itself):

'Through Jesus Christ your Son our Lord, who is alive and reigns with you in the unity of the Holy Spirit, one God, now and for ever'. [But if the Son is addressed: 'for you are alive and reign with the Father in the unity of the Holy Spirit, one God, now and for ever'.]

*Shorter Ending* (for the prayers Over the Offerings and Post-Communion): 'Through (Jesus) Christ our Lord'. [But if the Son is addressed: 'for you are alive and reign, now and for ever'.]

15 **EUCHARISTIC READINGS: SUNDAYS AND HOLY DAYS** are all in italics.

The *first* line of readings is CW (see paragraph 36 below). This Lectionary was based on the Roman Lectionary in which, S John's Gospel being used particularly in Eastertide, the three Synoptic Gospels take it in turn to dominate the Sundays of the Year (Year A, Matthew; B, Mark; C, Luke). The Roman original has been 'improved' several times by Anglican committees. **Where it is desired to abbreviate a CW reading, R: might be helpful (see below).**

This ORDO assumes that users will prefer the OT readings which will relate thematically to the Sunday Gospel (CW repeats them from R:) rather than the alternative 'continuous' OT readings. 'Typology' is the Bible's own way of using itself intertextually (I Cor 10:1–5; I Pet 3:20, etc.).

The *second* line is the original Roman provision, preceded *R:* (the psalm provision gives the psalm number according to the Anglican system of numbering psalms, but does not specify the detailed uses and combinations of verses).

Advantages in using the Roman version: (a) it will be practical to use books, of R.C. origin, in which the lessons are printed in full; (b) the R: readings generally represent a tighter selection of verses. Whether the differences between CW and R: are slight or greater, the use of R: will constitute a variation 'not of substantial importance' in terms of Canon B.5; and CW itself allows 'the minister' to 'depart from the Lectionary provision for pastoral reasons or preaching or teaching purposes' during 'Ordinary Time', after 'due consultation with the PCC'. (PCCs could pass a resolution 'that this Council has received such due consultation as may be necessary for the Incumbent at his discretion to depart from authorised lectionary provision.')

In the Roman rite, Solemnities have *two* readings before the Gospel; Festa only *one*. Where this ORDO prints two, it is because Rome offers them as alternatives. CW, on the other hand, offers *two* readings even for some 'Lesser Festivals'; i.e. Memorials.

16 **EUCHARISTIC READINGS: WEEKDAY LECTIONARY.** CW continues the authorisation ASB gave to the Roman weekday Eucharistic lectionary; its readings may be used both on Ferias *and* on Memorials. They are printed in full, in italics, although those who wish to use these readings daily at mass will find it simpler to follow the Liturgical Commission's advice and use copies of the small, cheap Roman 'Weekday Missal', containing these readings, than to have to mark up lessons in a Bible each day. See page i for further advice. Psalms follow the CW verse numbers.

Roman Psalms: the complexity of juggling the different versification systems in the Vulgate, King James, BCP and CW Psalters is too much for your compiler. Accordingly, just the psalm number (BCP numeration) is given for the Roman Psalms: which verses are used, how they are combined, and when the Response comes, will have to be discovered from liturgical books.

17 **THE CREED** is to be used on Sundays and Solemnities and *may* be used at special more solemn occasions. The 'Apostles' Creed', the ancient baptismal confession of the Apostolic Roman See (which , together with Quicunque Vult, is also allowed by CW), is particularly recommended by Rome during the baptismal seasons of Lent and Easter and when there are many children present. When it is used, Rome insists that *Carnis Resurrectionem* must be translated *Resurrection of the Flesh* (compare our Article IV). CW institutionalizes an *ad hoc* Vatican custom of omitting *Filioque* when ecumenical considerations urge this.

18 **PREFACES.** ASB and PHG moved, with Rome, in the direction of a generous supply of prefaces; CW only gives a minimum. It is intended that this will be

supplemented, before 2005, by '*Times and Seasons*' (a volume to replace LHWE and PHG). Meanwhile (see para 10 above) Rome offers 'extended prefaces' and ASB offers 'short prefaces' (to use the CW terminology) for such occasions as the Dedication, the Holy Family, the Chrism mass, the Transfiguration, Angels, Ss Joseph and John Baptist, our Lady, different categories of Saints, and variety during Christmastide and Eastertide. (In any case, *Times and Seasons* will only have the same legal status as LHWE, ASB, PHG and the Roman Rite have: see para 10.) So clergy should feel happy to continue to use ASB, PHG, and Roman prefaces. (CW p. 816 reveals that the House of Bishops still considers Canon B5 to cover the use of unauthorised prefaces, and this is confirmed by unauthorised Episcopal additions to the Altar Edition of CW.) R: now has two prefaces for Martyrs.

On Memorials which lack a proper preface, the Common Preface is used (in Advent and Easter, the Seasonal Preface) *or* the appropriate Preface of the Saint.

19 **POST SANCTUS.** Before the 1960s, in both the Roman and Anglican rites, there was but one unchanging 'Consecration Prayer' or 'Canon', so that this part of the service constituted a moment of familiarity, commonality, and invariability deeply sanctified by Tradition. But since CW follows Rome in now offering a dozen or so alternative EuPrs, the authorities in both communions have in effect abrogated this tradition, and transferred discretion to the officiating presbyter.

Does this discretion, combined with the canonical discretion to 'make and use variations' (see Para 10 above), entitle him to use EuPrs not authorised by General Synod or to improve CW EuPrs by introducing ancient, ecumenical and ARCIC verbs such as 'become' and 'offer'? Canons B.5.1, B.5.5 and B.1.3.iii make clear that the celebrant's 'discretion' (see para 10 above) *does* extend to the whole Eucharistic Prayer.

On 26 i 1988, the House of Bishops expressed the view that the use of Eucharistic rites which were once 'canonically authorised' but whose 'authorisation' had 'lapsed' would be a variation 'not of substantial importance' and therefore, in their pastoral judgement, legal. While the Bishops clearly only had in mind some of the temporary rites briefly authorised since 1965, this principle obviously and *a fortiori* also covers 'where well established' the first of the four Roman Eucharistic Prayers, which was frequently used in the Church of England between 597 and 1559. Roman rubrics strongly urge the use of this EuPr on all Sundays; the Octaves of Christmas and Easter; the Apostles and Saints listed in it; the Epiphany and Ascension; and Ritual masses. The Tudor English translation authorised by Rome may be sought from the Compiler. In the judgement of liturgical experts, if this venerable prayer, brought by S Augustine to Canterbury in 597, lacks Twentieth Century Synodical 'legality', it has the 'authority' of nearly a millenium of Anglican use. There are clearly no theological objections to the contents of this Prayer since the House of Bishops (GS Misc 632) has spoken of Anglicans finding 'that they can, with good conscience, say a heartfelt Amen at the end of the [Roman] Eucharistic Prayer.'

The 1988 'statement', so one Diocesan Bishop points out, also covers ASB EuPrIII, which has a more satisfactory *oblatio* that CW'B', its successor.

It has been suggested that CW EuPr G should not be ignored by Catholics. It breaks new ground in providing a post-consecration intercession into which episcopal names (see para 21) could be inserted. This intercession could be popped into other CW EuPrs.

20 **SAINTS IN THE EUCHARISTIC PRAYER.** The CW Eucharistic Prayers B, E, F, G invite mention by name of Saints, and they are easily inserted into the other Prayers. Rome and Orthodoxy agree that diachronic 'permanence through history' is 'brought into focus' by the mention of the Saints in the Canon. The Ecumenical (Roman and Orthodox) custom since early centuries has been at every mass to name our Lady, and

always to do so using her ecumenically agreed official doctrinal title **Mother of God** (*Theotokos*, Ephesus, 431, and Chalcedon, 451; some may be attracted by the ARCIC suggestion of translating this 'Mother of God Incarnate'). The older Byzantine and Latin prayers add another official ecumenical title: **and Ever-Virgin** (*aeiparthenos*, Chalcedon, 451, and Constantinople, 553). Mention of others, in addition to our Lady, (e.g. the Forerunner; Apostles; Patrons; Saints of the Day) varies from rite to rite.

21 **THE BISHOP.** The fundamental sacramental unit of Christ's Church is neither a 'National' Church or Province or 'Communion', nor a parish, but a unity of Bishop, *Presbyterium*, and People. So, when a priest offers mass apart from his Bishop, he does so as the Bishop's representative. The Orthodox and Roman Churches agree that it is 'essential' to show this by including his name in the Eucharistic Prayer. This is not merely a prayer *for* the Bishop but an expression of full ecclesial communion *with* him. Where CW formulae are used, at appropriate points after the Consecration the following (see Prayer G) can be interpolated: **Remember, Lord, your Church in every land. Reveal her unity, guard her faith, and preserve her in peace: together with . . .**

A priest says: . . . **our bishop (or whatever) N** adding, if appropriate, **and his assistant bishop N** or, if there are several of them, **and his assistant bishops**.

22 **COMMUNION:** LHWE and PHG print Roman introductions to the Our Father; and the Embolism ('Deliver us, Lord . . .') after the Our Father, as in the Roman rite, is printed in PHG. CW permits the Peace after the Our Father, as in the Roman rite. The (nonR:) CW formulae at the Fraction are only mandatory on Sundays and Principal Holy Days: could this be the moment quietly to dump them? The ASB/CW Zwinglianization of *ECCE Agnus Dei* could be got round in parish leaflets thus: "The priest invites the faithful to receive Jesus, the Lamb of God; they reply . . ."

23 **POSTCOMMUNION.** CW provides, together with the Collects referred to in paragraph 14, post-Communion collects, many of which will be found either eloquent or verbose according to differing tastes. Not one of them is a post-Communion in those same early sacramentaries which provided so many of Cranmer's collects. CW, however, envisages the use of 'another suitable prayer'; which could be found in the Roman selection, or the old one in the 'English Missal'. They replace, *or* are in addition to, '. . . send us out into the world . . .'.

24 **CONCLUSION OF THE MASS.** (i) On Solemnities and Festa outside Lent, and at Requiems, a solemn blessing is encouraged. The deacon or priest says: **Bow your heads and pray for God's blessing**; the blessing follows; and then the dismissal.

(ii) On Sundays and Weekdays in Lent, Prayers Over The People have been optionally restored in the Roman Rite. They are available for 'Green' Sundays. The deacon or priest says: **Bow your heads for God's blessing**; the Prayer is said, followed immediately by **'. . . and the blessing . . .'**; then the dismissal. The new latin Missal provides new texts; until translations are available, the English Missal could be used.

(iii) Otherwise, Mass ends with *The Lord be with you* and its response, the Blessing, and the Dismissal with its response. This applies to Requiems. When a liturgical function immediately follows the Mass, this Conclusion is omitted.

25 **EMBERS & ROGATIONS.** (The Weekday Missal has Votives For Productive Land and the Blessing of Man's Labour.) We indicate the CW Ember Weeks; but some Bishops have moved them so that they precede Diocesan Ordinations.

Ember and Rogation Masses may be said on Ferias and Optional Memorials; on Solemnities, Festivals, and General Memorials the expression of Ember and Rogation themes is confined to the Intercession, unless they are Class 1 or Class 2 Votives (see table).

The seasonal colour is used at Ember and Rogation Masses.

26 **RITUAL MASSES, REQUIEMS, VOTIVES.** The table opposite indicates when these may and may not be said.

(a) When a Wedding includes a **Nuptial Mass:** On Sundays and Solemnities, the Mass of the Day is said. But one of the Wedding readings may be included, except from Maundy Thursday to Easter Sunday and on Solemnities of Obligation. If the Parochial community is not present at a Wedding on a 'Green' Sunday or a Sunday after Christmas, the entire Nuptial Mass may be said. The ancient 'Nuptial Blessing' is traditionally said over the newly-weds immediately after the Our Father of the Wedding Mass. Consigned now by CW to oblivion for Political Incorrectness, versions of it will be found in R: and BCP (*O God who by thy mighty power . . .*) and ASB (Additional Prayer 35, on page 299.)

(b) **Our Lady on Saturday** (*in Sabbato*): (i) since at least the Eighth Century liturgical reforms associated with the name of Alcuin of York, our Lady has in the West been particularly commemorated on Saturday (on the Sabbath God the Creator rests from His labour in Mary's womb before His Great New Deed of Creation on His Eighth Day; Mary is the faithful Daughter of Zion, whose Faith begins the New – as Abraham's did the Old – Covenant; in her own Eschatological Rest she prefigures the Sabbath Rest to which God's Pilgrim people is journeying). Post Vatican II legislation confined this usage to when, after Epiphany and Trinity, there is no Solemnity, Festum, or Memorial for General Use. But since IGMR now 'commends' the observance *peculiari modo*, it should be the norm on free Saturdays after Epiphany and Trinity. (As a Class 2 votive – see page xxi – it may be used until December 16, after January 1, and after Low Sunday in Eastertide, and on Memorials for General Use.) (see p. 39 for the Immaculate Heart.) New Marian masses have just been issued.

(ii) Variety may be secured by using the "Collection of Masses of the BVM", issued by Rome particularly for use in Marian shrines (where, during pilgrimages, votives from the Collection may also be said on any weekday of Advent, Christmas after January 1, and Lent) and on Saturday. On particular days, the 'Mass' line gives information about suitable masses from this Collection. The Compiler (front of volume) can supply a sample mass. *Invariability may be secured from CW pp. 511–2 & 310–1.*

(iii) But, of course, the Feria, or an occuring optional Memorial, may be observed.

(c) **The Sacred Heart on Friday:** see p. 39.

(d) **Votive Masses** may be of the mysteries of the Lord or in honour of the BVM, Angels, any Saint, All Saints; and may be said on any feria when there is not a Memorial for General Use (with the exception of the Immaculate Conception, masses referring to events in the lives of the Lord and His Mother may not be used as votives). *Votive offices*, for a public cause or out of devotion, may be used on *any* day except Solemnities; Sundays of Advent, Lent, or Easter; Ash Wednesday; Palm Sunday to Low Sunday; and 2 November.

| | MASSES ‘FOR VARIOUS OCCASIONS’, & VOTIVES | | | REQUIEMS | | |
|---|---|---|---|---|---|---|
| | CLASS 1<br>Permitted or ordered by the Bishop when they have an unusually serious pastoral need or use; and also **RITUAL MASSES:** e.g. at Baptism, Confirmation or Ordination. | CLASS 2<br>When they have a real pastoral need or use; e.g., a First Friday: the Sacred Heart; Rogations. BVM on Saturday | CLASS 3<br>Chosen by the Celebrant for the Devotion of the people. | CLASS 1<br>at Funerals | CLASS 2<br>After hearing the news of a death, on the occasion of the final burial, and on the first Anniversary | CLASS 3<br>‘Daily’ masses for the Dead. |
| Solemnities ‘of obligation’; Sundays of Advent; Sundays of Lent; Sundays from Easter to Trinity Sunday inclusive; Maundy Thursday to Easter. | NO | NO | NO | NO | NO | NO |
| Solemnities NOT ‘of obligation’; Ash Wednesday; Monday, Tuesday and Wednesday in Holy Week; Easter Week All Souls’ Day. | NO | NO | NO | YES | NO | NO |
| Ordinary (‘green’) Sundays; Sundays of Christmas; Epiphany Sundays; Festa. | YES | NO | NO | YES | NO | NO |
| Weekdays December 17–24; the Octave of Christmas; Weekdays of Lent. | YES | NO<br>but see para 26b ii | NO | YES | YES | NO |
| Memorials for General Use; Weekdays of Advent up to December 16; Weekdays of Christmas after January 1; Weekdays of the Easter Season after Low Sunday. | YES | YES | NO | YES | YES | NO |
| Ordinary (‘green’) weekdays of the year; Epiphany weekdays; and Memorials for Optional Use. | YES | YES | YES | YES | YES | YES |

# Divine Office

**This ORDO is arranged on the assumption that clergy will 'say daily the Morning *and* Evening Prayer [at least!] either privately or openly' (1662); 'Bishops, priests and deacons . . . must give due importance to Morning and Evening Prayer . . . and be careful not to omit them except for a grave cause' (Liturgy of the Hours).**

27 Versions of the Opus Dei formally prescribed or permitted by Synod in England:

(1) Sarum (1542);

(2) BCP (1662);

(3) 'A Service of the Word' structured in conformity with CW pp. 24–27. These regulations were authorised so that (GS 1342 p. 3) their 'provisions would now give legal "cover" to the use of forms of Daily Office' such as the Roman Breviary ('Liturgy of the Hours') and 'Celebrating Common Prayer'; except that on Sundays and Principal Holy Days when such an Office is the principal service (i.e. in Churches where mass is not said), an Act of Penance, a sermon, and a Creed need to be added to a form which does not already possess them. IT MUST BE CLEARLY NOTED that the forms given in CW pp. 30–45 are purely '*examples* of forms which comply'; they are not mandatory *or even recommended* and take *no* priority over forms which the minister may borrow from elsewhere or devise himself.

Similarly (as one of the Bishops who sat on the Liturgical Commission and helped to write it has explained) *Common Worship: Daily Prayer* is no more than an 'outworking' of 'A Service of the Word' – as is the RC Divine Office.

28 **OFFICE HYMNS**, at Morning and Evening Prayer, are an ancient and integral part of the Divine Office. They now *precede the variable psalms* and state the theme of the Office.

This ORDO provides traditional Office Hymns from the old English Sarum Breviary and the current Latin Office Book, with a very little supplementation, according to the English Hymnal, which covers most needs. *We also give New English Hymnal numbers. But the NEH gives a much poorer selection than EH; we do the best we can with it while recommending EH for those who desire to use the traditional hymns in their daily office.*

Hymns for the 'Green' seasons and the Commons are in the table on page xxiii. Hymns for Advent, Christmas, Lent and Easter are indicated in the *Notes before those Seasons*.

Hymns for some other days are in the body of the ORDO; H: 5 (NEH 6) means that 5 is the English Hymnal number; 6 the New English Hymnal number. If no provision is made for Morning Prayer, the evening hymn is to be used; and vice versa.

29 **PSALMS:** arranged as given in CW. But any arrangement of the psalms is equally lawful. CW includes a psalter; but it was not passed by General Synod and has no more authority than any other translation. Nevertheless the Compiler has tried consistently to give verse numbers according to CW. 'The Revised Psalter' of 1964 (BCP sensitively adjusted by biblical scholars in collaboration with T.S. Eliot and C.S. Lewis) is considered by many the best English version.

# Office Hymns

**PER ANNUM** (The 'Green' Seasons after Epiphany and Pentecost)

| | Morning Prayer | | Evening Prayer | |
|---|---|---|---|---|
| | EH | NEH | EH* | NEH |
| Sunday | 50 | 53 or 149 | 51/164 | 150 or 54 |
| Monday | 52 or 632 | 149 or 151 | 58/81 | 61, 241, 248, or 152 |
| Tuesday | 165 | | 59/264 | |
| Wednesday | 54 | | 60/262 | |
| Thursday | 55, 53 or 254 | | 61/269 | |
| Friday | 56 | | 62/265 | |
| Saturday | 57 | | 49/280 | |
| BVM on Saturday | 213, 214, or 215 | 180, 181 or 183 | | |

**COMMONS** for the entire year.
**N.B.** On days which are memorials, R: allows *either* the weekday hymns (according to season), *or* these hymns from the Commons.

| | | | | |
|---|---|---|---|---|
| BVM | 214&215 | 181&183 | 213 | 180 |
| Apostles, Evangelists | 174 (R: Proper) | ‡ | 176 | 214 |
| in Eastertide | 124 pt 2 | ‡ | 123 pt 2 | 100 vv4–end |
| Several Martyrs | 175† or 183 | 213† | 182 | 218 |
| One Martyr | 180 or 185 | 217 | 181 | 218 |
| A Virgin Martyr | 180 or 185 | ‡ | 191 | 222 |
| A Virgin | ‡ | ‡ | 192 | 222 |
| A Holy Man | ‡ | ‡ | 189 | 223 |
| A Holy Woman | ‡ | ‡ | 193 | 222 |
| [Group Commem] | ‡ | ‡ | [253: 1&7–13] | [223] |

* The first hymn is from the Seventh Century Weekly Cycle celebrating the Days of Creation; the second is a suggested alternative.
† *Correct to* The Martyrs' glorious deeds . . .
‡ Use the Evening Hymn.

(None of the Roman hymns for 'Pastors' is to be found in Anglican hymnals. EH 188(NEH 220), the traditional hymn for 'Confessors', is now confined to S Martin, for whom it was composed.)

**VOTIVE OFFICES:** as on the day. See paragraph 26 (d).

The Church does not use the psalms in an individualistic way, or academically as pieces of historical Hebrew poetry; but corporately and Christologically according to the *sensus messianicus* (cf. Mt 22: 41–46; Lk 24: 44; Acts 2: 25–28 & 34–35; Hebrews passim). The Fathers received and explained the Psalter as a prophecy of Christ and the Church, and in the psalms, heard Christ crying to the Father, or the Father speaking with the Son, or the voice of the Church ('Christ prays for us as our Priest; in us as our Head; He is prayed to as our God'). Thus, in praying the psalms, the Body of Christ enters into the relationship between Son and Father.

So it is irrelevant whether the 'mood' of a psalm suits that of a particular worshipper at a particular moment. Nevertheless, the modern Roman Office, no less than Anglican equivalents, avoids some 'bloodthirsty' places because of their 'psychological difficulty'.

30 **OFFICE READINGS.** From Advent 3 to the Baptism, and from Palm Sunday to Trinity, CW expects 'authorised' readings to be used. Otherwise . . .

*In the middle column* the readings of the text are based on CW. ('Second Service' provides the 2 EP, and 'Third Service' the MP, on Sundays; on weekdays we use the CW 'Office Lectionary' for MP and the 'Second Office . . . Lectionary' for EP.) *In the third column* the readings are in the tradition of the 1922 (still legal) and 1961 lectionaries, designed to accompany the BCP. (Weekday CW material: GS 1341A etc.)

Technically, CW covers interchanging readings between MP, EP, and Mass, but the distribution of readings as given in this ORDO is to be recommended.

When a reading begins with a personal pronoun the reader may substitute the appropriate noun.

Verses printed within (parentheses) are permitted additions to the appointed passages. Verse numbers followed by 'a' or 'b' indicate the first or second part of the verse. Verse numberings generally follow the *(New) Revised Standard Version*. When other versions are used, such adaptations may be made as are necessary.

31 **CANTICLES & FINAL ANTHEMS.** The ancient Canticles of the Western Church (R: and BCP) are: MP *Benedictus* EP *Magnificat* and *Nunc Dimittis*. MP includes the *Te Deum* on all Sundays outside Lent, and on Solemnities and Festa. By long custom encouraged by an Archbishop of Canterbury, this Office concludes with an anthem to our Lady (Celebrating Common Prayer pp. 265–7).

32 **RITUAL.** Rome still anticipates the Sign of the Cross at *O God make speed* . . . , and the beginnings of the Gospel Canticles; the Cross on the mouth at *O Lord open* . . . ; and, **together with Byzantium expects the congregation to be standing for the proclamation of a Gospel reading!** PHG encourages a service of Light before EP, the ancient *Lucernarium*. It is not always realised that, since MP and EP occupy the time of the Temple morning and evening offerings of incense, its traditional use at the *Benedictus* and *Magnificat* is more than just a piece of highchurchery. EAD urges consideration also of 'a proper focus on the Blessed Sacrament, exposed for adoration.' Elliot (Int P38) tells you how to do it.

# Resources

33 **'TRADITIONAL LANGUAGE' LITURGY.** While the Prayer Book Communion may be used as it is printed, for many years it was universally modified (e.g. omission of long exhortations). Nearly all the customary modifications of the 1662 eucharistic rite, including the 'Interim Rite', have now been given legal 'cover' by recent legislation.

With this rite one may add to the BCP propers the bulk of the additional *collects and propers from the 1928 Prayer Book* (and Old Testament readings from the old Series I), which were authorised by General Synod in 2000.

As far as *Series One and Two* are concerned, on 26 i 1988 the House of Bishops 'agreed in regarding the continued use, where well established, of any form of service which has, at any time since 1965, been canonically authorised (notwithstanding the fact that such authorisation was not renewed after it lapsed) as not being of 'substantial importance' within the meaning of Canon B5.4' . . . a creatively cheeky use of Canon Law.

34 **'LENT • HOLY WEEK • EASTER:** Services and Prayers', (LHWE) 'commended by the House of Bishops' provides forms of traditional liturgy for the period from Ash Wednesday to Pentecost. This may be used under the Diocesan's authority (Canon B4) or by decision of the Parish Priest (Canon B5). Since (LHWE) 'the Services . . . are set out so that they can be used as they stand. Alternatively, they may be used as source material . . . Every part of these services is optional . . .', it is clearly not illegal to borrow from other Churches and Rites.

Many priests have found the existence of LHWE an influential pastoral tool in recommending traditional Lenten and Holy Week rites to congregations unfamiliar with them. The texts provided for Holy Week are in fact the Roman texts with mostly insignificant alterations. Some of these changes slightly improve the Roman (ICEL) wording; unfortunately, LHWE lacks the detailed rubrical directions required (e.g.) for the traditional rites surrounding the Paschal Candle; and, for example, has seen fit to eliminate such memorable pieces of liturgical poetry as *O felix culpa*.

On Good Friday, the earlier tradition, preserved by the Roman rite, is for the intercessions to come between the Passion and the Veneration of the Cross; LHWE makes 'The Proclamation of the Cross' precede the Intercessions.

35 **'THE PROMISE OF HIS GLORY'** (PHG) contains a great deal of liturgical material beyond the scope of this ORDO. It provides Mass (R:) and Office for the Holy Family, and the (R:) Eucharistic readings for the Solemnities of Our Lady (Dec 8 and Jan 1); but in its movement towards the three-year Lectionary it has now been superseded by CW. This ORDO draws attention to such PHG material, from All Saints to the Presentation, as remains relevant.

36 **CALENDAR LECTIONARY AND COLLECTS 2000** finally sanctioned the three-year Roman Sunday and Festival Eucharistic Lectionary. This had already been 'improved', and the 'improved' version called the Revised Common Lectionary. Before General Synod promulgated it, it 'improved' it some more (although not as much as some pressure groups desired). There is NO *single* version of this Lectionary with readings printed out in full which is authorised by General Synod. *Any* translation of the Bible may be used. Mowbray/Cassell have published a version with NRSV texts; Hodder and Stoughton favour the NIV; etc; but none of these possesses any exclusive 'official' status.

CW accommodates Evangelical dislike of the Deuterocanonical books by providing alternatives to readings from them (a recent custom; 1549 and 1662 denied such alternatives). This ORDO assumes that users have no problems with those Deuterocanonical books which the C of E and the Roman Catholic Church both receive.

37 **SUNDAY MISSAL; WEEKDAY MISSAL.** The cheapest and simplest way of using the Roman Sunday readings (which are much the same as those now authorised in CW) is by purchasing a small Collins 'Sunday Missal'. The Collins 'Weekday Missal' prints in full the readings of the CW Daily Eucharistic Lectionary, propers for all the Saints in the Roman Universal Calendar, and a small Supplement of the main National Saints.

38 **CEREMONIES OF THE MODERN ROMAN RITE** by Msgr P.J. Elliot. This gives full, intelligent, and sensitive advice about the performance of Mass and Office in the Western tradition; it is modern, yet sensitive to the desire to do God's Work in a decent and orderly way not totally divorced from earlier traditions. It is the modern replacement for both 'Fortescue' and our own 'Ritual Notes'. It includes information about what to do with the Bishop! It costs £21.95 (+£2.20 p/p in the UK). It may be bought from Faith House Bookshop. (The same author's follow-up of 1998 is called "Liturgical Question Box".)

39 **AKATHIST HYMN:** that great explosion of Byzantine wit and of Sixth Century devotion to our Lady is suitable, as the late Fr Colin Stephenson of Walsingham used to urge, for use in the Mary Month of May. PPL warmly encourages it. (During the Jubilee Year of 2000 it was used in Rome on October 1 and December 8). Two English translations (by Bishop Kallistos Ware and Roger Green) are suitable. A limited number of copies is available from The Publications Secretary ESBVM, 11 Drove Acre Road, OXFORD OX4 3DF; at £1.35 each including p&p (cheques to ESBVM).

40 **COLLECTION OF MASSES:** see paragraph 26b ii.

The following observance of the Principal Joys of Mary by daily votives has received strong episcopal encouragement in the Diocese of Exeter. The bracketed numbers are the Compiler's suggestions as to which votives in the 'Collection' (above) fit.

Sunday: Nativity of BVM (20)
Monday: Annunciation (2)
Tuesday: Nativity of the Lord (4, 5, 19)
Wednesday: Adoration of the Magi (6)
Thursday: Purification of BVM (7)
Friday: Compassion of BVM (11, 12)
Saturday: Assumption of BVM (29)

41 **A MANUAL OF ANGLO-CATHOLIC DEVOTION** by the Bishop of Ebbsfleet contains a wealth of traditional resources.

42 ***THE DIRECTORY ON POPULAR PIETY AND THE LITURGY***, a Vatican production, offers 'principles' and takes us through the liturgical year.

# Appendix 1: Particular days

**JANUARY 1:** The Vatican observes World Peace Day. Leo the Great pointed out that the association of Peace with Christmastime is based as much on dogma as on sentiment. The Old Covenant community, defined by Circumcision, is replaced by Christ, the Father's One New Creation, into whom we are incorporated by Baptism. All peoples are called to this Unity and Peace. See the readings at the Office for Mary, Mother of God.

## JANUARY 18 (PHG) OR □ FEBRUARY 22 (R:)

### The { Confession (PHG) / □ Chair (R:) } of S Peter, Apostle

| | | | |
|---|---|---|---|
| W | MP | | Ezek 34:11–16 |
| | | Ps: 30, 34 | Jn 21:15–22 |
| | Mass | *Gl; R: Pref of Apostles; CW, of a Saint CRP* | |
| | | *Ps 23, 1 Pet 5:1–4; Mt 16:13–19* | |
| | EP | H: 226 (NEH 171) vv 3&6 | Ezek 3:4–11 |
| | | Ps: 71, 145 | Acts 11:1–18 (= R:) |

The *Week of Prayer for Christian Unity* began in 1908 (among Anglicans who sought unity around the See of Peter) as the *Chair of Unity Octave.* It linked the Feasts of S Peter's Chair (January 18) and S Paul's Conversion (January 25). In 1969 Rome suppressed the former feast because it duplicated the Fourth Century Feast of the Chair (i.e. 'Episcopal Consecration') of S Peter in February (which R: retains). PHG put S Peter back at the start of our annual Prayer for Unity and, despite the lack of interest of CW, he survives there in some Diocesan Calendars. Even those who prefer the more ancient date and title in February might like to begin the Week of Prayer with a votive mass and office of S Peter.

MP commemorates the Pastoral Charge to Peter; in the Gospel at mass Peter's Confession of Christ leads to the granting of the keys; and EP shows Peter unlocking the Church's doors to the Gentiles.

At mass, the texts in the Missal for February 22 may conveniently be used on either day. PHG suggests the ASB Collect on p. 780 (a more prolix version of the Roman).

## SUNDAY IN THE CHAIR OF UNITY OCTAVE

PHG follows the old English R.C. practice in allowing a mass for Unity on this Sunday (in green vestments). The Missal has texts towards the end; PHG on pp. 246 ff with Collects on pp. 366 f.

R: = CW = PHG Sunday Mass: *Gl; Cr; Pref of Unity, PHG p. 257 (= R:)*
*Ps 100, 122; Zeph 3:16–end; Eph 4:1–6 or Col 3:9–17 or 1 Jn 4:9–15; Jn 11:45–52 or Jn 17:11b–19 (20–23)*

## MOTHERING SUNDAY (LENT 4)

On 'Mothering' or 'Refreshment' Sunday, rose colour is sometimes used; together with the organ and flowers.

Mothering Sunday can be combined with Lent if its theme is **Our Lady of Sorrows**. For texts, see Missal September 15. CW *Readings: Exod 2:1–10; 2 Cor 1:3–7 or Col 3:12–17; Ps 34:11–20; 127:1–4; Jn 19:25–27 or Lk 2:33–35; Preface PHG p. 278 (second pref).*

## HARVEST

CW offers

| | |
|---|---|
| *Year A* | *Deuteronomy 8:7–18* or *Deuteronomy 28:1–14*;<br>*Psalm 65*;<br>*2 Corinthians 9:6–15*;<br>*Luke 12:16–30* or *Luke 17:11–19*. |
| *Year B* | *Joel 2:21–27*;<br>*Psalm 126*;<br>*1 Timothy 2:1–7* or *1 Timothy 6:6–10*;<br>*Matthew 6:25–33*. |
| *Year C* | *Deuteronomy 26:1–11*;<br>*Psalm 100*;<br>*Philippians 4:4–9* or *Revelation 14:14–18*;<br>*John 6:25–35*. |

## REMEMBRANCE SUNDAY

PHG recommended the original R: Sunday lections (inappropriately 'improved' by CW) as suitable themes for Remembrance. CW also provides a votive for Peace. In many places the traditional practice of a Solemn Requiem on this day is continued, with appropriate propers related to the Resurrection Hope and the duty of Prayer for the Dead. CW considers the Collects for the Third Sunday before Advent most suitable for Remembrance Sunday.

## THE BISHOP

On the Anniversary of the Pope's Inauguration and the 'Episcopal Ordination' (Consecration) or Translation of the Diocesan or the Provincial Bishop, a class 2 Votive (p. xxi) may be said. Texts in the Missal, or CW p. 237. (In the Collect, change 'your servant now to be *enthroned*' to 'your chosen servant *N*'.)

## THE MONARCH

Office and Mass: Josh 1:1–10; Prov 8:1–16; Rom 13:1–10; Rev 21:22–22:4; Ps 20; 101; 121; Mt 22:16–22; Lk 22:24–30.

# Appendix 2: Local days

## THE DEDICATION OF THE LOCAL CHURCH

is a Solemnity observed on the date of the church's Consecration; if this Solemnity falls on a Sunday in Advent, Lent or Easter the seasonal notes will indicate how to transfer it. (The Dedication of the Cathedral is a Festum.)

When the Day of Consecration is unknown, CW allows the first Sunday in October. R: and CW suggest the Sunday before All Saints, in order to focus on the unity between the Church on Earth and the Church in Heaven. See Introduction paragraph 5 (External Solemnities, etc.). Clergy who serve several (country) churches may observe their Dedications as they get around them Sunday by Sunday 'on suitable dates chosen locally' (CW).

Hymns: 1 & 2 EP: 169 (NEH 204); MP 170 (NEH 205)
*Mass: Gl; Cr; R: Pref of Dedication (ASB 26)*

| | | | | | |
|---|---|---|---|---|---|
| **R:** | | Mass | *II Chron 5:6–11 & 13–6:2 (in Eastertide, Acts 7:44–50) I Cor 3:9–13 & 16–17; Jn 4:19–24* | | |
| **CW** | W | 1st EP of foll; | | II Chron 7:11–16 | Gen 28:10–end |
| | | | Ps: 24 | Jn 4:19–29 | Rev 21:9–16 |
| | W | MP | | Hag 2:6–9 | I Chron 29:6–11 |
| | | | Ps: 48 | Heb 10:19–25 | Eph 2:8–end |
| | | Mass | *Year A: I Kings 8:22–30 or Rev 21:9–14; Ps 122; Heb 12:18–24; Mt 21:12–16.* | | |
| | | | *Year B: Gen 28:11–18 or Rev 21:9–14; Ps 122; 2 Pet 2:1–10; Jn 10:22–29.* | | |
| | | | *Year C: I Chron 29:6–19; Ps 122; Eph 2:19–22; Jn 2:13–22.* | | |
| | | 2 EP | Year A | Jer 7:1–11 | I Kgs 8:22–30 |
| | | | Ps: 132 | I Cor 3:9–17 | Heb 10:19–25 |
| | | | Years B & C | Jer 7:1–11 | |
| | | | Ps: 132 | Lk 19:1–10 | |

## THE DEDICATION OF THE CATHEDRAL

is a Festum throughout the Diocese: no 1 EP or Creed at mass, but otherwise as above.

## THE PATRON OF A CHURCH, CITY OR TOWN

is a Solemnity; Gloria and Creed are said at Mass, a first EP is said. The readings used in the Office should be the CW Proper Readings given by the middle column of the ORDO, supplemented by readings for the first EP from the list below, or else readings from the Commons. Or the generous provision in the Weekday Missal may be found helpful.

Appropriate readings should be selected if neither the ORDO nor this Appendix nor the Weekday Missal make adequate provision. August 6 is traditionally the Title of Churches dedicated to Christ; August 15 of those dedicated to S Mary.

If this Solemnity falls on a Sunday in Advent, Lent or Easter, the seasonal notes will indicate how to transfer it. See Introduction, paragraph 5, External Solemnity.

**THE PRINCIPAL PATRON OF A DIOCESE** is a Solemnity *or* Festum. Anglican Diocesan Calendars tend not to use this term, but it is often clear that particular Saints are so regarded (e.g. Chichester: Ss Richard and Wilfrid; Truro: Ss Piran and Petroc). When more than one Saint is clearly regarded as of more than 'Memorial' status, they should all probably be regarded as Co-Principal Patrons. When such Calendars tend to assume that these Saints can displace a 'Green' Sunday, they may be regarded as Solemnities (1 EP; Gl and Cr at Mass). Rome and EAD prefer such Patrons only to be Festa; no 1 EP; Gl only.

**THE TITLE OF THE LOCAL CHURCH** is a Solemnity.

**THE TITLE OF THE CATHEDRAL** is not observed outside the Cathedral unless (which tends particularly to be true in 'Celtic' areas) he/she – may be regarded as also the Diocesan Patron.

WHEN A SOLEMNITY REQUIRES A FIRST EVENING PRAYER (CW):

**HYMNS** are the same as for the Second EP.

| | Psalm | OT Reading | NT Reading |
|---|---|---|---|
| S Paul | 149 | Isa 49:1–13 | Acts 22:3–16 |
| Presentation | 118 | I Sam 1:19b–28 | Heb 4:11–16 |
| S Mark | 19 | Isa 52:7–10 | Mk 1:1–15 |
| Ss P and James | 25 | Isa 40:27–31 | Jn 12:20–26 |
| S Matthias | 147 | Isa 22:15–22 | Phil 3:13b–4:1 |
| Visitation | 45 | Songs 2:8–14 | Lk 1:26–38 |
| S Barnabas | 1 & 15 | Isa 42:5–12 | Acts 14:8–28 |
| S Thomas | 27 | Isa 35 | Heb 10:35–11:1 |
| S Mary Magdalen | 139 | Isa 25:1–9 | II Cor 1:3–7 |
| S James | 144 | Deut 30:11–20 | Mk 5:21–43 |
| Transfiguration | 99 & 110 | Exodus 24:12–18 | Jn 12:27–36a |
| S Bartholomew | 97 | Isa 61:1–9 | II Cor 6:1–10 |
| Holy Cross Day | 66 | Isa 52:13–53:12 | Eph 2:11–22 |
| S Matthew | 34 | Isa 33:13–17 | Mt 6:19–34 |
| S Michael etc | 91 | II Kgs 6:8–17 | Mt 18:1–6 & 10 |
| S Luke | 33 | Hos 6:1–3 | II Tim 3:10–17 |
| Ss S and Jude | 124, 125, & 126 | Deut 32:1–4 | Jn 14:15–26 |
| S Andrew | 48 | Isa 49:1–9a | I Cor 4:9–16 |

# Appendix 3

## CW COMMONS

Arranged for use at mass; but available to be used at the Office when, for example, a Patron is to be celebrated.

*coincides with or overlaps Roman reading. †Reading supplied from R:

| | 1st READING | | | | |
|---|---|---|---|---|---|
| | OT: Outside Eastertide | NT: Within Eastertide | PSALMS | 2nd READING | GOSPEL |
| MARTYRS | II Chron 24:17–21* | Rev 12:10–12a* | 31:1–5* | Rom 8:35–39* | Mt 10:16–22* |
| | Wisd 4:10–15 | | 126* | II Cor 4:7–15* | Mt 10:28–39* |
| | Isa 43:1–7 | | 3; 11 | II Tim 2:3–7(8–13)* | Jn 12:24–26* |
| | Jer 11:18–20 | | 44:19–24 | I Pet 4:12–19* | Jn 15:18–21* |
| | | | | Heb 11:32–40 | Mt 16:24–26 |
| BISHOPS AND PASTORS | I Sam 16:1 & 6–13* | Acts 20:28–35* | 15*; 96* | I Cor 4:1–5* | Jn 10:11–16* |
| | Isa 6:1–8* | | 110* | II Cor 4:1–10* | Jn 21:15–17* |
| | Jer 1:4–10* | | 1; 16:5–11 | II Cor 5:14–20* | Mt 11:25–30 |
| | Ezek 3:16–21* | | | I Pet 5:1–4* | Mt 24:42–46 |
| | Mal 2:5–7 | | | | |

| | 1st READING | | | | |
|---|---|---|---|---|---|
| | OT: Outside Eastertide | NT: Within Eastertide | PSALMS | 2nd READING | GOSPEL |
| DOCTORS | I Kgs 3:(6–10)11–14*<br>Wisd 7:7–10 & 15–16*<br>Ecclus 39:1–10*<br>Prov 4:1–9 | Acts 13:26–33† | 19:7–10*<br>37:30–35*<br>119:89–96*<br>119:97–104<br>34:11–17 | I Cor 1:18–25*<br>I Cor 2:1–10*<br>I Cor 2:9–16*<br>Eph 3:8–12*<br>II Tim 4:1–8*<br>Titus 2:1–18 | Mt 5:13–19*<br>Mt 23:8–12*<br>Mk 4:1–9*<br>Mt 13:52–58<br>Jn 16:12–15 |
| VIRGINS | Song S 8:6–7*<br>Hos 2:14–15 & 19–20* | Rev 19:1 & 5–9* | 45†; 149† | II Cor 10:17–11.2* | Mt 19:3–12* |
| HOLY MEN AND WOMEN | Gen 12:1–14*<br>Mic 6:6–8*<br>Ecclus 2:7–13(14–17)*<br>Prov 8:1–11 | Rev 21:(1–4)5–7* | 33:1–5<br>32; 119:1–8;<br>139:1–4(5–12);<br>145:8–14 | Eph 3:14–19*<br>Eph 6:11–18*<br>Jas 2:14–17*<br>I Jn 4:7–16*<br>Heb 13:7–8 & 15–16 | Mt 25:1–13*<br>Mt 25:14–30*<br>Jn 15:1–8*<br>Jn 17:20–26*<br>Mt 19:16–21 |
| RELIGIOUS<br>As for Virgins; and— | I Kgs 19:9–18*<br>Prov 10:27–32<br>Isa 61:10–62.5 | Acts 4:32–35* | 34:1–8*<br>112:1–9*<br>131*<br>119:57–64<br>123 | Phil 3:7–14*<br>I Jn 2:15–17 | Mt 11:25–30*<br>Mt 19:3–12<br>Lk 9:57–62*<br>Lk 12:32–37*<br>Mt 19:23–30 |
| MISSIONARIES | Isa 52:7–10<br>Isa 61:1–3a<br>Ezek 34:11–16<br>Jonah 3:1–5 | Acts 2:14 & 22–36<br>Acts 13:46–49<br>Acts 16:6–10<br>Acts 26:19–23 | 67; 87;<br>97; 100;<br>117 | Rom 15:17–21<br>II Cor 5:11–6:2 | Mt 9:35–38<br>Mt 28:16–20<br>Mk 16:15–20<br>Lk 5:1–11<br>Lk 10:1–9 |
| Those who worked for the UNDER-PRIVILEGED | Isa 58:6–11* | Acts 4:32–35† | 82;<br>146: 5–10 | I Jn 3:14–18*<br>Heb 13:1–3 | Mt 5:1–12*<br>Mt 25:31–46* |
| MARRIED | Tobit 8:4–7*<br>Prov 31:10–31* | Rev 19:1 & 5–9† | 128*<br>127 | I Pet 3:1–9* | Mk 3:31–35*<br>Lk 10:38–42* |
| RULERS | I Sam 16:1–13a<br>I Kgs 3:3–14 | Rev 3:14 & 20–22† | 72:1–7<br>99 | I Tim 2:1–6 | Lk 14:27–33*<br>Mk 10:42–45 |
| SCHOLARS | Prov 8:22–31<br>Ecclus 44:1–15 | Rev 21:5–7† | 36:5–10<br>49:1–4 | Phil 4:7–8* | Mt 13:44–46 & 52*<br>Jn 7:14–18 |

## ***Office of the Dead*** (a selection)

| | | | |
|---|---|---|---|
| MP | Ps: 40, 42 | Isa 25:6–9<br>Phil 3:10–21 | Isa 38:10–20<br>I Cor 15:51–end |
| EP | H: 350 vv 1 & 4–7 (NEH 327)<br>Ps: 121, 130 | Lam 3:22–26 & 31–33<br>Jn 14:1–6 | Isa 43:1–7<br>Rev 1:9–18 |

# Appendix 4

## 'LESSER FESTIVALS' AND 'COMMEMORATIONS'

### in The Christian Year: Calendar, Lectionary and Collects=Common Worship.

This list contains two distinct categories:

(a) the *Roman type* names, followed (mostly without description) by: are those (only) of the CW 'lesser festivals' for which CW provides optional proper readings. Some, but not all, of these suggested readings coincide with Roman optional suggestions for the same Saint; those which do are marked †.

(b) the *Italic* names, with brief descriptions, are those recommended, as 'commemorations': i.e. for naming in the prayers of intercession and thanksgiving. The Liturgical Commission admitted that it had not been 'scrupulous in reflecting on questions of orthodoxy or even baptismal status' with regard to some of these. Your compiler, see front of volume, may be able to provide information about some of them. 'RefM' means 'Reformation Martyr'.

(BRACKETS) distinguish those who have not been canonised or enjoyed a traditional cultus in the Latin or Byzantine rites. Your compiler accepts that different ecclesiological presuppositions will lead different users to regard some of these as having been definitively raised to the altars of the Church; or as suited to a real but restricted cultus ('Beati'); or as orthodox Christians judged to have had cardinal and theological virtues to a heroic degree and deserving therefore a private cultus ('Venerabiles'); or as still needing to have the Holy Sacrifice offered for them. (Those listed for 'commemoration' on the CW list who have been canonised, or enjoyed a long-standing traditional cultus, are mostly omitted from this list since they are incorporated into the main body of the ORDO as having (CW) 'an established celebration in the wider church'.)

JAN:
2 Basil and Gregory: II Tim 4:1–8; Mt 5:13–19
2 *Seraphim, Monk*
2 (*Vedanayagam Samuel Azariah, Bishop*)
10 (*William Laud, Bishop, Martyr*)
11 (*Mary Slessor, Missionary*)
12 Aelred: Ecclus 15:1–6
13 Hilary: I Jn 2:18–25†; Jn 8:25–32
13 (*George Fox*)
17 Antony: Phil 3:7–14; Mt 19:16–26†
17 (*Charles Gore, Bishop*)
19 Wulfstan: Mt 24:42–46
20 *Richard Rolle, Religious*
21 Agnes: Rev 7:13–17
24 Francis de Sales: Prov 3:13–18; Jn 3:17–21
28 Thomas Aquinas: Wisd 7:7–10 & 15–16; I Cor 2:9–16; Jn 16:12–15
30 Charles: Ecclus 2:12–17; I Tim 6:12–16

FEB:
3 Anskar: Isa 52:7–10; Rom 10:11–15
14 Cyril and Methodius: Isa 52:7–10; Rom 10:11–15
15 (*Thomas Bray, Priest*)
17 (*Janani Luwum, Bishop, Martyr:* Ecclus 4:20–28; Jn 12:24–32)
23 Polycarp: Rev 2:8–11†
27 (*George Herbert, Priest:* Mal 2:5–7; Mt 11:25–30; Rev 19:5–9

MAR:
1 David: II Sam 23:1–4; Ps 89:19–22 & 24
7 Perpetua, etc.: Rev 12:10–12a; Wisd 3:1–7
8 (*Geoffrey Studdert Kennedy, Priest*)
8 (*Edward King, Bishop:* Heb 13:1–8)
17 Patrick: Ps 19:1–4 & 13–16; Lk 10:1–12 & 17–20
21 (*Thomas Cranmer,* Bishop, RefM.)
24 (*Walter Hilton, Religious*)
24 (*Oscar Romero, Bishop, Martyr*)
26 (*Harriet Monsell, Religious*)
31 (*John Donne, Priest*)

APR: 1 (*Frederick Denison Maurice, Priest*)
9 (*Dietrech Bonhoeffer, Martyr*)
10 (*William Law, Priest:* I Cor 2:9–16; Mt 17:1–9)
10 (*William of Ockham*)
11 (*George Augustus Selwyn, Bishop*)
16 (*Isabella Gilmore, Deaconess*)
19 Alphege: Heb 5:1–4
21 Anselm: Wisd 9:13–18; Rom 5:8–11
27 (*Christina Rossetti*)
29 Catherine: Prov 8:1 & 6–11; Jn 17:12–26
30 (*Pandita Mary Ramabai*)

MAY: 2 Athanasius: Ecclus 4:20–28; Mt 10:24–27
8 (*Julian:* I Cor 13:8–13; Mt 5:13–16)
16 (*Caroline Chisholm*)
19 Dunstan: Mt 24:42–46; Exod 31:1–5
20 (*Alcuin, Deacon, Abbot:* Col 3:12–16; Jn 4:19–24)
24 (*John and Charles Wesley, Priests:* Eph 5:12–20)
25 Bede: Ecclus 39:1–10
26 Augustine: I Thess 2:2b–8; Mt 13:31–33
26 (*John Calvin, Priest*)
28 (*Lanfranc, Bishop*)
30 (*Josephine Butler:* Isa 58:6–11; I Jn 3:18–23; Mt 9:10–13
30 (*Apolo Kivebulaya, Priest*)

JUNE: 1 Justin: Jn 15:18–21; I Macc 2:15–22; I Cor 1:18–25
5 Boniface: Acts 20:24–28
6 (*Ini Kopuria, Religious*)
8 (*Thomas Ken, Bishop:* II Cor 4:1–10; Mt 24:42–46)
9 Columba: Titus 2:11–15
14 (*Richard Baxter, Priest*)
15 (*Evelyn Underhill*)
16 Richard: Jn 21:15–19
16 (*Joseph Butler, Bishop*)
17 (*Samuel, Priest, and Henrietta Barnett*)
18 (*Bernard Mizeki, Martyr*)
19 (*Sundar Singh of India*)
22 Alban: II Tim 2:3–13; Jn 12:24–26
23 Etheldreda: Mt 25:1–13
28 Irenæus: II Pet 1:16–21

JULY: 1 (*John and Henry Venn, Priests*)
11 Benedict: I Cor 3:10–11; Lk 18:18–22
14 (*John Keble, Priest:* Lam 3:19–26; Mt 5:1–8)
15 Swithun: Jas 5:7–11 & 13–18
18 (*Elizabeth Ferard, Deaconess*)
19 Gregory, and Macrina: I Cor 2:9–13; Wisd 9:13–17
20 (*Bartolomé de las Casas, Bishop*)
27 (*Brooke Foss Westcott, Bishop*)
30 (*William Wilberforce:* Job 31:16–23; Gal 3:26–29 & 4:6–7; Lk 4:16–21)

AUG: 5 Oswald: I Pet 4:12–19; Jn 16:29–33
7 (*John Mason Neale, Priest*)
8 Dominic: Ecclus 39:1–10
9 (*Mary Sumner:* Heb 13:1–5)
10 Laurence: II Cor 9:6–10†
11 Clare: Song S 8:6–7
11 (*John Henry Newman, Priest*)
13 (*Jeremy Taylor, Bishop:* Titus 2:7–8 & 11–14)
13 (*Florence Nightingale*)
13 (*Octavia Hill*)
20 Bernard: Rev 19:5–9
20 (*William and Catherine Booth*)
27 Monica: Ecclus 26:1–3 & 13–16
28 Augustine: Ecclus 39:1–10; Rom 13:11–13
30 (*John Bunyan:* Heb 12:1–2; Lk 21:21 & 34–36)
31 Aidan: I Cor 9:16–19

SEPT: 2 (*The Martyrs of Papua New Guinea*)
3 Gregory: I Thess 2:3–8
4 Cuthbert: Ezek 34:11–16; Mt 18:12–14
6 (*Allen Gardiner, Missionary*)
9 (*Charles Fuge Lowder, Priest*)
13 John Chrysostom: Mk 5:13–19; Jer 1:4–10
15 Cyprian: I Pet 4:12–19; Mt 18:18–22
16 Ninian: Acts 13:46–49; Mk 16:15–20
16 (*Edward Bouverie Pusey, Priest*)
17 Hildegard: I Cor 2:9–13; Lk 10:21–24
20 (*John Coleridge Patteson, Bishop and Comps Martyrs:* II Chron 24:17–21; Acts 7:55–60
25 (*Lancelot Andrewes, Bishop:* Isa 6:1–8)
25 *Sergei of Radonezh, Religious*
26 (*Wilson Carlile, Priest*)
27 Vincent de Paul: I Cor 1:25–31†; Mt 25:34–40

OCT: 1 (*Anthony Ashley Cooper*)
4 Francis: Gal 6:14–18†; Lk 12:22–34
6 (*William Tyndale, RefM:* Prov 8:4–11; II Tim 3:12–17
9 (*Robert Grosseteste, Bishop*)
10 Paulinus: Mt 28:16–20
10 (*Thomas Traherne*)
11 (*James the Deacon*)
12 Wilfrid: Lk 5:1–11; I Cor 1:18–25
12 (*Elizabeth Fry*)
12 (*Edith Cavell*)
13 Edward the Confessor: II Sam 23:1–5; I Jn 4:13–16
15 Teresa of Avila: Rom 8:22–27†
16 (*Nicholas Ridley, Bishop, and Hugh Latimer, Bishop, RefMs*)
17 Ignatius: Phil 3:7–12; Jn 6:52–58
19 (*Henry Martyn:* Mk 16:15–20; Isa 55:6–11)
26 (*Alfred the Great:* II Sam 23:1–5; Jn 18:33–37)
26 Chad/Cedd: I Tim 6:11b–16
29 (*James Hannington, Bishop and Martyr:* Mt 10:28–39)
30 (*Martin Luther, Priest, Religious*)

NOV: 3 (*Richard Hooker, Priest:* Jn 16:12–15; Ecclus 44:10–15)
6 (*William Temple, Bishop*)
7 Willibrord: Isa 52:7–10; Mt 28:16–20
9 (*Margery Kempe*)
10 Leo: I Pet 5:1–11
11 Martin: I Thess 5:1–11; Mt 25:34–40†
13 (*Charles Simeon, Priest:* Mal 2:5–7; Col 1:3–8; Lk 8:4–8)
14 (*Samuel Seabury, Bishop*)
16 Margaret: Prov 31:10–12 & 20 & 26–31; I Cor 12:13–13:3; Mt 25:34–46
17 Hugh: I Tim 6:11–16
18 Elizabeth: Mt 25:31–46; Prov 31:10–31
19 Hilda: Isa 61:10–62:5
20 Edmund: Prov 20:28 & 21:1–4 & 7
20 (*Priscilla Lydia Sellon, Religious*)
23 Clement: Phil 3:17–4:3; Mt 16:13–19
25 (*Isaac Watts*)

DEC: 1 (*Charles de Foucauld, Hermit*)
4 (*Nicholas Ferrar, Deacon*)
6 Nicolas: Isa 61:1–3; I Tim 6:6–11; Mk 10:13–16
7 Ambrose: Isa 41:9b–13; Lk 22:24–30
13 Lucy: Wisd 3:1–7; II Cor 4:6–15
13 (*Samuel Johnson*)
17 John of the Cross: I Cor 2:1–10†; Jn 14:18–23
17 (*Eglantine Jebb*)
29 Thomas Becket: Mt 10:28–33; Ecclus 51:1–8
31 (*John Wyclif, Priest*)

## OIL IN INITIATION

1. The main thrust of the ancient Western, and particularly Roman, tradition is to use two distinct sets of terms:
   (a) line[i]re or ung(u)ere (or simply tangere) – to *smear* oil on; and
   (b) (con)signare – to 'seal' with the *sign* of (usually) the Cross.
2. The use of oil may feature at three points:
   (i) Before the act of Baptism, when the Oil of the Catechumens, often nowadays called the Oil of Baptism, is used. Historically, 1(a) terms were used, and the candidates were smeared on their *chests* and *backs* (in the modern Roman Rite, only on their chests) *not* on (the one place required in *Common Worship*!) their heads.
   Concepts of exorcism or of the Christian Athlete can be associated with this.
   (ii) Immediately after the act of baptism. Historically, a presbyter smeared (1(a)) *the top of the head* (*not* the forehead) of the new Christian with Chrism. This is still Roman practice.
   (iii) In Confirmation, when the Bishop sealed (1(b)) the *forehead* of the candidates, usually (but see 3, below) having dipped his thumb in Chrism. This is still Roman practice.
3. One way of reading the evidence is to see 2(ii) as a preliminary to 2(iii); the presbyter (as S. Ambrose's description appears to suggest) poured generously and smeared oil from the top of the head downwards, and the Bishop then thumbed the sign of the Cross on the already oily forehead. When the current Western practice of splitting 'Baptism' and 'Confirmation' results in 2(ii) and 2(iii) having several years between them, one could, catechetically, explain 2(ii) in 'Baptism' as a 'pointer' to 2(iii) in 'Confirmation'.
4. SUMMARY. If it is desired to use CW texts as they stand:
   (i) CW Section "Signing with the Cross":
   – Make the sign of the Cross on the **chest**. If using oil, use the "Oil of Baptism".
   (ii) CW Section "Baptism," after the words ". . . inheritance of the Saints in glory. Amen.":
   – Do **not** make the sign of the Cross. If using oil, simply smear Chrism on the **top** of the head, **saying nothing**.
   (iii) The sign of the Cross on the forehead is proper to Confirmation alone.

**Advent 2004 until Christ the King 2005 inclusive:**

CW and the ROMAN SUNDAY LECTIONARY . . . . . . . . . . . . . . . . . . . *CYCLE A*

*This year's readings are dominated by S Matthew's Gospel.*

DAILY EUCHARISTIC AND OFFICE LECTIONARIES . . . . . . . . . . . *CYCLE 1*

# ADVENT AND DECEMBER

## UNTIL DECEMBER 16

1 Nothing may displace the Sunday Mass and Office. Any Solemnity (e.g. Dedication or Patron) is transferred to the Monday. Festa and Memorials are suppressed. (CW orders a Festum to be so transferred to Monday, and allows Dedication and Patronal festivals except on Advent 1.)

2 Altars are not decorated with *flowers* except on Solemnities, Festa, and Advent 3; and apart from these days the *organ* and other instruments are only played at liturgical services to sustain singing.

3 **Office Hymns. Until 16 December: EH: MP 2 EP 1.** ***NEH: MP 2 EP 1.***

4 On the Sundays of Advent, *Te Deum* is said at MP even though the *Gloria* is not used at Mass.

5 A seasonal form of the **Penitential Rite** (Introduction 12) is given in PHG p. 128, 2a (=R:).

6 Of the two prefaces provided in the Roman missal, Advent (I) is to be used from Advent Sunday to 16 December. This **preface** is the first of the 'extended' CW prefaces. On memorials, *either* the *seasonal* preface is used, *or* that of the Saint.

7 November 29 is, in Anglican Calendars, a Day of Intercession for the Missionary Work of the Church.

## DECEMBER 17–24

8 On December 17 the Great Antiphons begin. They are found at EH 734 and NEH 503, and they are all now a day later than the medieval/BCP dates given in EH and NEH. They are said before and after the Magnificat at EP. (PHG suggests other uses for these Antiphons.) *The CW EP readings relate to these Antiphons.*

9 In the Roman rite, the second Advent **preface** is now used. This preface is the second of the 'extended' CW prefaces.

10 **Office Hymns: EH: MP 14 EP 5.** ***NEH: MP 19 EP5.***

11 On the remaining weekdays of December, the propers in the Daily Eucharistic Lectionary are according to the *date in the month.*

12 On the remaining weekdays of December, Memorials are indicated [within square brackets] which means the following: Mass and Office of the Feria. The Memorial may be *either* totally ignored; *or* its Collect may be said *after* the Collect of the day at MP and EP, and *instead* of the Collect of the day at Mass.

13 Advent 4 is the Sunday of the Fathers of the Old Testament, and of Our Lady seen as the climax of God's ancient Covenant and Scriptures. The ancient Western celebration of January 1 as the Solemnity of Mary, Mother of God (Theotokos), is not a duplication of this, since it concentrates more on Our Lady as guarantee of the dogmatic truths of the Incarnation: Christ, Man and God; one Person, two Natures. (PHG encourages the R: mass readings of this Solemnity.)

## IMMACULATE CONCEPTION OF THE BVM

**December 8, 2004, is the Sesquicentenary of the proclamation by Bl Pius IX of the Dogma of the Immaculate Conception.**

1 'The Immaculate Conception was a feast (and a doctrine) first developed in the West in the Anglo-Saxon England of the early eleventh century on an older and rather different Byzantine basis.' (Gregory Dix). (It had to fend off assaults by Norman Romanizers who pointed out that it was not observed by the Papal Court.)

2 'Anglicans and Roman Catholics can agree in much of the truth that [the dogma of the Immaculate Conception is] designed to affirm; . . . the affirmation . . . that Mary was conceived without original sin is based on recognition of her unique role within the mystery of the Incarnation. By being thus prepared to be the mother of our Redeemer, she also becomes a sign that the salvation won by Christ was operative among all mankind before his birth.' (ARCIC 1981).

3 While CW only offers the Commons, we follow PHG, which provides the (R:) mass readings and the full provision for MP and EP (Collect 89) as being 'appropriate to the season of Advent'. 'In the night of the Advent expectation, Mary began to shine like a true *Stella Matutina*. For just as the Morning Star, together with the Dawn, precedes the rising of the Sun, so Mary from the time of her Immaculate Conception preceded the coming of the Saviour, the rising of the Sun of Righteousness.' (JP2). PPL urges a Novena.

4 The *Office Hymns* now used are not in EH or NEH but may be obtained from the Compiler. The Common Hymns are 213, 214, 215 (NEH 180, 181, 183). EH 229 vv 1–3 & 7 is appropriate.

S NICOLAS, BISHOP, PATRON: Mass: Isa 61:1–3; I Tim 6:6–11; Mk 10:13–16
1 EP: Ezek 34:11–16, Mt 25:14–30 MP: Isa 6:1–8, I Cor 4:1–6
2 EP: Isa 52:7–10; I Tim 4:1–5 Psalms, 1, 15, 23 (CW and PHG.)

## NOVEMBER 2004 *R: CW Year A; Weekday Lectionaries Year 1*

✠ *SUNDAY* — **ADVENT 1**

**28** P — MP — Ps: 44 — Mic 4:1–7; I Thess 5:1–11 — Isa 1:1–20; Mt 24:1–28

R: Ps I — Mass — *no Gl; Cr; Pref of Advent (1)*
*CW: Isa 2:1–5; Ps 122; Rom 13:11–14; Mt 24:36–44*
*R: Isa 2:1–5; Ps 122; Rom 13:11–14; Mt 24:37–44 (The Day of the Lord)*

EP — Ps: 9 — Isa 52:1–12; Mt 24:15–28 — Isa 2:10–end; I Thess 5

*MONDAY* — *Feria*

**29** P — MP — Ps: 70, 75 — Isa 1:1–20; I Thess 1 — Isa 3:1–15; Mk 1:1–20

Mass — *of Sunday or the day in Advent; no Gl or Cr; Pref of Advent (1)*
*Isa 4:2–end; Ps 122; Mt 8:5–11*

EP — Ps: 94 — Gen 12:1–3; 13:2–end; Heb 11:1–10 — Isa 4:2–end; Rev 6

*TUESDAY* — **S Andrew Apostle (Scotland Solemnity)**

**30** R — MP — Ps: 47; 147:1–12 — Ezek 47:1–12 or Ecclus 14:20–27; Jn 12:20–32 — Isa 49:1–9a; Jn 1:35–42

Mass — *Gl; R: Pref of Apostles; CW, of Saints**
*CW: Isa 52:7–10; Ps 19:1–6; Rom 10:12–18; Mt 4:18–22*
*R: Rom 10:9–18; Ps 19; Mt 4:18–22*

EP — Ps: 87, 96 — Zech 8:20–23; Jn 1:35–42 — Ezek 47:1–12; Jn 12:20–32

## DECEMBER

*WEDNESDAY* — *Feria*

**1** P — MP — Ps: 28, 76 — Isa 2:1–11; I Thess 2:13–end — Isa 6; Mk 2:1–22

Mass — *as Monday (**Charles de Foucauld Rel**)*
*Isa 25:6–10a; Ps 23; Mt 15:29–37*

EP — Ps: 44 — Gen 16; Gal 4:21–27 — Isa 8:16 — 9:7; Rev 8

*THURSDAY* — *Feria*

**2** P — MP — Ps: 62, 82 — Isa 2:12–end; I Thess 3:1–13 — Isa 9:8 — 10:4; Mk 2:23 — 3:12

Mass — *as Monday*
*Isa 26:1–6; Ps 118:18–27a; Mt 7:21 & 24–27*

EP — Ps: 11, 12 — Gen 17:15–22; Lk 1:68–79 — Isa 10:5–23; Rev 9

*FRIDAY* — *S Francis Xavier Pr*

**3** W — MP — Ps: 40 — Isa 3:8–15; I Thess 4:1–12 — Isa 10:24 — 11:9; Mk 3:13–end

Mass — *of the Saint (First Friday: Sacred Heart; see p. 39)*
*Isa 29:17–end; Ps 27:1–4 & 16–17; Mt 9:27–31*

EP — Ps: 42, 43 — Gen 18:1–15; Rom 12:9–18 — Is 11:10 — 12 end; Rev 10

*SATURDAY* — *Feria (S John of Damascus Pr Dr)*

**4** P (or W) — MP — Ps: 9 — Isa 4:2–end; I Thess 4:13–end — Isa 13:1 — 14:2; Mk 4:1–20

Mass — *as Monday (or of the Saint) (**Nicolas Ferrar Dcn Rel**)*
*(First Saturday: Immaculate Heart of Mary; see p. 39)*
*Isa 30:19–21 & 23–26; Ps 146:4–9; Mt 9:35–10:1 & 6–8*

P — 1 EP of foll — Ps: 123, 130 — Gen 18:16–end; Mt 9:2–13 — Isa 14:3–27; Rev 11

* Anniversary of the Episcopal Ordination in 2000 of Andrew, third bishop of Ebbsfleet.

| Day | Colour | Office | Psalms / Mass | Readings | Alternative |
|---|---|---|---|---|---|
| ✠ *SUNDAY* | | | **ADVENT 2** | | |
| **5** | P | MP | Ps: 80 | Amos 7 | Isa 5:1–6 |
| | | | | Lk 1:5–20 | Mt 24:29–end |
| R: Ps II | | Mass | *no Gl; Cr; Pref of Advent (1)* | | |
| | | | *CW: Isa 11:1–10; Ps 72:1–7 & 18–19; Rom 15:4–13; Mt 3:1–12* | | |
| | | | *R: Isa 11:1–10; Ps 72; Rom 15:4–9; Mt 3:1–12 (Our Baptism in the Spirit)* | | |
| | P | 2 EP | | I Kgs 18:17–39 | Isa 5:18–end |
| | | | Ps: 11; (28) | Jn 1:19–28 | 2 Tim 3:14–4:8 |
| *MONDAY* | | | *Feria (S Nicolas B (see p. xxxvi) EAD: Obligatory)* | | |
| **6** | P (or W) | MP | Ps: 70 [75] | Isa 5:1–13 | Isa 17 |
| | | | | I Thess 5:1–11 | Mk 4:21–end |
| | | Mass | *of Sunday or the day in Advent; no Gl or Cr; Pref of Advent (1) (or of the Saint)* | | |
| | | | *Isa 35; Ps 85:7–end; Lk 5:17–26* | | |
| | | EP | | Gen 19:15–29 | Isa 18 |
| | | | Ps: 94 | Mk 13:14–end | Rev 12 |
| *TUESDAY* | | | *S Ambrose B Dr* | | |
| **7** | W | MP | Ps: 50 | Isa 5:14–25 | Isa 19:1–17 |
| | | | | I Thess 5:12–end | Mk 5:1–20 |
| | | Mass | *of the Saint* | | |
| | | | *Isa 40:1–11; Ps 96:1 & 10–end; Mt 18:12–14* | | |
| | | | ***IMMACULATE* CONCEPTION OF THE BVM (PHG) (see page xxxvi)** | | |
| | W | 1 EP | | Ecclus 24:17–22 | ◁ |
| | | | Ps: 113, 147:12–20 | Rom 8:28–30 | ◁ |
| *WEDNESDAY* | | | | | |
| **8** | W | MP | | Isa 61:10 – 62:5 | ◁ |
| | | | Ps: 46, 87 | I Cor 1:26–30 | ◁ |
| | | Mass | *Gl; Cr; Proper Pref (or ASB 6 or CW, Annunciation)* | | |
| | | | *Gen 3:9–15 & 20; Eph 1:3–6 & 11–12; Lk 1:26–38* | | |
| | | 2 EP | | Zeph 3:14–17 | ◁ |
| | | | Ps: 122, 127 | Rev 11:19 & 12:1–6 & 10 | ◁ |
| *THURSDAY* | | | *Feria* | | |
| **9** | P | MP | Ps: 62, 82 | Isa 7:1–19 | Isa 24 |
| | | | | II Thess 2:1–3:15 | Mk 6:1–13 |
| | | Mass | *as Monday* | | |
| | | | *Isa 41:13–20; Ps 145:1 & 8–13; Mt 11:11–15* | | |
| | | EP | | Gen 24:1–7 & 10–27 | Isa 28:1–13 |
| | | | Ps: 11, 12 | Jn 4:1–26 | Rev 15 |
| *FRIDAY* | | | *Feria (Ember Day)** | | |
| **10** | P | MP | Ps: 40 | Isa 7:10–end | Isa 28:14–end |
| | | | | II Thess 2:13–3:5 | Mk 6:14–29 |
| | | Mass | *as Monday* | | |
| | | | *Isa 48:17–19; Ps 1; Mt 11:16–19 (**Our Lady of Guadeloupe**)* | | |
| | | EP | | Gen 24:50–end | Isa 29:1–14 |
| | | | Ps: 42, 43 | Jn 4:27–42 | Rev 16 |
| *SATURDAY* | | | *Feria (Ember Day)* (S Damasus I Pp)* | | |
| **11** | P (or W) | MP | Ps: 9 | Isa 8:1–15 | Isa 29:15–end |
| | | | | II Thess 3:6–end | Mk 6:30–end |
| | | Mass | *as Monday (or of the Saint)* | | |
| | | | *Ecclus 48:1–4 & 9–11; Ps 80:1–4 & 18–19; Mt 17:10–13* | | |
| | †P | 1 EP of Advent 3 | | Gen 25:19–end | Isa 30:1–18 |
| | | | Ps: 123, 130 | Lk 15:11–end | Rev 17 |

* Ember Masses see Introduction paragraph 25.

† Rose colour is sometimes used this evening and tomorrow.

## DECEMBER 2004 *R: CW Year A; Weekday Lectionaries Year 1*

| | | | | | |
|---|---|---|---|---|---|
| ✠ *SUNDAY* | | | **ADVENT 3** | | |
| **12** | P* | MP | Ps: 68:1–19 | Zeph 3:14–20 | Isa 25:1–9 |
| | | | | Phil 4:4–7 | Mt 25:1–30 |
| R: Ps III | | Mass | *no Gl; Cr; Pref of Advent (1)* | | |
| | | | *CW: Isa 35:1–10; Ps 146:4–10; Jas 5:7–10; Mt 11:2–11* | | |
| | | | *R: Isa 35:1–6a & 10; Ps 146; Jas 5:7–10; Mt 11:2–11 (S John Baptist)* | | |
| | | 2 EP | | Isa 5:8–30 | Isa 26:1–13 |
| | | | Ps: 12; (14) | Acts 13:13–41 | I Tim 1:12 – 2:7 |
| *MONDAY* | | | *S Lucy V M* | | |
| **13** | R | MP | Ps: 70, 75 | Isa 8:16–9:1 | Isa 30:19–end |
| | | | | II Pet 1:1–11 | Mk 7:1–23 |
| | | Mass | *of the Saint (**Samuel Johnson**)* | | |
| | | | *Num 24:2–7 & 15–17; Ps 25:3–8; Mt 21:23–27* | | |
| | | EP | | Gen 26:34 – 27:17 | Isa 31 |
| | | | Ps: 94 | Lk 3:1–14 | Rev 18 |
| *TUESDAY* | | | *S John of the Cross Pr Dr* | | |
| **14** | W | MP | Ps: 50 | Isa 9:1b–7 | Isa 38:1–20 |
| | | | | II Pet 1:12–end | Mk 7:24 – 8:10 |
| | | Mass | *of the Saint* | | |
| | | | *Zeph 3:1–2 & 9–13; Ps 34:1–6 & 21–22; Mt 21:28–32* | | |
| | | EP | | Gen 27:18–40 | Isa 40:1–11 |
| | | | Ps: 144 | Acts 4:32–5:12 | Rev 19 |
| *WEDNESDAY* | | | *Feria* | | |
| **15** | P | MP | Ps: 28, 76 | Isa 9:8–17 | Isa 40:12–end |
| | | | | II Pet 2:1–10*a* | Mk 8:11 – 9:1 |
| | | Mass | *no Gl or Cr; Pref of Advent (1)* | | |
| | | | *Isa 45:6b–8 & 18:21–26; Ps 85:7–end; Lk 7:18b–23* | | |
| | | EP | | Gen 29:1–14 | Isa 41 |
| | | | Ps: 44 | Mt 12:1–14 | Rev 20 |
| *THURSDAY* | | | *Feria* | | |
| **16** | P | MP | Ps: 62, 82 | Isa 9:18–10:4 | Isa 42:1–17 |
| | | | | II Pet 2:10b–end | Mk 9:2–32 |
| | | Mass | *as Wednesday* | | |
| | | | *Isa 54:1–10; Ps 30:1–5 & 11–end; Lk 7:24–30* | | |
| | | EP | | Gen 29:15–30 | Isa 42:18 – 43:13 |
| | | | Ps: 11, 12 | Titus 1:1–9 | Rev 21:1–14 |
| *FRIDAY* | | | *Feria* **(O Sapientia: see Notes pp. xxxv–xxxvi)** | | |
| **17** | P | MP | Ps: 113 | Jer 30:12–22 | Isa 43:14 – 44:5 |
| | | | | Heb 10:23–39 | Mk 9:33–end |
| | | Mass | *of the day, December 17. No Gl or Cr; Pref of Advent (2): see p. xxxv (**Eglantine Jebb**)* | | |
| | | | *Gen 49:2 & 8–10; Ps 72:1–5 & 18–19; Mt 1:1–17* | | |
| | | EP | | Ecclus 24:1–9 | Isa 44:6–23 |
| | | | Ps: 90, 111 | I Cor 2:1–13 | Rev 21:15 – 22:5 |
| *SATURDAY* | | | *Feria (O Rex)* | | |
| **18** | P | MP | Ps: 114 | Isa 42:1–12 | Isa 44:24 – 45:13 |
| | | | | Eph 6:10–20 | Mk 10:1–31 |
| | | Mass | *of Dec 18; see Friday (Obit, 1999, of Michael, Second bishop of Ebbsfleet)* | | |
| | | | *Jer 23:5–8; Ps 72:1 & 6–8 & 18–19, Mt 1:18–24* | | |
| | | 1 EP of Advent 4 | | Ex 3:1–6 | Isa 45:14–end |
| | | | Ps: 106 | Acts 7:20–36 | Rev 22:6–end |

* Rose colour sometimes used today.

| Day | Colour | Office | | | |
|---|---|---|---|---|---|
| ✠ *SUNDAY* | | | **ADVENT 4** *(O Radix)* | | |
| **19** | P | MP | Ps: 144 | Mic 5:2–5a | Isa 32:1–18 |
| | | | | Lk 1:26–38 | Mt 25:31–end |
| R: Ps IV | | Mass | *no Gl; Cr; Pref of Advent (2)* | | |
| | | | *CW: Isa 7:10–16; Ps 80:1–8 & 18–20; Rom 1:1–7; Mt 1:18–25* | | |
| | | | *R: Isa 7:10–14; Ps 24; Rom 1:1–7; Mt 1:18–24 (our Lady)* | | |
| | | 2 EP | | Song of S 2:8–14 | Isa 35 |
| | | | Ps: 50 | Rom 15:7–13 | II Pet 3:1–14 |
| *MONDAY* | | | *Feria (O Clavis)* | | |
| **20** | P | MP | Ps: 116:1–8 | Isa 11:11–end | Isa 46 |
| | | | | Rev 20:11–21:8 | Mk 10:32–end |
| | | Mass | *of December 20. No Gl or Cr; Pref of Advent (2) (**Our Lady of the Annunciation [2]**)* | | |
| | | | *Isa 7:10–14; Ps 24:1–6; Lk 1:26–38* | | |
| | | EP | H: 14 | Isa 22:20–23 | Isa 47 |
| | | | Ps: 89:1–34 | Rev 3:7–13 | Jude 1–16 |
| *TUESDAY* | | | *Feria (O Oriens) [□ S Peter Canisius Pr Dr]* | | |
| **21** | P | MP | Ps: 116:10–end | Isa 28:9–22 | Isa 48 |
| | | | | Rev 21:9–21 | Mk 11:1–26 |
| | | Mass | *of December 21; see Monday* | | |
| | | | *(Anniversary of the Episcopal Ordination in 1996 of David, Bishop in Wales)* | | |
| | | | *Zeph 3:14–18; Ps 33:1–14 & 11–12 & 19–end; Lk 1:39–45* | | |
| | | EP | | Num 24:15b–19 | Isa 50:4–10 |
| | | | Ps: 27 | Rev 22:10–21 | Jude 17–end |
| *WEDNESDAY* | | | *Feria (O Rex)* | | |
| **22** | P | MP | Ps: 146, 147 | Isa 29:13–end | Isa 51:1–16 |
| | | | | Rev 21:22 – 22:5 | Mk 11:27 – 12:12 |
| | | Mass | *of December 22; see Monday* | | |
| | | | *I Sam 1:24–end; Ps 113; Lk 1:46–56* | | |
| | | EP | | Jer 30:7–11a | Isa 51:17 – 52:12 |
| | | | Ps: 118 | Acts 4:1–12 | II Pet 1 |
| *THURSDAY* | | | *Feria (O Emmanuel) [□ S John de Kety Pr ]* | | |
| **23** | P | MP | Ps: 148, 150 | Isa 33:17–22 | Isa 52:13 – 53 end |
| | | | | Rev 22:6–11 | Mk 12:13–34 |
| | | Mass | *of December 23; see Monday* | | |
| | | | *Mal 3:1–4 & 4:5–6; Ps 25:3–9; Lk 1:57–66* | | |
| | | EP | | Isa 7:10–14 | Isa 54 |
| | | | Ps: 80 | Mt 1:18–23 | II Pet 2 |
| *FRIDAY* | | | *Feria (in the morning)* | | |
| **24** | P | MP | Ps: 137, 138 | Isa 32:1–8 | Isa 56:1–8 |
| | | | | Rev 22:12–21 | Mk 12:35 – 13:13 |
| | | Mass | *of December 24; see Monday* | | |
| | | | *II Sam 7:1–5 & 8–11 & 16; Ps 89:2 & 19–27; Lk 1:67–79* | | |

**CHRISTMAS EVE, CHRISTMAS DAY**
**Notes for Christmastide See page 5**

✠
# 24-25 NATIVITY OF THE LORD

*CHRISTMAS EVE and CHRISTMAS DAY*

All the masses of Christmas—*including* the Vigil Mass (see note 1 below) — are celebrated in white vestments, with Gloria, Creed (Kneel for the *Incarnatus*), and Preface of the Incarnation (see note 4 below).

| | | | | |
|---|---|---|---|---|
| ***EVE*** | Evening ('Vigil') Mass: | *Isa 62:1–5;Ps 89:3–4 & 15–16 & 26 &28; Acts 13:16–17 & 22–25 Mt(1–17) 18–end* | | |
| | 1 EP | | Zech 2 (R: Isa 11:1–10) | Zech 2:10–end |
| | | Ps: 85 | Rev 1:1–8 | Titus 2:11–14 |
| ***NIGHT*** | Midnight Mass: | *CW = R: Isa 9:2–7; Ps 96; Titus 2:11–14; Lk 2:1–14* | | |
| ***DAY*** | MP | Ps: 110, 117 | Isa 62:1–5 | Isa 9:2–7 |
| | | | Mt 1:18–25 | Lk 2:1–20 |
| | Mass at Dawn: | *CW: Isa 62:6–12; Ps 97; Titus 3:4–7; Lk 2 (1–7) 8–20* <br> *R: Isa 62:11–12; Ps 97; Titus 3:4–7; Lk 2:15–20* | | |
| | Mass of the Day: | *CW: Isa 52:7–10; Ps 98; Heb 1:1–4 (5–12); Jn 1:1–14* <br> *R: Isa 52:7–10; Ps 98; Heb 1:1–6; Jn 1:1–18 or 1–5 & 9–14* | | |
| | 2 EP | | Isa 65:17–25 | Isa 35 |
| | | Ps: 8 | Phil 2:5–11 | I Jn 4:7–end |

## NOTES FOR CHRISTMASTIDE AND EPIPHANY

1 **The Eve.** The Vigil mass of Christmas is the first of the four masses of Christmas, and is celebrated festally as such. Its Collect in the Roman Rite is the ancient one which CW (in a translation which is better than R:) mistakenly assigns to the Advent mass in *purple* vestments said in the *earlier* part of the 24th. This Collect is also used at 1 EP.

2 **Penitential Rite.** Seasonal forms (Introduction, Paragragh 12) are given in PHG: *Christmas* p. 196, 1; *Epiphany* p.233, a and b (all=R:).

3 **Collects.** *Eve*: see Note 1. *Midnight*: CW gives the Roman Collect in a better translation than R:. *Dawn*: the R: Collect, which is not in CW, is also used at MP. *Day*: CW continues to offer Cranmer's elegant composition.

The ancient Christmas Collect *Deus qui humanae substantiae...* was introduced by 1928 for Christmas II, transferred by ASB and CW to Christmas I, (where it will unfortunately be in competition with the Holy Family) and is now the Roman Collect for Christmas Day itself. Of the available translations, 1928 is by far the least bowdlerized, but CW is better than R:.

On *ferial days* from Christmas until the Sunday after Ephiphany, R: has a different Collect for each day (PHG pp. 350 ff also provides considerable variety). Anglican custom expects the Christmas Day and Epiphany Collects to be used until the following Sundays, and otherwise the Collect of the previous Sunday to be used. Your compiler recommends that it is best *either* to use the daily Roman Collects: *or* to stay with *Almighty God who wonderfully created...* until Epiphany, and thereafter to use the Epiphany Collect. **Memorials:** see page xxxvi note 12.

4 **Prefaces.** The CW 'extended' Preface is a lengthened version of the Roman Preface. R: offers two more Christmas Prefaces. PHG gives us a version of the Roman Epiphany Preface on p.238 (b); and the Roman Preface for the Baptism on p. 231. On the Feasts of Christmas Week, the Christmas Prefaces are used. On memorials after January 1, the Preface of the Season or of the Saint is used.

5 **Evening Prayer.** The great festival of the Incarnation should dominate its octave. Accordingly, from S Stephen to the Holy Innocents, Rome, endorsed by PHG but not CW, has *MP only* of the Festum; EP of Christmastide (H:17 NEH 19). *Your Order follows this usage*, while giving readings for the Saints *in the right-hand column* for those who follow the other practice, or who need to treat these Saints as Patronal Solemnities. (The readings in both columns are CW.)

6 **Office hymns until Epiphany: EH: MP 18 EP 17 *NEH: MP 20 EP 19.***

| Day | | | | | |
|---|---|---|---|---|---|
| ✠ *SUNDAY* | | | **CHRISTMAS 1 (CW) (S Stephen, see p. 7)** | | |
| **26** | W | MP | Ps: 105:1–9 | Isa 35:1–6 | Isa 41:8–20 |
| | | | | Gal 3:23–29 | Col 1:1–20 |
| R. Ps I | | Mass | *Gl; Cr; Pref of Christmas* | | |
| | | | *CW: Isa 63:7–9; Ps 148; Heb 2:10–18; Mt 2:13–23* | | |
| | | 2 EP | H: 17 | Isa 49:7–13 | Isa 12 |
| | | | Ps: 132 | Phil 2:1–11 | Phil 2:1–11 |
| *OR* | | | **HOLY FAMILY (ROMAN & PHG)** | | |
| | W | MP | Ps: 132 | Isa 35 | ◁ |
| | | | | Col 1:1–20 | ◁ |
| | | Mass | *Gl; Cr; Pref of Christmas* | | |
| | | | *Ecclus 3:2–6 & 12–14; Ps 128; Col 3:12–21; Mt 2:13–15 & 19–end* | | |
| | | 2 EP | H: 46 (NEH 45) | Isa 41:21–end | ◁ |
| | | | Ps: 84, 122 | Lk 2:22–40 or Phil 2:1–11 | ◁ |
| *MONDAY* | | | **S John, Apostle and Evangelist** | | |
| **27** | W | MP | Hymn from Common | Exod 33:12–end | ◁ |
| | | | Ps: 21, 147:13–20 | I Jn 2:1–11 (=R:) | ◁ |
| | | Mass | *Gl; Pref of Christmas* | | |
| | | | *CW: Exod 33:7–11a; Ps 117; I Jn 1; Jn 21:19b–25* | | |
| | | | *R: I Jn 1:1–4; Ps 97; Jn 20:2–8* | | |
| | | | | | [EP of the Saint |
| | | EP of Christmas | H: 17 (NEH 19) | Isa 41:8–16 | Ps 97: Isa 6:1–8 |
| | | | Ps: 45 | Jn 12:27–33 | 1 Jn 5:1–12] |
| *TUESDAY* | | | **Holy Innocents** | | |
| **28** | R | MP | H: 34 (NEH 218) | Baruch 4:21–27 | ◁ |
| | | | Ps: 36, 146 | Mt 18:1–10 | ◁ |
| | | Mass | *Gl; Pref of Christmas* | | |
| | | | *CW: Jer 31:15–17; Ps 124; I Cor 1:26–29; Mt 2:13–18* | | |
| | | | *R: I Jn 1:5 – 2:2; Ps 124; Mt 2:13–18* | | |
| | | | | | [EP of the Saints: |
| | W | EP of Christmas | H: 17 (NEH 19) | Isa 41:17–20 | Ps 123, 128: Isa 49:14–25 |
| | | | Ps: 132 | Jn 12:34–37 | Mk 10:13–16] |
| *WEDNESDAY* | | | **In the Octave of Christmas** | | |
| **29** | | | [*S Thomas a Becket B and M*] *(see p. xxxvi note 12)* | | |
| | W | MP | H: 18 (NEH 20) | Isa 12 | Isa 55 |
| | | | Ps: 20, 149 | Jn 7:37–52 | Jn 1:14–18 |
| | | Mass | *Gl; Pref of Christmas* | | |
| | | | *1 Jn 2:3–11; Ps 96:1–4; Lk 2:22–35* | | |
| | | EP of Christmas | H: 17 (NEH 19) | II Sam 23:13–17b | Isa 60:1–12 |
| | | | Ps: 61, 99 | Rev 1:1–8 | Mt 11:2–6 |
| *THURSDAY* | | | **In the Octave of Christmas** | | |
| **30** | W | MP | H: 18 (NEH 20) | Isa 25:1–9 | Isa 60:13–end |
| | | | Ps: 45, 147:1–12 | Jn 7:53 – 8:11 | Jn 3:16–21 |
| | | Mass | *Gl; Pref of Christmas* | | |
| | | | *1 Jn 2:12–17; Ps 96; Lk 2:36–40* | | |
| | | EP of Christmas | H: 17 (NEH 19) | I Kgs 17:17–24 | Isa 61 |
| | | | Ps: 97, 98 | Rev 1:9–20 | Mt 16:13–20 |
| *FRIDAY* | | | **In the Octave of Christmas** [*S Silvester Pp*] | | |
| **31** | W | MP | Ps: 132, 117 | Isa 26:1–8 | Isa 62 |
| | | | | Jn 8:12–19 | Jn 6:41–58 |
| | | Mass | *Gl; Pref of Christmas* (***John Wyclif***) | | |
| | | | *1 Jn 2:18–21; Ps 96:1 & 11–end Jn 1:1–18* | | |
| *EITHER* | | 1 EP of The Holy Name of Jesus* | | Jer 23:1–6 | Num 6:22–26 |
| | | | Ps: 148 | Col 2:8–15 | Lk 21:25–36 |
| *OR* | | 1 EP of Mary Mother of God (R)* | | Gen 17:1–12a & 15–16 | ◁ |
| | | | Ps: 90 | Col 2:8–15 | ◁ |

from tomorrow's EP.

## DECEMBER 2004

According to R:, S Stephen is omitted this year because the Holy Family takes precedence. If, however, he is Patron, he takes precedence over the Sunday.

According to CW, he is either observed on the Sunday *or* transfered to Wednesday.

The provision is printed below for local decision.

| | | | **S Stephen, First Martyr** | | |
|---|---|---|---|---|---|
| | R | MP | H: 31 (NEH 218) | Jer 26:12–15 | ◁ |
| | | | Ps: 13, 31:1–8, 150 | Acts 6(=R:) | ◁ |
| | | Mass | *Gl; Pref of Christmas* | | |
| | | | *CW: from: II Chron 24:20–22; Acts 7:51–60; Ps 119:161–168; Gal 2:16b–20; Mt 10:17–22* | | |
| | | | *R: Acts 6:8–10 & 7:54–9; Ps 31; Mt 10:17–22* | | |
| | | | | | [EP of the Saint<br>Ps 57, 86; Gen 4:1–10<br>Mt 23:34–end] |

## JANUARY 2005

| *SATURDAY* | | | **THE MOST HOLY NAME OF JESUS (CW)** | | |
|---|---|---|---|---|---|
| **1** | W | MP | H: 238 (NEH 291) | Gen 17:1–13 | Deut 10:12 – 11:1 |
| | | | Ps: 103, 150 | Rom 2:17–29 | Rom 2:17–end |
| | | Mass | *Gl; Cr; Pref of Incarnation* | | |
| | | | *Num 6:22–27; Ps 8; Gal 4:4–7; Lk 2:15–21* | | |
| | | 2 EP | H:237 (NEH 153) | Deut 30: (1–10) 11-20 | Deut 30 |
| | | | Ps: 115 | Acts 3:1–16 | Col 2:8–15 |
| *OR* | | | **MARY MOTHER OF GOD (ROMAN)** | | |
| | W | MP | H:214 (NEH 181) | Mic 5:2–5a | ◁ |
| | | | Ps: 103 | Heb 2:9–17(=R:) | ◁ |
| | | Mass | *Gl; Cr; Pref I of BVM (. . . as we celebrate the Motherhood . . .)* | | |
| | | | *Num 6:22–27; Ps 67; Gal 4:4–7; Lk 2:16–21 (given by PHG & CW)* | | |
| | | 2 EP | H:613:1 & 3–6 | | |
| | | | (NEH 33) | Baruch 4:36–5:4 | ◁ |
| | | | Ps: 115 | Eph 2:11–22 | ◁ |

## EPIPHANY

In the Roman Rite, Epiphany is transferred to the Sunday in places where it is *not* 'of obligation'. English Roman Catholics observe it 'of obligation' on Thursday. According to CW, the Epiphany *is* of obligation and *may* be transferred to Sunday January 2 'for pastoral reasons'. Accordingly, we print here the Epiphany and Christmas II provisions, for local decision.

Rome now provides a *Vigil mass of Epiphany*; its Collect should be used at 1 EP. (We beseech/beg thee/you, Lord; may the splendour of thy/your majesty pour its light into our hearts, so that we may be able to pass through the darkness of this world and come to the country of everlasting glory.)

| ✠ | | | **EPIPHANY OF THE LORD (see Notes p. 5)** | | |
|---|---|---|---|---|---|
| | | 1 EP | H: 38 (NEH 46) | Isa 49:1–13 | Isa 42:1–9 |
| | | | Ps: 96, 97 | Jn 4:7–26 | Rom 15:8–21 |
| | W | MP | H: 40 (NEH 48) | Jer 31:7–14 | Isa 49:1–13 |
| | | | Ps: 132, 113 | Jn 1:29–34 | Lk 3:15–22 |
| | | Mass | *Gl; Cr; Pref of Epiphany* | | |
| | | | *CW: Isa 60:1–6; Ps 72: (1–9) 10–15; Eph 3:1–12; Mt 2:1–12* | | |
| | | | *R: Isa 60:1–6; Ps 72; Eph 3:2–3a & 5–6; Mt 2:1–12* | | |
| | | 2 EP | H: 38 (NEH 46) | Isa 60:1–9 (10–22) (= R:) | Isa 60 |
| | | | Ps: 98, 100 | Jn 2:1–11 | Jn 2:1–11 |

✠ **CHRISTMAS II (January 2)**

R: Ps II W MP H: 18 (NEH 20) Jer 31:15–17 Isa 41:1–21–end
Ps: 87 2 Cor 1:3–12 1 Jn 1:1 – 2:6
Mass *Gl; Cr; Pref of Christmas*
*CW: Ecclus 24:1–12; Ps 147:13–21; Eph 1:3–14; Jn 1:(1–9)10–18*
*R: Ecclus 24:1–4 & 8–12; Ps 147; Eph 1:3–6 & 15–18; Jn 1:1–5(6–8)9–14*
*(Christ the Wisdom of God)*
EP H: 17 (NEH 19) Isa 41:21 – 42:4 Isa 12
Ps: 135 Col 1:1–14 Phil 2:1–11

**WEEKDAYS BEFORE AND AFTER EPIPHANY**

| CW; and Roman Rite if Epiphany was on THURSDAY. | Date | Roman Rite if Epiphany was transferred to SUNDAY. | BCP |
|---|---|---|---|
| X | Monday 3 | A (Name of Jesus) | X |
| Y | Tuesday 4 | B | Y |
| Z | Wednesday 5 | C | Z |
| W | Thursday 6 | D | – |
| A | Friday 7 | E (□S Raymond de Penyafort, pr) | E |
| B | Saturday 8 | F (Sacred Heart, p. 39) | F |

**THE HOLY NAME OF JESUS** is restored as an optional memorial on January 3. (*Philippians 2:1–11; Ps 8; Lk 2:21–24*). New propers are available from the Compiler (or CW – January 1 – could be used). R: does not offer Proper hymns.

*WEEKDAYS BEFORE AND AFTER EPIPHANY*

*Feria*

**W** MP Ps: 89:5–18, 146 Gen 12:1–7
Heb 11:1–12
Mass *CW; of Sunday. Weekday Missal: 'Masses for Weekdays of the Christmas Season'*
*no Gl or Cr; Pref of Christmas*
*I Jn 2:22–28; Ps 98:1–4; Jn 1:19–28*
EP 1 Kgs 19:1–8
Ps: 66 Jn 6:35–51

*Feria*

**X** W MP Ps: 111, 147:1–11 Gen 28:10–end Isa 64
Heb 11:13–22 Mt 2
Mass *as above*
*I Jn 2:29 – 3:6; Ps 98:2–7; Jn 1:29–34*
EP 1 Kgs 19:9–18 Isa 65:1–16
Ps: 46, 48 Jn 10:7–17 I Thess 2:1–16

*Feria*

**Y** W MP Ps: 112, 148 Exod 3:1–12 Isa 65:17–end
Heb 11:23–31 Mt 3:1–4:11
Mass *as above*
*I Jn 3:7–10; Ps 98:1 & 8–end; Jn 1:35–42*
EP Josh 3:14 – 4:7 Isa 66:1–9
Ps: 89:1–4, 19–29 Jn 14:6–14 I Thess 2:17 – 3:end

*Feria*

**Z** W MP Ps: 113, 149 Josh 1:1–9 Isa 66:10–end
Heb 11:32 – 12:2 Mt 4:12 – 5:16
Mass as above
*I Jn 3:11–21; Ps 100; Jn 1:43–end*
EP Jonah 2:2–9
Ps: 100 Jn 9:1–12 & 35–38

| | | | | | |
|---|---|---|---|---|---|
| | | | *Feria* | | |
| **A** | W | MP | H: 40 (NEH 48) | Isa 52:3–6 | Hos 2:14–3 end |
| | | | Ps: 99, 150 | Jn 2:1–11 | Mt 5:17–end |
| | | Mass | CW: *of Epiphany; R: from 'Masses for weekdays of the Christmas season'. No Gl or Cr; Pref of Christmas or Epiphany. I Jn 3:22–4:6; Ps 149:1–5; Mt 4:12–17 & 23–end (Printed in Weekday Missal as 'Readings for 2-12 January: 7 January or Monday after Epiphany'.)* | | |
| | | EP | H: 38 (NEH 46) | Deut 8:1–3 | Hos 4:1–11 |
| | | | Ps: 47, 48 | Rev 2:1–7 | I Thess 4:1–12 |
| | | | *Feria* | | |
| **B** | W | MP | H: 40 (NEH 48) | Isa 59:15–21 | Hos 5:8–6:6 |
| | | | Ps: 97,146 | Jn 4:46–54 | Mt 6:1–18 |
| | | Mass | *as above* | | |
| | | | *I Jn 4:7–10; Ps 72:1–8; Mk 6:34–44* | | |
| | | EP | H: 38 (NEH 46) | Exod 17:1–7 | Hos 8 |
| | | | Ps: 145 | Rev 2:8–17 | I Thess 4:13–5:11 |
| | | | *Feria* | | |
| **C** | W | MP | H: 40 (NEH 48) | Isa 63:1–5 | Hos 9 |
| | | | Ps: 66, 147:13–end | Jn 5:1–15 | Mt 6:19—end |
| | | Mass | *as above* | | |
| | | | *I Jn 4:11–18; Ps 72:1 & 10–13; Mk 6:45–52* | | |
| | | EP | H: 38 (NEH 46) | Isa 45:14–19 | Hos 10 |
| | | | Ps: 81 | Rev 2:18–29 | I Thess 5:12–end |
| | | | *Feria* | | |
| **D** | W | MP | H: 40, (NEH 48) | Isa 65:1–9 | Hos 11 |
| | | | Ps: 24, 148 | Jn 6:1–14 | Mt 7 |
| | | Mass | *as above* | | |
| | | | *I Jn 4:19–5:4; Ps 72:1 & 17–end; Lk 4:14–22* | | |
| | | EP | H: 38 (NEH 46) | Jer 23:1–8 | Hos 12 |
| | | | Ps: 98 | Rev 3:1–6 | II Thess 1 |
| | | | *Feria* | | |
| **E** | W | MP | H:40 (NEH 48) | Isa 65:13–16 | Hos 13:1–14 |
| | | | Ps: 57, 147:1–12 | Jn 6:15–27 | Mt 8:1–17 |
| | | Mass | *as above* | | |
| | | | *I Jn 5:5–13; Ps 147:13–end; Lk 5:12–16* | | |
| | | EP | H: 38 (NEH 46) | Isa 55:3–9 | Hos 14 |
| | | | Ps: 36, 46 | Rev 3:7–22 | II Thess 2 |
| | | | *Feria* | | |
| **F** | W | MP | H: 40 (NEH 48) | Isa 66:1, 2, 22, 23 | Joel 1 |
| | | | Ps: 21, 148 | Gal 3:23 – 4:7 | Mt 8:18–end |
| | | Mass | *as above* | | |
| | | | *I Jn 5:14–end; Ps 149:1–5; Jn 3:22–30* | | |
| | | | **Saturday Evening before the Baptism of the Lord:** | | |
| | | 1 EP of foll | H: 47 | Isa 61 | ◁[Joel 2:1–14] |
| | | | Ps: 36 | Titus 2:11–14 & 3:4–7 | ◁[II Thess 3] |

| | | | | | |
|---|---|---|---|---|---|
| ✠ *SUNDAY* | | | **BAPTISM OF THE LORD BCP EPIPHANY 1* (see Notes p. 5)** | | |
| **9** | W | MP | | Exod 14:15–22 | Isa 49:13–23 |
| | | | Ps: 89:19–29 | I Jn 5:6–9 | Mt 7:1–13 |
| R:Ps III | | Mass | *Gl; Cr on Sunday; R: Proper Pref; CW, of Epiphany* | | |
| | | | *CW: Isa 42:1–9; Ps 29; Acts 10:34–43; Mt 3:13–17* | | |
| | | | *R: Isa 42:1–4 & 6–7; Ps 29; Acts 10:34–38; Lk 3:13–17* | | |
| | | 2 EP | H: NEH 58 (EH 38) | Josh 3:1–8 & 14–17 | Isa 61 |
| | | | Ps: 46; 47 | Heb 1:1–12 | Mt 2 |

**'ORDINARY TIME' – 'PER ANNUM' – 'THE GREEN SEASON' – BEGINS**

**1st WEEK of YEAR**

| | | | | | |
|---|---|---|---|---|---|
| *MONDAY* | | | *Feria* | | |
| **10** | G | MP | Ps: 93, 99, 150 | Isa 40:1–17 | Joel 2:15–end |
| | | | | Rev 1:1–8 | Mt 9:1–17 |
| R:Ps I | | Mass | *of Sunday; no Gl or Gr; Comm Pref (**William Laud BM**)* | | |
| | | | *Heb 1:1–6; Ps 97:1–2 & 6–10; Mk 1:14–20* | | |
| | | EP | | Gen 37:1–11 | Joel 3 |
| | | | Ps: 47, 48 | Rom 1:1–17 | Gal 1 |
| *TUESDAY* | | | *Feria* | | |
| **11** | G | MP | Ps: 97, 146 | Isa 40:18–end | Amos 1 |
| | | | | Rev 1:9–16 | Mt 9:18–34 |
| | | Mass | *as Monday (**Mary Slessor**)* | | |
| | | | *Heb 2:5–12; Ps 8; Mk 1:21–28* | | |
| | | EP | | Gen 37:12–end | Amos 2 |
| | | | Ps: 145 | Rom 1:18–end | Gal 2 |
| *WEDNESDAY* | | | *Feria (S Aelred of Rievaulx Ab)* | | |
| **12** | G (or W) | MP | Ps: 66, 147:13–21 | Isa 41:1–16 | Amos 3 |
| | | | | Rev 1:17 – 2:7 | Mt 9:35–10:23 |
| | | Mass | *as Monday (or of the Saint) (**Benedict Biscop Ab**)* | | |
| | | | *Heb 2:14–end; Ps 105:1–9; Mk 1:29–39* | | |
| | | EP | | Gen 39:1–20 | Amos 4 |
| | | | Ps: 81 | Rom 2:1–17 | Gal 3 |
| *THURSDAY* | | | *Feria (S Hilary B Dr; SCOTLAND; S Kentigern B)* | | |
| **13** | G (or W) | MP | Ps: 24, 148 | Isa 41:17–end | Amos 5 |
| | | | | Rev 2:8–17 | Mt 10:24–end |
| | | Mass | *as Monday (or of the Saint) (**George Fox**)* | | |
| | | | *Heb 3:7–14; Ps 95:1 & 8–end; Mk 1:40–end* | | |
| | | EP | | Gen 39:21 – 40:22 | Amos 6 |
| | | | Ps: 72, 98 | Rom 3:1–20 | Gal 4:1–5:1 |
| *FRIDAY* | | | *Feria* | | |
| **14** | G | MP | Ps: 57, 147:1–12 | Isa 42:(1–9) 10–end | Amos 7 |
| | | | | Rev 2:18–29 | Mt 11 |
| | | Mass | *as Monday* | | |
| | | | *Heb 4:1–5 & 11; Ps 78:3–8; Mk 2:1–12* | | |
| | | EP | | Gen 41:1–24 | Amos 8 |
| | | | Ps: 36, 46 | Rom 3:21–31 | Gal 5:2—end |
| *SATURDAY* | | | *Our Lady on Saturday† or the Feria* | | |
| **15** | W (or G) | MP | Ps: 21, 149 | Isa 43:1–13 | Amos 9 |
| | | | | Rev 3:1–6 | Mt 12:1–21 |
| | | Mass | *(Our Lady of Perpetual Succour)* | | |
| | | | *Heb 4:12–16; Ps 19:7–end; Mk 2:13–17* | | |
| | G | 1 EP of foll | | Gen 41:25–45 | Obadiah |
| | | | Ps: 8, 20 | Rom 4 | Gal 6 |

* PPL and PHG urge the use of the Asperges on this day. Introduction paragraph 12.

† For 'Our Lady on Saturday' see Introduction Paragraph 26 (b), and Hymns page xxiii.

| Day | Colour | Service | | | |
|---|---|---|---|---|---|
| ✠ *SUNDAY* | | | **2nd SUNDAY and WEEK of YEAR; EPIPHANY 2** | | |
| **16** | G | MP | Ps: 145:1–12 | Jer 1:4–10<br>Mk 1:14–20 | Isa 43:14 – 44:5<br>Eph 1 |
| R:Ps II | | Mass | *Gl; Cr; Sunday Pref*<br>*CW: Isa 49:1–7; Ps 40:1–12; I Cor 1:1–9; Jn 1:29–42*<br>*R: Isa 49:3 & 5–6; Ps 40; I Cor 1:1–3; Jn 1:29–34 (The Lamb of God)* | | |
| | | 2 EP | Ps: 96 | Ezek 2:1–34<br>Gal 1:11–24 | Isa 44:6–23<br>Mk 1:35–end |
| *MONDAY* | | | *S Antony Ab* | | |
| **17** | W | MP | Ps: 93, 99, 150 | Isa 43:14 – 44:8<br>Rev 3:7–13 | Jonah 1 & 2<br>Mt 12:22–end |
| | | Mass | *of the Saint (**Charles Gore B**)*<br>*Heb 5:1–10; Ps 110:1–4; Mk 2:18–22* | | |
| | | EP | Ps: 47, 48 | Gen 41:46–49 & 41:53 – 42:5<br>Rom 5:1–11 | Jonah 3 & 4<br>I Cor 1:1–25 |
| *TUESDAY** | | | *Feria (Confession or Chair of S Peter: see Intro Appendix 1)* | | |
| **18** | G | MP | Ps: 97, 146 | Isa 44:9–23<br>Rev 3:14–end | Micah 1<br>Mt 13:1–23 |
| | | Mass | *as Monday (or of the Saint) (**Richard Rolle**)*<br>*Heb 6:10–end; Ps 111; Mk 2:23–end* | | |
| | | EP | Ps: 145 | Gen 42:6–28<br>Rom 5:12–end | Micah 2<br>I Cor 1:26 – 2 end |
| *WEDNESDAY* | | | *Feria (S Wulfstan B (Compulsory in EAD))* | | |
| **19** | G (or W) | MP | Ps: 66, 147:13–end | Isa 44:24 – 45:7<br>Rev 4:1–8 | Micah 3<br>Mt 13:24–43 |
| | | Mass | *as Tuesday (or of the Saint)*<br>*Heb 7:1–3 & 15–17; Ps 110:1–4; Mk 3:1–6* | | |
| | | EP | Ps: 81 | Gen 43:1–3 & 11–18 & 26–31<br>Rom 6:1–14 | Micah 4:1–5:1<br>I Cor 3 |
| *THURSDAY* | | | *Feria (S Fabian Pp M; □ S Sebastian M)* | | |
| **20** | G (or R) | MP | Ps: 57, 148 | Isa 45:8–17<br>Rev 4:9 – 5:5 | Micah 5:2–end<br>Mt 13:44–end |
| | | Mass | *as Tuesday (or of the Saint) (**Richard Rolle**)*<br>*Heb 7:25 – 8:6; Ps 40:7–10 & 17–end; Mk 3:7–12* | | |
| | | EP | Ps: 72, 98 | Gen 44:1–7<br>Rom 6:15–end | Micah 6<br>I Cor 4:1–17 |
| *FRIDAY* | | | *S Agnes V M* | | |
| **21** | R | MP | Ps: 24, 147:1–12 | Isa 45:18–end<br>Rev 5:6–end | Micah 7<br>Mt 14 |
| | | Mass | *of the Saint*<br>*Heb 8:6–end; Ps 85:7–end; Mk 3:13–19* | | |
| | | EP | Ps: 36, 46 | Gen 45:1–15<br>Rom 7:1–12 | Nahum 1<br>I Cor 18:5–end |
| *SATURDAY* | | | *Our Lady on Saturday or the Feria (S Vincent Dcn M)* | | |
| **22** | W (or G or R) | MP | Ps: 21, 149 | Isa 46<br>Rev 6 | Nahum 2<br>Mt 15:1–28 |
| | | Mass | *Our Lady, the Feria, or the Saint*<br>*Heb 9:2–3 & 11–14; Ps 47:1–8; Mk 3:20–21* | | |
| | G | 1 EP of foll | Ps: 8, 20 | Gen 45:16 – 46:7<br>Rom 7:13–end | Nahum 3<br>I Cor 6 |

* Chair of Unity Octave: Intro Appendix I.

| | | | | | |
|---|---|---|---|---|---|
| ✠ *SUNDAY* | | | **3rd SUNDAY and WEEK of YEAR; EPIPHANY 3; BCP SEPTUAGESIMA** | | |
| **23** | G | MP | Ps: 113 | Amos 3:1–8 | Gen 1:1 – 2:3 |
| | | | | I Jn 1:1–4 | Jn 1:1–18 |
| R:Ps III | | Mass | *Gl; Cr; Sunday Pref Christian Unity see Introduction Appendix 1* | | |
| | | | *CW: Isa 9:1–4; Ps 27:1 & 4–12; I Cor 1:10–18; Mt 4:12–23* | | |
| | | | *R: Isa 8:23 – 9:3; Ps 27; I Cor 1:10–13 & 17; Mt 4:12–17 (18–23) (The Light of the World)* | | |
| | | 2 EP | | Eccles 3:1–11 | Gen 2:4–end |
| | | | Ps: 33 | I Pet 1:3–12 | Rev 4 |
| *MONDAY* | | | *S Francis de Sales B Dr* | | |
| **24** | W | MP | Ps: 93, 99, 150 | Isa 47 | Gen 3 |
| | | | | Rev 7:1–8 | Mt 15:29 – 16:12 |
| | | Mass | *of the Saint* | | |
| | | | *Heb 9:15 & 24–end; Ps 98:1–7; Mk 3:22–30* | | |
| | | EP | | Gen 49:28 – 50:14 | Gen 4:1–16 |
| | | | Ps: 47, 48 | Rom 8:1–17 | Rom 1 |
| *TUESDAY* | | | **Conversion of S Paul, Apostle** | | |
| **25** | W | MP | H: 226 vv4 & 6 | Ezek 3:22–27 | Isa 56:1–8 |
| | | | Ps: 66, 147:13–21 | Phil 3:1–14 | Gal 1:11–end (=R:)] |
| | | Mass | *of the Saint; Gl; R; Pref of Apostles; CW, of Saints* | | |
| | | | *CW: from Jer 1:4–10; Ps 67; Acts 9:1–22; Mt 19:27–30* | | |
| | | | *R: Acts 22:3–16 or 9:1–22; Ps 117; Mk 16:15–18* | | |
| | | EH | H: NEH 154 | Ecclus 39:1–10 | Jer 1: 4–10 |
| | | | Ps: 119:41–56 | Col 1:24 – 2:7 | Phil 3:1–14 |
| *WEDNESDAY* | | | *Ss Timothy and Titus Bs* | | |
| **26** | W | MP | Ps: 66, 147:13–end | Isa 49:1–12 | Gen 8:1–14 |
| | | | | Rev 8 | Mt 17:1–23 |
| | | Mass | *of the Saints* | | |
| | | | *CW: Isa 61:1–3a; Ps 100; II Tim 2:1–8 or Titus 1:1–5; Lk 10:1–9* | | |
| | | | *R: II Tim 1:1–18 or Titus 1:1–5; Ps 96; Lk 10:1–9* | | |
| | | | *[Heb 10:11–18; Ps 110:1–4; Mk 4:1–20]* | | |
| | | EP | | Num 6:1–8 | Gen 8:15–9:17 |
| | | | Ps: 81 | Rom 8:28–end | Rom 3 |
| *THURSDAY* | | | *Feria (☐ S Angela Merici V)* | | |
| **27** | G (or W) | MP | Ps: 57, 148 | Isa 49:13–23 | Gen 11:1–9 |
| | | | | Rev 9:1–12 | Mt 17:24–18:14 |
| | | Mass | *as Sunday; no Gl or Cr; Common Pref (or of the Saint)* | | |
| | | | *Heb 10:19–25; Ps 24:1–6; Mk 4:21–25* | | |
| | | EP | | Num 22:21–35 | Gen 11:27 – 12:10 |
| | | | Ps: 72, 98 | Rom 10:1–17 | Rom 4 |
| *FRIDAY* | | | *S Thomas Aquinas Pr Dr* | | |
| **28** | W | MP | Ps: 24, 147:1–12 | Isa 50 | Gen 13 |
| | | | | Rev 9:13–end | Mt 18:15–end |
| | | Mass | *of the Saint* | | |
| | | | *Heb 10:32–39; Ps 37:3–6 & 40–end; Mk 4:26–34* | | |
| | | EP | | Num 28:16–31 | Gen 14 |
| | | | Ps: 36, 46 | Rom 11:1–12 | Rom 5 |
| *SATURDAY* | | | *Our Lady on Saturday or the Feria* | | |
| **29** | W (or G) | MP | Ps: 21, 149 | Isa 51:1–18 | Gen 15 |
| | | | | Rev 10 | Mt 19:1–15 |
| | | Mass | *of Our Lady or the Feria* | | |
| | | | *Heb 11:1–2 & 8–19; Canticle: Lk 1:69–73; Mk 4:35–end* | | |
| | G | 1 EP of foll* | | Josh 1:1–9 | Gen 16 |
| | | | Ps: 8, 20 | Rom 11:13–25 & 33–end | Rom 6 |

The *Presentation*, according to CW, may be celebrated *either* on Sunday January 30 *or* on Wednesday February 2. In either case it is, for CW, a Solemnity with a 1 EP and the Creed at Mass. (According to R: it is observed on Wednesday, with *no* 1 EP: and, additionally, an 'External Solemnity' – all Masses and Offices including a 1 EP - may be observed on the *preceding* Sunday – January 30.) We print the entire provision separately for insertion according to local decision.

| | | **Presentation of the Lord** | | |
|---|---|---|---|---|
| | [IEP | Ps: 118 | I Sam 1:19b–28 | Exod 13:11–16 |
| | | | Heb 4:11–16 | Gal 4:1–7] |
| W | MP | Ps: 48; 146 | Exod 13:1–16 (=R:) | I Sam 1:21–end |
| | | | Rom 12:1–5 | Heb 10:1–10 |
| | Mass | *Ceremonies*; Gl; Pref of Presentation (Missal or CW)* | | |
| | | *CW: Mal 3:1–5; Ps 24:(1–6)7–10; Heb 2:14–18; Lk 2: 22–40* | | |
| | | *R: Mal 3:1–4; Ps 24; Heb 2:14–18; Lk 2: 22–32 (33–40)* | | |
| | (2)EP | IIL 208 (NEH156*) | Hag 2:1–9 | Hag 2:1–9 |
| | | Ps: 122, 132 | Jn 2:18–22 | Rom 12:1–5 |

* In H: NEH156, NEH seems curiously intent on eliminating *Theotokos*. The Presentation ceremonies traditionally take place before the main mass (R: & PHG pp. 283 ff); PHG envisages they might follow it (pp. 280ff). R: and PHG both envisage the omission of the Penitential Rite.

If the Presentation is (CW) observed on SUNDAY, Psalms at the Office will be:

| | | |
|---|---|---|
| Monday | MP 75,76 | EP 77 |
| Tuesday | MP 78:1–20 | EP 78:21–55 |
| Wednesday | MP 78:56–end | EP 79 |

## J A N U A R Y — *R: CW Year A. Weekday Lectionaries Year 1*

| Day | Colour | Office | | | |
|---|---|---|---|---|---|
| ✠ *SUNDAY* | | | **4th SUNDAY and WEEK of YEAR; EPIPHANY 4 *OR* PRESENTATION; BCP SEXAGESIMA** | | |
| **30** | G | MP | Ps: 71:1–6 & 15–17 | Hag 2:1–9 | Gen 3 |
| | | | | I Cor 3:10–17 | I Cor 10: 1–13 |
| R:Ps IV | | Mass | *Gl; Cr; Sunday Pref* | | |
| | | | *CW: I Kgs 17:8–16; Ps 36:5–10; I Cor 1:18–31; Jn 2:1–11* | | |
| | | | *R: Zeph 2:3 & 3:12–13; Ps 146; I Cor 1:26–31; Mt 5:1–12 (Our Nothingness)* | | |
| | | 2 EP | | Gen 28:10–22 | Gen 4:1–16 |
| | | | Ps: 34 | Philemon 1–16 | I Jn 3:1–15 |
| *MONDAY* | | | *S John Bosco Pr* | | |
| **31** | W | MP | Ps: 93, 99, 150 | Isa 51:9–end | Gen 17:1–22 |
| | | | | Rev 11:1–14 | Mt 19:16 – 20:16 |
| | | Mass | *of the Saint* | | |
| | | | *Heb 11:32–end; Ps 31:19–end; Mk 5:1–20* | | |
| | | EP | | Josh 4:1–11 | Gen 18 |
| | | | Ps: 47, 48 | Rom 13 | Rom 7 |

## F E B R U A R Y

| Day | Colour | Office | | | |
|---|---|---|---|---|---|
| *TUESDAY* | | | *Feria (IRELAND S Brigid V FESTUM)* | | |
| **1** | G (or W) | MP | Ps: 97, 146 | Isa 52:1–12 | Gen 19:1–3 & 12–29 |
| | | | | Rev 11:15–end | Mt 20:17–end |
| | | Mass | *of Sunday;* no Gloria or Creed; Common Pref (or of the Saint)* | | |
| | | | *Heb 12:1–4; Ps 22:25b–end; Mk 5:21–43* | | |
| | | EP | | Josh 6:1–21 | Gen 21 |
| | | | Ps: 145 | Rom 14:1–18 | Rom 8:1–17 |
| *WEDNESDAY* | | | *Feria (PRESENTATION, see p. 13)* | | |
| **2** | G | MP | Ps: 66, 147:13–end | Isa 54:1–10 (11–end) | Gen 22:1–19 |
| | | | | Rev 12:1–6 | Mt 21:1–22 |
| | | Mass | *as Tuesday** | | |
| | | | *Heb 12:4–7 & 11–15; Ps 103:1–2 & 13–18; Mk 6:1–6* | | |
| | | EP | | Josh 23 | Gen 23 |
| | | | Ps: 81 | Rom 14:19 – 15:6 | Rom 8:18–end |
| *THURSDAY* | | | *Feria (S Blaise B M; S Anskar B)* | | |
| **3** | G (or R or W) | MP | Ps: 80 | Isa 55 | Gen 24:1–28 |
| | | | | Rev 12:7–end | Mt 21:23–end |
| | | Mass | *as Tuesday (or of the Saint)** | | |
| | | | *Heb 12:18–19 & 21–24; Ps 48:1–3 & 8–10; Mk 6:7–13* | | |
| | | EP | | Josh 24 | Gen 24:29–end |
| | | | Ps: 81 | Rom 15:7–22 | Rom 9 |
| *FRIDAY* | | | *Feria (Ss Gilbert of Sempringham, Simon Stock, Stephen Harding, Pr Rel Founders)* | | |
| **4** | G (or W) | MP | Ps: 82, 83 | Isa 56:1–8 | Gen 25:7–11 & 19–end |
| | | | | Rev 13:1–10 | Mt 22:1–33 |
| | | Mass | *as Tuesday (or of the Saints)* (First Friday; Sacred Heart; see p. 39)* | | |
| | | | *Heb 13:1–8; Ps 27:1–6 & 9–12; Mk 6:14–29* | | |
| | | EP | | Judg 13:2–25 | Gen 27:1–40 |
| | | | Ps: 84 | Rom 15:23–end | Rom 10 |
| *SATURDAY* | | | *S Agatha V M* | | |
| **5** | R | MP | Ps: 85, 86 | Isa 57:3–end | Gen 27:41–28 end |
| | | | | Rev 13:11–end | Mt 22:34 – 23:12 |
| | | Mass | *of the Saint (First Saturday; Immaculate Heart: see p. 39)* | | |
| | | | *Heb 13:15–17 & 20–21; Ps 23; Mk 6:30–34* | | |
| | G | 1 EP of foll | | Judg 14 | Gen 29:1–20 |
| | | | Ps: 87, 88 | Phil 1:1–14 | Rom 11 |

* According to CW, on the weekdays after the Presentation (whenever it is observed), Collect and Post Communion are from 'the Fifth (sic) Sunday before Lent.' (February 2 is the Anniversary of the Episcopal Ordination in 1994 of Martyn, Bishop of Beverley.)

## NOTES FOR LENT

1 The faithful are encouraged to see Lent as their preparation for the *Paschal* Mystery of the Death and Resurrection of the Lord, the Easter Triduum, rather than as a mere imitation of the Forty Days in the Wilderness. Preachers might notice that CW texts now follow Rome in expecting congregations to understand the word 'Paschal'. Those who are to be baptized and/or confirmed at Easter are prepared for the Sacraments, and the rest of the faithful express their penitence sacramentally and in communal Services of Penitence (LHWE pp. 38 ff). Ash Wednesday is a day of fasting and abstinence (p. xiv).

2 *On Sundays in Lent,* any Solemnity (e.g. Dedication or Patron) is transferred to the Monday; Festa and Memorials are suppressed. (CW also allows a Festum to be transferred to Monday, and permits a Dedication or Patronal Festival on Sundays 2, 3, and 4).

3 *On Weekdays in Lent,* Solemnities and Festa are observed; Memorials are indicated [within square brackets] which means the following: Mass and Office are of the Feria. The memorial may be *either* totally ignored *or* its collect may be said *after* the Collect of the day at MP and EP, and *instead* of the Collect of the day at Mass. (The new R: Calendar for England has moved S Chad from 2 March to 26 October; and S Cuthbert from 20 March to 4 September: to get them out of Lent. CW permits this optionally. Local Saints will prefer to have a non-Lenten date found for them: e.g. as of a Translation.)

4 **Office Hymns: EH: Sundays: MP 65 EP 66; Ferias: MP 67 or 68 EP 69. *NEH: MP 59 EP 60.***

5 Altars are not decorated with *flowers* except on Solemnities, Festa, and Lent 4, Refreshment Sunday; and apart from these days the organ and other instruments are only played at liturgical services to sustain poor singing. All use of *Alleluia* is avoided.

6 *Prefaces:* R: provides, in the Weekday Missal, four Lenten Prefaces, the first of which beautifully brings out the character of Lent as preparation for the *Pascha*, followed now in this by the (less generously provided) CW prefaces. R: also encourages marking Lent 1 with the Litany at the Entrance of the Mass.

7 **Sunday Themes and Readings**

(a) On *Lent 1*, CW and Rome remember the Temptation in the Wilderness.

(b) On *Lent 2*, Rome recalls the Transfiguration (Lent calls us to a participation in the Lord's own Paschal Transfiguration). CW transferred this perception to the Sunday *before* Lent.

(c) On *Lent 3, 4, and 5* CW and Rome reflect an ancient Christian association of Lent with Eschatological, Paschal, and Redemptive themes. Rome (see also CW) allows (even in Years B and C) the Year A Gospels (together with their associated readings and proper prefaces) which are given below. These are the readings anciently used in the preparation of candidates for Baptism and Confirmation. They may also be used on weekdays. (Compare also the Byzantine rite.)

**Roman Sundays in Year A**

3 Living Water [The Samaritan Woman]
*Exod 17:3–7; Rom 5:1–2 & 5–8; Jn 4:5–42* (*or 5–15 & 19–26 & 39–42*)

4 Enlightenment [the Man Blind from Birth]
*I Sam 6:1 & 6–7 & 10–13; Eph 5:8–14; Jn 9:1–41* (*or 1 & 6–9 & 13–17 & 34–38*)

5 New Life [Lazarus]
*Ezek 37:12–14; Rom 8:8–11; Jn 11:1–45* (*or 3–7 & 17–27 & 33b–45*)

8 Customary ways of observing Lent include: *Thursdays* Eucharistic Adoration *Fridays* Way of the Cross and penitential celebrations *Saturdays* Rosary. PPL urges also: venerating relics of the Cross; reading the Passion; the *Via Matris*.

| | | | | | |
|---|---|---|---|---|---|
| ✠ *SUNDAY* | | | **5th SUNDAY and WEEK of YEAR; CW NEXT BEFORE LENT BCP QUINQUAGESIMA** | | |
| **6** | G | MP | Ps: 72 | Exod 34:29–35 | Gen 12:1–9 |
| | | | | II Cor 4:3–6 | I Cor 12:4–end |
| R:Ps I | | Mass | *Gl; Cr; Sunday Pref*<br>*CW: Exod 24:12–18; Ps 2 or 99; II Pet 1:16–21; Mt 17:1–9*<br>*R: Is 58:7–10; Ps 112; I Cor 2:1–5; Mt 5:13–16 (The Church: A Light in the Darkness)* | | |
| | | 2 EP | | Ecclus 48:1–10 | Gen 6:5–end |
| | | | Ps: 84 | Mt 17:(1–8) 9–23 | Lk 17:20–end |
| *MONDAY* | | | *Feria* | | |
| **7** | G | MP | Ps: 18:1–25 | Deut 6:1–15 | Gen 31:1–9 & 14–21 |
| | | | | Jn 1:1–18 | Mt 23:13–end |
| | | Mass | *of Sunday; no Gl or Cr; Common Pref*<br>*Gen 1:1–19; Ps 104:1–2 & 6–13 & 26; Mk 6:53–end* | | |
| | | EP | | Ruth 1 | Gen 31:22 – 32:2 |
| | | | Ps: 18:26–end | Mt 5:1–12 | Rom 12 |
| *TUESDAY* | | | *Feria (□ S Jerome Emiliani; □ S Josephine Bakhita V; □ Bl Pius IX Pp)* | | |
| **8** | G (or W) | MP | Ps: 20 | Deut 6:16–end | Gen 32:3–30 |
| | | | | Jn 1:19–34 | Mt 24:1–28 |
| | | Mass | *as Monday (or of the Saint)*<br>*Gen 1:20 – 2:4a; Ps 8; Mk 7:1–13* | | |
| | | EP | | Ruth 2 | Gen 33 |
| | | | Ps: 21 | Mt 5:13–16 | Rom 13 |
| ✠ *WEDNESDAY* | | | **ASH WEDNESDAY** | | |
| **9** | P | MP | Ps: 38 | Dan 9:3–6 & 17–19 | Isa 58 |
| | | | | I Tim 6:6–19 | Mk 2:13–22 |
| R:Ps IV | | Mass | *of the day; the penitential rite is omitted; Blessing & imposition of Ashes takes place after the Homily; R: Pref 4 of Lent; CW, Pref 1 of Lent*<br>*CW: Joel 2:1–2 & 12–17; Ps 51:1–18; II Cor 5:20b – 6:10; Mt 6:1–6 & 16–21*<br>*R: Joel 2:12–18; Ps 51; II Cor 5:20 – 6:2; Mt 6:1–6 & 16–18* | | |
| | | EP | | Isa 1:10–18 [R: Isa 58:1–12] | Dan 9:3–19 |
| | | | Ps: 102 *or* 102:1–18 | Lk 15:11–32 | Heb 3:12 – 4:13 |
| *THURSDAY* | | | *Feria [S Scholastica V* ]* | | |
| **10** | P | MP | Ps: 25 | Deut 7:6–11 | Gen 35:1–20 |
| | | | | Jn 1:35–end | Mt 24:29–end |
| | | Mass | *as Monday*<br>*Deut 30:15–end; Ps 1; Lk 9:22–25* | | |
| | | EP | | Ruth 3 | Gen 37 |
| | | | Ps: 27 | Mt 5:17–20 | Rom 14 |
| *FRIDAY* | | | *Feria [□ Our Lady of Lourdes; World Day for the Sick EAD: Compulsory ]* | | |
| **11** | P | MP | Ps: 39 | Deut 7:12–16 | Gen 39 |
| | | | | Jn 2:1–12 | Mt 25:1–30 |
| | | Mass | *of the day; Pref of Lent*<br>*Isa 58:1–9a; Ps 51:1–5 & 17–18; Mt 9:14–15* | | |
| | | EP | | Ruth 4 | Gen 40 |
| | | | Ps: 69 | Mt 5:21–26 | Rom 15 |
| *SATURDAY* | | | *Feria* | | |
| **12** | P | MP | Ps: 13, 124 | Deut 7:17–end | Gen 41:1–40 |
| | | | | Jn 2:13–end | Mt 25:31–end |
| | | Mass | *of the day; Pref of Lent*<br>*Isa 58:9b–end; Ps 86:1–7; Lk 5:27–32* | | |
| | P | 1 EP of foll | | I Sam 1:1–20 | Gen 41:41–end |
| | | | Ps: 31 | Mt 5:27–37 | Rom 16 |

* See p. 15 Para 3.

| Day | Colour | Office | Psalms / Mass | Readings | Alternative readings |
|---|---|---|---|---|---|
| ✠ *SUNDAY* | | | **LENT 1 see Notes for Lent** | | |
| **13** | P | MP | Ps: 119:1–16 | Jer 18:1–11 | Gen 13 |
| | | | | Lk 18:9–14 | Lk 15:1–10 |
| R:Ps I | | Mass | *Cr; R: Proper Pref; CW, of Lent* | | |
| | | | *CW: Gen 2:15–17 & 3:1–7; Ps 32; Rom 5:12–19; Mt 4:1–11* | | |
| | | | *R: Gen 2:7–9 & 3:1–7; Ps 51; Rom 5:12 (13–16) 17–19* | | |
| | | | *Mt 4:1–11 (Christ The Second Adam)* | | |
| | | 2 EP | | Deut 6:4–9 & 16–25 | Gen 8:15 – 9:17 |
| | | | Ps: 50:1–15 | Lk 15:1–10 | Mk 14:1–26 |
| *MONDAY* | | | **Ss Cyril, Monk, and Methodius, B, Patrons of Europe** | | |
| **14** | W | MP | [Ps: 26, 32] | [Deut 8] | [Gen 42] |
| | | | | [Jn 3:1–21] | [Mt 26:1–30] |
| | | Mass | *of the Saints; Gl, no Cr; R: Pref of Patrons, CW of Saints (**S Valentine B & M**)* | | |
| | | | *Office Readings from Appendix 3, 'Missionaries'* | | |
| | | | *CW = R:: Acts 13:46–49; Ps 117; Lk 10–1–9* | | |
| | | | *[Lev 19:1 2 & 11–18; Ps 19:7–end; Mt 25:31–end]* | | |
| | | EP | | [I Sam 2:1–10] | [Gen 43] |
| | | | [Ps: 102] | [Mt 5:38–end] | [Phil 1] |
| *TUESDAY* | | | *Feria [S Sigfrid B ]* | | |
| **15** | P | MP | Ps: 56 | Deut 9:4–12 | Gen 44 |
| | | | | Jn 3:22–end | Mt 26:31–56 |
| | | Mass | *of the day; Pref of Lent (**Thomas Bray Pr**)* | | |
| | | | *Isa 55:10 & 11; Ps 34:4–6 & 21–22; Mt 6:7–15* | | |
| | | EP | | I Sam 3 – 4:1a | Gen 45:1–15 |
| | | | Ps: 38 | Mt 6:1–6 | Phil 2 |
| *WEDNESDAY* | | | *Feria (Ember Day)** | | |
| **16** | P | MP | Ps: 3, 6 | Deut 9:13–21 | Gen 45:16 – 46:7 |
| | | | | Jn 4:1–26 | Mk 26:57–end |
| | | Mass | *as Tuesday* | | |
| | | | *Jonah 3; Ps 51:1–5 & 17–18; Lk 11:29–32* | | |
| | | EP | | I Sam 9:15–10:1 & 6–8 | Gen 46:26 – 47:12 |
| | | | Ps: 90 | Mt 6:(7–15) 16–18 | Phil 3 |
| *THURSDAY* | | | *Feria [□ Seven Holy Founders of the Servite Order ]* | | |
| **17** | P | MP | Ps: 25 | Deut 9:23 – 10:5 | Gen 47:13–end |
| | | | | Jn 4:27–42 | Mt 27:1–26 |
| | | Mass | *as Tuesday (**Janani Luwum, B, M**)* | | |
| | | | *Esther 14:1–5 & 12–14; Ps 138; Mt 7:7–12* | | |
| | | EP | | I Sam 11:12 – 12:6 | Gen 48 |
| | | | Ps: 27 | Mt 6:19–24 | Phil 4 |
| *FRIDAY* | | | *Feria (Ember Day)** | | |
| **18** | P | MP | Ps: 39 | Deut 10:12–end | Gen 49:1–32 |
| | | | | Jn 4:43–end | Mt 27:27–56 |
| | | Mass | *as Tuesday* | | |
| | | | *Ezek 18:21–28; Ps 130; Mt 5:20–26* | | |
| | | EP | | I Sam 15:10–28 | Gen 49:33–50 end |
| | | | Ps: 69 | Mt 6:25–end | Col 1:1–20 |
| *SATURDAY* | | | *Feria (Ember Day)** | | |
| **19** | P | MP | Ps: 13, 124 | Deut 11:18–28 | Exod 1:1–14 & 22–2:10 |
| | | | | Jn 5:1–18 | Mt 27:574–28 end |
| | | Mass | *as Tuesday* | | |
| | | | *Deut 26:16–end; Ps 119:1–8; Mt 5:43–end* | | |
| | P | 1 EP of foll | | I Sam 16:1–13 | Exod 2:11–22 |
| | | | Ps: 31 | Mt 7:1–6 (7–12) | Col 1:21 – 2:7 |

* Ember Masses Introduction paragraph 25.

| Day | Col. | Office | | | |
|---|---|---|---|---|---|
| ✠ *SUNDAY* | | | **LENT 2** | | |
| **20** | P | MP | Ps: 74 | Jer 22:1–9<br>Mt 8:1–13 | Gen 18:1–16<br>Lk 15:11–end |
| R:Ps II | | Mass | *Cr; Pref of Lent*<br>*Gen 12:1–4a; Ps 121; Rom 4:1–5 & 13–17; Jn 3:1–17*<br>*R: Gen 12:1–4a; Ps 33; II Tim 1:8b–10; Mt 17:1–9 (The Transfiguration)* | | |
| | | 2 EP | Ps: 135 | Num 21:4–9<br>Lk 14:27–33 | Gen 11:1–9<br>Mk 14:27–52 |
| *MONDAY* | | | *Feria* [□ *S Peter Damian B Dr* ] | | |
| **21** | P | MP | Ps: 26, 32 | Jer 1<br>Jn 5:19–29 | Exod 2:23–3 end<br>Jn 1:1–28 |
| | | Mass | *of the day. Pref of Lent*<br>*Daniel 9:4–10; Ps 79:8–9 & 12 & 14; Lk 6:36–38* | | |
| | | EP | Ps: 102 | I Sam 17:1–16 & 25–50<br>Mt 7:13–20 | Exod 4:1–23<br>Col 2:8 – 3:11 |
| *TUESDAY* | | | □ **The Chair of S Peter Ap** | | |
| **22** | W | MP | [Ps: 56] | [Jer 2:1–13 (14–28)]<br>[Jn 5:30–end] | [Exod 4:27 – 6:1]<br>[Jn 1:29–end] |
| | | Mass | *the Festum. See Intro Appendix 1*<br>*[Isa 1:10 & 16–20; Ps 50:8 & 16–end; Mt 23:1–12]* | | |
| | | EP | [Ps: 38] | [I Sam 17:58 – 18:16]<br>[Mt 7:21–end] | [Exod 6:2–13 & 7:1–7]<br>[Col 3:12 – 4:1] |
| *WEDNESDAY* | | | *Feria* [*S Polycarp B M*] | | |
| **23** | P | MP | Ps: 3, 6 | Jer 3:6–22<br>Jn 7:1–13 | Exod 7:8–end<br>Jn 2 |
| | | Mass | *as Monday*<br>*Jer 18:18–20; Ps 31:4–5 & 14–18; Mt 20:17–28* | | |
| | | EP | Ps: 90 | I Sam 24<br>Mt 8:1–17 | Exod 8:1–19<br>Col 4:2–end |
| *THURSDAY* | | | *Feria* | | |
| **24** | P | MP | Ps: 25 | Jer 4:5–28<br>Jn 7:14–36 | Exod 8:20 – 9:12<br>Jn 3:1–21 |
| | | Mass | *as Monday*<br>*Jer 17:5–10; Ps 1; Lk 16:19–end* | | |
| | | EP | Ps: 27 | II Sam 1:1–16<br>Mt 8:18–27 | Exod 9:13–end<br>Philemon |
| *FRIDAY* | | | *Feria* | | |
| **25** | P | MP | Ps: 39 | Jer 5<br>Jn 7:37–52 | Exod 10:1–20<br>Jn 3:22–end |
| | | Mass | *as Monday*<br>*Gen 37:3–4 & 12–13 & 17–28; Ps 105:16–22; Mt 21:33–43 & 45–46* | | |
| | | EP | Ps: 69 | II Sam 1:17–end<br>Mt 8:28–end | Exod 10:21 – 11:end<br>Eph 1 |
| *SATURDAY* | | | *Feria* | | |
| **26** | P | MP | Ps: 13, 124 | Jer 6:(1–8) 9–19<br>Jn 7:53 – 8:11 | Exod 12:1–20<br>Jn 4:1–26 |
| | | Mass | *asa Monday*<br>*Micah 7:14–15 & 18–20; Ps 103:1–4 & 9–12; Lk 15:1–3 & 11–end* | | |
| | P | 1 EP of foll | Ps: 31 | II Sam 2:1–7<br>Mt 9:1–8 | Exod 12:21–36<br>Eph 2 |

## FEBRUARY

*R: CW Year A. Weekday Lectionaries Year 1*

| | | | | | |
|---|---|---|---|---|---|
| ✠ *SUNDAY* | | | **LENT 3** | | |
| **27** | P | MP | Ps: 46 | Amos 7:10–17 | Gen 18:17–end |
| | | | | II Cor 1:1–11 | Lk 18:1–14 |
| R:Ps III | | Mass | *Cr; Pref of Lent* | | |
| | | | *CW: Exod 17:1–7; Ps 95; Rom 5:1–11; Jn 4:5–42* | | |
| | | | *R: Exod 17:3–7; Ps 95; Rom 5:1–2 & 5–8; Jn 4:5–42 (see p. 15)* | | |
| | | | *(The Samaritan Woman: Living Water)* | | |
| | | 2 EP | | Josh 1:1–9 | Gen 24 |
| | | | Ps: 40 | Eph 6:10–20 | Mk 14:53–end |
| *MONDAY* | | | *Feria* | | |
| **28** | P | MP | Ps: 26, 32 | Jer 7:1–15 (16–20) | Exod 12:37–end |
| | | | | Jn 8:12–30 | Jn 4:27–end |
| | | Mass | *of the day. Pref of Lent (**Foundation of the SSC**)* | | |
| | | | *II Kings 5:1–15; Ps 42:1–2 and 43:1–4; Lk 4:24–30* | | |
| | | EP | | II Sam 5:1–5 | Exod 13:1–16 |
| | | | Ps: 102 | Mt 9:9–17 | Eph 3 |

## MARCH

| | | | | | |
|---|---|---|---|---|---|
| *TUESDAY* | | | **S David B (Festum, SOLEMNITY in Wales)** | | |
| **1** | W | MP | [Ps: 56] | [Jer 7:21 – 8:7] | [Exod 13:17 – 14:14] |
| | | | | [Jn 8:31–47] | [Jn 5:1–23] |
| | | Mass | *of the Saint; Gl; Cr in Wales only. Office Readings from Appendix 3* | | |
| | | | *[Song of the Three vv 2 & 11–20*; Ps 25:3–10; Mt 18:21–35]* | | |
| | | EP | | [II Sam 5:6–16] | [Exod 14:15–end] |
| | | | [Ps: 38] | [Mt 9:18–26] | [Eph 4:1–16] |
| *WEDNESDAY* | | | *Feria (Chad, see Oct 26)* | | |
| **2** | P | MP | Ps: 3, 6 | Jer 8:8 – 9:6 | Exod 15:1–26 |
| | | | | Jn 8:48–end | Jn 5:24–end |
| | | Mass | *as Monday* | | |
| | | | *Deut 4:1 & 5–9; Ps 147:13–end; Mt 5:17–19* | | |
| | | EP | | II Sam 6:1–9 | Exod 15:27 – 16:35 |
| | | | Ps: 90 | Mt 9:27–34 | Eph 4:17–30 |
| *THURSDAY* | | | *Feria* | | |
| **3** | P | MP | Ps: 25 | Jer 10:11–end | Exod 17 |
| | | | | Jn 9:1–17 | Jn 6:1–21 |
| | | Mass | *as Monday* | | |
| | | | *Jer 7:23–28; Ps 95:1–2 & 6–end; Lk 11:14–23* | | |
| | | EP | | II Sam 7:1–17 | Exod 18 |
| | | | Ps: 27 | Mt 9:35 – 10:4 | Eph 4:31 – 5:21 |
| *FRIDAY* | | | *Feria [□ S Casimir ]* | | |
| **4** | P | MP | Ps: 39 | Jer 11:1–20 | Exod 19 |
| | | | | Jn 9:18–end | Jn 6:22–40 |
| | | Mass | *as Monday* | | |
| | | | *Hos 14:2–10; Ps 81:6–10 & 13 & 16; Mk 12:28–34* | | |
| | | EP | | II Sam 7:18–end | Exod 20:1–21 |
| | | | Ps: 69 | Mt 10:5–15 | Eph 5:22 – 6:9 |
| *SATURDAY* | | | *Feria [S Piran, Patron, in Cornwall ]* | | |
| **5** | P | MP | Ps: 13, 124 | Jer 13:1–11 (12–17) | Exod 22:20 – 23:17 |
| | | | | Jn 10:1–21 | Jn 6:41–end |
| | | Mass | *as Monday* | | |
| | | | *Hos 5:15 – 6:6; Ps 51:1–2 & 17–end; Lk 18:9–14* | | |
| | †P | 1 EP of foll | | II Sam 9 | Exod 23:20–end |
| | | | Ps: 31 | Mt 10:16–23 | Eph 6:10–end |

* Apocryphal/Deuterocanonical Books, "Prayer of Azariah and Song of the three young men/Jews/Children". King James-based and Vulgate-based Bibles have different verse systems; we follow the former.

† Rose colour is sometimes used this evening and tomorrow; similarly, the organ and flowers. For Mothering Sunday, Introduction Appendix 1.

✠ *SUNDAY* **LENT 4**
**6** P MP Ps: 19 Isa 43:1–7 Exod 1:8–14 & 22–2:10
Eph 2:8–14 Lk 18:35 – 19:10
R:Ps IV Mass *Cr; Pref of Lent. MOTHERING SUNDAY p. xxvii*
*CW: I Sam 16:1–13; Ps 23; Eph 5:8–14; Jn 9:1–41*
*R: I Sam 16:1 & 6–7 & 10–13; Ps 23; Eph 5:8–14; Jn 9:1–41 (see page 15)*
*(The Man Blind from Birth: Enlightenment)*
2 EP Mic 7 Gen 24:29–end
Ps: 31:1–8(9–16) James 5 Mk 15:1–21

*MONDAY* *Feria [Ss Perpetua and Felicity Ms ]*
**7** P MP Ps: 26, 32 Jer 14 Exod 24
Jn 6:1–15 Jn 7:1–24
Mass *of the day. Pref of Lent**
*Isa 65:17–21; Ps 30:1–5 & 8 & 11–end; Jn 4:43–end*
EP II Sam 11:1–5 & 14–17 & 26–27 Exod 25:1–22
Ps: 102 Mt 10:24–33 I Tim 1:1–17

*TUESDAY* *Feria [□ S John of God Rel; S Felix B ]*
**8** P MP Ps: 56 Jer 16:10 – 17:4 Exod 28:1–4 & 29:1–9
Jn 6:16–27 Jn 7:25–end
Mass *as Monday (**Edward King B; Geoffrey Studdert Kennedy Pr**)*
*Ezek 47:1–9 & 12; Ps 46:1–8; Jn 5:1–3 & 5–16*
EP II Sam 12:1–8a & 13 Exod 29:38 – 30:16
Ps: 38 Mt 10:34–end I Tim 1:18–2 end

*WEDNESDAY* *Feria [□ S Frances of Rome Rel ]*
**9** P MP Ps: 3, 6 Jer 17:19 – 18:12 (19:1–6) Exod 32
Jn 6:27–40 Jn 8:1–30
Mass *as Monday*
*Isa 49:8–15; Ps 145.8–18; Jn 5:17–30*
EP II Sam 18:1–16 & 24–end Exod 33
Ps: 90 Mt 11:1–16 I Tim 3

*THURSDAY* *Feria* **[SCOTLAND: □ S John Ogilvie Pr M Festum]**
**10** P MP Ps: 25 Jer 22:13–23 Exod 34
Jn 6:41–51 Jn 8:31–end
Mass *as Monday*
*Exod 32:7–14; Ps 106:19–23; Jn 5:31–47*
EP II Sam 22:1–37 & 47–end Exod 35:20 – 36:7
Ps: 27 Mt 11:7–15 I Tim 4

*FRIDAY* *Feria*
**11** P MP Ps: 39 Jer 23:1–8 Exod 40:17–end
Jn 6:52–59 Jn 9
Mass *as Monday*
*Wisd 2:1 & 12–22; Ps 34:15–end; Jn 7:1–2 & 10 & 25–30*
EP II Sam 23:1–7 Lev 6:8–end
Ps: 69 Mt 11:16–24 I Tim 5

*SATURDAY* *Feria*
**12** P MP Ps: 13, 124 Jer 23:9–32 Lev 19:1–18 & 30–end
Jn 6:60–end Jn 10:1–21
Mass *as Monday*
*Jer 11:18–20; Ps 7:1–2 & 8–10; Jn 7:40–52*
†P 1 EP of foll II Sam 24:18–end Lev 25:1–24
Ps: 13, 130 Mt 11:25–end I Tim 6

* Anniversary of the Episcopal Ordination in 2002 of Keith, Second Bishop of Richborough.
† Before this EP, crosses, statues and pictures may be veiled in purple.

**MARCH** *R: CW Year A. Weekday Lectionaries Year 1*

| Day | | | | | |
|---|---|---|---|---|---|
| ✠ *SUNDAY* | | | **LENT 5*** | | |
| **13** P | | MP | Ps: 86 | Jer 31:27–37 | Exod 2:23 – 3:20 |
| | | | | Jn 12:20–33 | Mt 20:17–28 |
| R:Ps I | | Mass | *Cr; Pref of Lent (CW: Pref of Fifth Sunday onwards)* | | |
| | | | *CW: Ezek 37:1–14; Ps 130; Rom 8:6–11; Jn 11:1–45* | | |
| | | | *R: Ezek 37:12–14; Ps 130; Rom 8:8–11; Jn 11:1–45 (see p. 15) (Lazarus: New Life)* | | |
| | | 2 EP | | Lam 3:19–33 | Exod 4:27 – 6:1 |
| | | | Ps: 30 | Mt 20:17–34 | Mk 15:22–39 |
| *MONDAY* | | | *Feria* | | |
| **14** P | | MP | Ps: 73 | Jer 24 | Num 6 |
| | | | | Jn 10:22–end | Jn 10:22–end |
| | | Mass | *of the day; Pref I of Passion (CW: Pref of Fifth Sunday onwards)* | | |
| | | | *Susanna 1–9 & 15–17 & 19–30 & 33–62 [or 41–62]; Ps 23; Jn 8:1–11* | | |
| | | EP | | Amos 2:6–end | Num 9:15–end & 10:29–end |
| | | | Ps: 26, 27 | Mt 12:1–14 | Titus 1:1 – 2:8 |
| *TUESDAY* | | | *Feria* | | |
| **15** P | | MP | Ps: 20, 122 | Jer 25:(1–7) 8–18 | Num 11:10–23 |
| | | | | Jn 11:1–27 | Jn 11:1–44 |
| | | Mass | *as Monday* | | |
| | | | *Num 21:4–9; Ps 102:1–3 & 16–23; Jn 8:21–30* | | |
| | | EP | | Amos 3:1–8 | Num 12 |
| | | | Ps: 61, 64 | Mt 12:15–21 | Titus 2:9 – 3:end |
| *WEDNESDAY* | | | *Feria* | | |
| **16** P | | MP | Ps: 55 | Jer 25:30–end | Num 13:1–3 & 17–end |
| | | | | Jn 11:28–44 | Jn 11:45–end |
| | | Mass | *as Monday* | | |
| | | | *Dan 3:14–20 & 24–25 & 28; Song of the Three 29–34; Jn 8:31–42* | | |
| | | EP | | Amos 4:1–12 | Num 14:1–25 |
| | | | Ps: 56, 62 | Mt 12:22–37 | II Tim 1 |
| *THURSDAY* | | | **S Patrick B (Ireland: Solemnity)** | | |
| **17** W | | MP | [Ps: 40, 54] | [Jer 26:1–16 & (17–end)] | [Num 16:1–35] |
| | | | | [Jn 11:45–end] | [Jn 12:1–19] |
| | | Mass | *of the Saint; Gl; Cr only in Ireland; Pref of Saints ; Office Readings from Appendix 3* | | |
| | | | *[Gen 17:3–9; Ps 105:4–9; Jn 8:51–end]* | | |
| | | EP | | [Amos 5:18–end] | [Num 16:36–17 end] |
| | | | [Ps: 42, 43] | [Mt 12:38–end] | [Ii Tim 2] |
| *FRIDAY* | | | *Feria [S Cyril of Jerusalem B Dr]* | | |
| **18** P | | MP | Ps: 69 | Jer 29:1 & 4–14 | Num 20 |
| | | | | Jn 12:37–end | Jn 12:20–end |
| | | Mass | *as Monday (R: now provides an alternative Collect for our Lady of Sorrows)* | | |
| | | | *Jer 20:10–13; Ps 18:1–6; Jn 10:31–end* | | |
| | W | | **S JOSEPH, HUSBAND OF THE BVM** | | |
| | | 1 EP of foll | | Hos 11:1–9 | ◁ |
| | | | Ps: 132 | Lk 2:41–52 | ◁ |
| *SATURDAY* | | | | | |
| **19** W | | MP | Ps: 25, 147:1–12 | Isa 11:1–10 | ◁ |
| | | | | Mt 13:54–58 | ◁ |
| | | Mass | *Gl; Cr; R: Proper Pref; CW, of a Saint* | | |
| | | | *CW: II Sam 7:4–16; Ps 89:26–36; Rom 4:13–18; Mt 1:18–25* | | |
| | | | *R: II Sam 7:4–5a & 12–14a & 16; Ps 89; Rom 4:13 & 16–18 & 22; Mt 1:16 & 18–21 & 24a or Lk 2:41–51a* | | |
| | R | 1 EP of foll | | Nahum 1:1–8 & 15 | Num 23:27 – 24 end |
| | | | Ps: 13, 130 | Mt 13:10–17 | II Tim 4 |

* Confusion may arise from the fact that this Sunday is no longer called 'Passion Sunday' in the Roman Rite, which has transferred this title to next Sunday (Palm Sunday). But the Roman Office allows the use of the 'Passion' Hymns on the Weekdays of this Week: MP 95 or 96 (NEH 78 or 517); EP 94 (NEH 79). CW continues talk of 'Passiontide'.

## HOLY WEEK AND THE END OF LENT

Lent lasts until the Evening of Maundy Thursday. The Mass of the Last Supper until the EP of Easter Sunday inclusively constitutes the Easter Triduum, which is of even greater antiquity than the Season of Lent.

1 From Palm Sunday onwards, Solemnities are transferred to after Low Sunday; Festivals and Memorials are suppressed.

2 **The Chrism Mass** provides the Oils for use at Baptism and Confirmation at Easter and thereafter. It should take place towards the end of Lent at a time when priests and peoples can easily gather. (Oils in Initiation: see p. xxxiv.)

In some places, the Oils are subsequently 'received' into Parish Churches, and their purpose explained. Before the Mass of the Lord's Supper is a popular time for this, but undeniably complicates the occasion. Earlier in Holy Week, or at MP on Good Friday or Holy Saturday, may be convenient occasions.

3 **Confessions and Penitential Celebrations** for the whole Christian community (LHWE pp. 38 ff) should take place at the end of Lent, *before* the Easter Triduum, but not immediately before the Mass of the Lord's Supper.

4 **PALM SUNDAY** The colour of the day is red. Palms are held during the Palm gospel and procession, but not during the Passion gospel. The processional cross is carried unveiled. After the procession, when the celebrant arrives at the altar, he reverences (and censes) it. Then he goes to his chair and Mass begins with the collect of the day. Rome allows, for pastoral reasons, one or both of the readings before the Passion to be omitted.

The Passion gospel may be read by three deacons or by laymen. If possible, the priest should read the part of Christ. The Passion may be read by the deacon of the Mass, or if necessary by the celebrant. Neither lights nor incense are used. At the beginning the greeting and signing of the book are omitted. At the end the book is not kissed, nor the reply given. LHWE permits the omission of the Creed.

5 **MAUNDY THURSDAY** Before the Evening, holy water stoups are emptied, the Blessed Sacrament taken to a private place of reservation, and lamps extinguished. Those who have concelebrated or communicated with the Bishop in the morning may celebrate concelebrate or communicate again in the evening.

6 The practice of attenuating the Office during the Triduum, mentioned by LHWE (p. 90), was discontinued by Rome in 1971.

| Day | Col. | Service | | | |
|---|---|---|---|---|---|
| ✠ *SUNDAY* | | | **PALM SUNDAY OF THE LORD'S PASSION** | | |
| **20** | R | MP | H: 95 or 96 (NEH 78) | Zech 9:9–12 | Exodus 11 |
| | | | Ps: 61, 62 | Lk 16:19–31 | Mt 26 |
| R:Ps II | | Mass | *Cr; Pref Proper (CW: 'from the Fifth Sunday of Lent')* | | |
| | | | *Gospel for Palms Ceremony: Mt 21:1–11* | | |
| | | | *CW: Isa 50:4–9a; Ps 31:9–16; Phil 2:5–11; Mt 26:14 – 27:66 or 27:11–54* | | |
| | | | *R: Isa 50:4–7; Ps: 22; Phil 2:6-11; Mt 26:14 – 27:66 or 27:11–54* | | |
| | | EP | H: 94 (NEH 79) | Isa 5:1–7 | Isa 52:13–53 end |
| | | | Ps: 80 | Mt 21:33–46 | Lk 19:29–end |
| *MONDAY* | | | **MONDAY IN HOLY WEEK** | | |
| **21** | P | MP | H: 95 or 96 (NEH 78) | Lam 1:1–12a | ◁ |
| | | | Ps: 41 | Lk 22:1–23 | Jn 14:1–14 |
| | | Mass | *of the day; R: Pref of Passion II; CW, Pref of Fifth Sunday onwards* | | |
| | | | *CW: Isa 42:1–9; Ps 36:5–11; Heb 9:11–15; Jn 12:1–11* | | |
| | | | **ASB = R: = LHWE: Isa 42:1–7; Ps 27:1–3 & 16–17; Jn 12:1–11* | | |
| | | EP | H: 94 (NEH 79) | Lam 2.8–19 | Lam 2:8–19 |
| | | | Ps: 25 | Col 1:18–23 | Jn 14:15–end |
| *TUESDAY* | | | **TUESDAY IN HOLY WEEK** | | |
| **22** | P | MP | H: 95 or 96 (NEH 78) | Lam 3:1–18 | Lam 3:1–30 |
| | | | Ps: 27 | Lk 22:24–53 (or 39–53) | Jn 15:1–16 |
| | | Mass | *as Monday* | | |
| | | | *CW: Isa 49:1–7; Ps 71:1–8 (9–14); I Cor 1:18–31; Jn 12:30–36* | | |
| | | | **ASB = R: = LHWE: Isa 49:1–6; Ps 71:1–6 & 15–16; Jn 13:21–33 & 36–38* | | |
| | | EP | H: 94 (NEH 79) | Lam 3:40–51 | Lam 3:40–51 |
| | | | Ps: 55:13–24 | Gal 6:11–18 | Jn 15:17–end |
| *WEDNESDAY* | | | **WEDNESDAY IN HOLY WEEK** | | |
| **23** | P | MP | H: 95 or 96 (NEH 78) | Wisd 1:16 – 2:1 & 2:12–22 | Isa 42:1–9 |
| | | | Ps: 102 | Lk 22:54–end | Jn 16:1–15 |
| | | Mass | *as Monday* | | |
| | | | *CW: Isa 50:4–9a; Ps 70: Heb 12:1–3; Jn 13:21–32* | | |
| | | | **ASB = R: = LHWE: Isa 50:4–9a; Ps 69:7–9 & 32–35; Mt 26:14–25* | | |
| | | EP | H: 94 (NEH 79) | Isa 63:1–9 | Num 21:4–9 |
| | | | Ps: 88 | Rev 14:18–15:4 | Jn 16:16–end |
| *THURSDAY* | | | **THURSDAY IN HOLY WEEK (Morning)** | | |
| **24** | P | MP | H: 95 or 96 (NEH 78) | Lev 16:2–24 | Exod 24:1–11 |
| | | | Ps: 42, 43 | Lk 23:1–25 | Jn 17 |
| | P | EP | H: 331 (NEH 308) vv 2–4 | Exod 11 | Levit 16:2–24 |
| | | | Ps: 39 | Eph 2:11–18 | ◁ or Jn 13:1–35 |

* Readings at Mass: ASB = R: = LHWE: are the originally Roman propers authorised by ASB p. 1074 and repeated in LHWE, printed in the Weekday Missal.

## THE EASTER TRIDUUM

1 **THE EASTER FAST**, more ancient than Lent, should be observed both on Friday and Saturday, until the Vigil.

2 **R:** the following anthem is said before Benedictus and Magnificat from EP on Maundy Thursday to Holy Saturday: **Christ humbled himself for us, and, in obedience, accepted death**. Good Friday add **even death on a cross**.
Holy Saturday add **Therefore God raised him to the heights and gave him the name which is above all other names**.

3 **MAUNDY THURSDAY** For the evening Mass of the Lord's Supper, white vestments are worn, the altar is decorated as on feasts, and the cross is veiled in white. Bells may

be rung at *Gloria in excelsis* and then are silent until the Easter Vigil. The Washing of Feet may follow the Sermon. The Creed is omitted. The Institution Narrative begins *Who in this night when . . .* It is appropriate that authorised lay people take Communion to the sick or elderly at Communion time. Immediately after the post-communion prayer the procession to the altar of repose follows, where the watch takes place. John 13–17 may be read. After midnight, flowers and candles are removed; one lamp or two candles are to be left burning. After the procession altars are privately stripped and crosses removed (or covered with a purple veil).

If there will be no Good Friday Liturgy in the same church, the Blessed Sacrament is replaced in the Tabernacle and Mass ends in the ordinary way.

4 **GOOD FRIDAY** The colour for the day is red. Public MP is encouraged. For the Solemn Liturgy, which should begin about 3 pm but may for pastoral reasons take place between noon and 9 pm, the sacred ministers wear Mass vestments throughout. The altar should be completely bare at the start of the service. Afterwards, it is stripped again, the Cross and four candles being left upon it.

The Passion According To John, Chapters 18 & 19, is, according to ancient tradition (preserved in CW and the Roman Rite) read in its entirety at the Solemn Liturgy. CW, and BCP allow it to be divided: MP Jn 18; Liturgy Jn 19:1–37; EP Jn 19:38–end.

The priest may remove his chasuble and shoes to venerate the Cross; and *Stabat Mater* (EH 115, NEH 97) or another piece about our compassionate Mother is added to the texts which may accompany the Veneration.

5 **HOLY SATURDAY BEFORE THE VIGIL** The *Anglican* tradition has been for a Liturgy of the Word – 'Antecommunion' or 'Altar Prayers' – in purple stole (and cope); MP; and EP; the 'Principal Service' readings should be used at the main Office attended by the faithful. *Rome* recommends the Office of Readings, and Morning Prayer, with the participation of the people – or at least 'some celebration of the Word of God, or some suitable act of devotion'. Representations of Christ crucified or entombed or visiting Hell, or of our Lady of Sorrows, may be placed in Church for the veneration of the faithful.

EP must be said, and veiled statues and pictures unveiled, before the Vigil.

6 **THE EASTER VIGIL** is the 'Solemnity of Solemnities', and the people (even those who will be away from their home parishes on holiday) are urged to see it as the greatest observance of the Christian Year and the foretaste of the Everlasting Easter; and as the Celebration of the Resurrection Night rather than as a service that happens at the end of Holy Saturday. The dignity and festive character of the Vigil may be enhanced if smaller groups and parishes celebrate it together. Both Rome and LHWE are adamant that there *must still only be one Paschal Candle*; LHWE adds that 'if it is desired to take Easter Candles back to other churches, they may be lit from the first candle at the end of the service and carried in procession out of the building'.

The Vigil should begin after nightfall and end before daybreak; the bonfire should, if possible, be big enough for its flames truly to scatter the darkness of this Night; and the Paschal Candle should be large. The marking of the Candle is compulsory.

The service of Light and Fire should precede the Vigil readings from the OT: for the Christian tradition, the OT is not a period of darkness but a divine dispensation illuminated and elucidated by Christ our Light: 'only in the light of Resurrection can we comprehend the unfolding revelation of the prophecies that point to the Paschal Mystery'. The 'Light of Christ' is proclaimed at: church door; mid-church; sanctuary.

The sacred ministers wear white Mass vestments throughout. At *Gloria in excelsis* bells are rung (and statues and pictures unveiled). At the Gospel incense is carried, but not candles. Before he shows the *Lamb of God* the priest may briefly address any new communicants. After the Mass, the Blessed Sacrament is replaced in the aumbry or tabernacle. Priests who celebrate or concelebrate the Vigil Mass may celebrate or concelebrate the Mass of Easter Day. Those who receive Holy Communion at the Vigil Mass may communicate again at Mass on Easter Day. But they *have* already fulfiled their Easter duty.

*THE EASTER TRIDUUM*

THURSDAY **MAUNDY THURSDAY EVENING**

**24** W Mass *Gl; R: Pref of Eucharist; CW, Proper Pref*
*CW: Exod 12:1–4(5–10) 11–14; Ps 116:1 & 10–end;*
*I Cor 11:23–26; Jn 13:1–17 & 31b–35*
*R: Exod 12:1–8 & 11–14; Ps 116:12–13 & 15–16bc & 17–18; I Cor 11:23–26; Jn 13:1–15*

(✠) FRIDAY **GOOD FRIDAY, IN THE LORD'S PASSION**

**25** R MP H: 95 or 96 (NEH 78) Lam 5:15–22 Gen 22:1–18
Ps: 69 Heb 10:1–10 see note, or ◁

The Solemn Liturgy

*Readings (CW = R:): Isa 52:13 – 53:12; Ps 22 (R:31:2 & 6 & 12–13 & 15–17 & 25); Heb 4:14–16 & 5:7–9; Jn 18 & 19 (see note)*

EP H: 94 (NEW 79) Gen 22:1–18 Isa 50.4–10
Ps: 130, 143 Col 1:18–23 see note; or I Pet 2:11–end

SATURDAY **HOLY SATURDAY**

**26** P CW 'Principal Service': Job 14:1–14 or Lam 3:1–9 & 19–24; Ps 31:1–4 & 15–16; I Pet 4:1–8; Mt 27:57–66 or Jn 19:38–42
CW 'Second Service': Ps 142; Hos 6:1–6; Jn 2:18–22
CW 'Third Service': Ps 116; Job 19:21–27; I Jn 5:5–12
1922: MP: Zech 9:9–12 & Lk 23:50–end; EP: Job 19:21–27 & Jn 2:13–22
R: MP: Hos 5:15d – 6:2; Office of Readings Heb 4:1–13; EP I Pet 1:18–21
Byzantium: Liturgy: I Cor 5:6–9 & Gal 3:13–14; Mt 27:62–66

**26–27** W *EASTER TIME*
**EASTER NIGHT: THE EASTER VIGIL**

There should be at least three readings before the Epistle and Gospel. The account of the Crossing of the Red Sea (Exodus) must always be read. (CW and LHWE make suggestions additional to those listed).

| | **Roman Rite** | **CW (or LHWE)** |
|---|---|---|
| 1. | *Gen 1:1 – 2:2 | *Gen 1:1 – 2:4a |
| | (or 1:1 & 26–31a) | (or 1:1–5 & 26–end: LHWE) |
| | | *Gen 7:1–5 & 11–18 & 8:6–18 & 9:8–13 |
| 2. | *Gen 22:1–18 | *Gen 22:1–18 |
| | (or 22:1–2 & 9a & 10–13 & 15–18) | (or 22:1–2 & 9–13 & 15–18: LHWE) |
| 3. | *Exodus 14:15–15:1 | *Exodus 14:10–31 & 15:20–21 |
| | | (or Exodus 14:15 – 15:1a: LHWE) |
| 4. | Isa 54:5–14 | (Isa 54:5–14: LHWE) |
| 5. | *Isa 55:1–11 | *Isa 55:1–11 |
| 6. | *Baruch 3:9–15 & 32 – 4:4 | *Baruch 3:9–15 & 32 – 4:4 |
| 7. | Ezek 36:16–17a & 18–28 | Ezek 36:24–28 |
| | | *Ezek 37:1–14 |
| | Romans 6:3–11 | Romans 6:3–11 |
| | Mt 28:1–10 | Mt 28:1–10 |

For Reading 7, R: allows, where baptisms are happening, Isa 12:2–6.
[In Churches where the Vigil is not observed, the Principal Eucharist on Easter Sunday morning is the Great Easter Liturgy; it may start with the blessing of the Paschal Candle (LHWE).
It fittingly includes Baptisms and Confirmations or else the Renewal of Baptismal Vows (ASB pp. 276–7 paragraphs 94 and 96–100 or, e.g., CW 'Initiation' pp. 127–8) after the Gospel; if so, the Creed is omitted.]

* Readings from the ancient Roman Vigil.

| ✠ *SUNDAY* | | **EASTER DAY IN THE LORD'S RESURRECTION** | | |
|---|---|---|---|---|
| **27** W (or G) | MP | Ps: 114, 117 | Exod 14:10–18 & 26 – 15:2<br>Rev 15:2–4 | Exod 12:1–14<br>Rev 1:4–18 |
| R:Ps I | Mass | *Gl; (R: Seq compulsory: EH 130 NEH 519) Cr; R: Pref I of Easter; CW, Pref of Easter.*<br>*CW: Acts 10:34–43; Ps 118*:1–2 & 14–24; Col 3:1–4; Jn 20:1–18 (or Mt 28:1–10)*<br>*R: Acts 10:34a & 37–43; Ps 118*:1–2 & 16ab–17 & 22–23; Col 3:1–4 (or I Cor :6b–8); Jn 20:1–9 (or Mt 28:1–10 or, at an Evening Mass, Lk 24:13–35)*<br>*[OT readings: see Note 9 below. For those who particularly desire an OT reading, CW provides Isa 65:17–25]* | | |
| | EP | Ps: 105, 66:1–11 | Song of S 3:2–5 & 8:6–7<br>Rev 1:12–18 | Exod 14:5–end<br>Jn 20:(1–10)11–23 |

* Ps 118, last of the Passover Hallel psalms, quoted by the Lord and in the Easter Kerygma. Verses 24 & 1 are anciently associated with the readings at Rome and Byzantium.

## NOTES FOR EASTER WEEK ONLY

1 During the octave of Easter, that is, from Easter Day *until the evening of Low Sunday*, two alleluias are added to the dismissals at the end of Mass, and at the end of Morning and Evening Prayer, and to the response. Throughout Eastertide, Alleluia is added to all Antiphons or 'Sentences' which do not already have it.

2 In R: from Easter Sunday MP to the EP of Low Sunday, before Benedictus and Magnificat, this antiphon is used: **This is the day which was made by the Lord: let us rejoice and be glad. Alleluia.**

3 Preface: In CW, the '*short* preface' is the ancient Western Easter preface, which comes down to us via BCP. According to ancient custom, R: orders this preface, *and no other*, to be used until Low Sunday inclusive (*but not thereafter*). Your Compiler urges its exclusive use during the Octave instead of the CW 'extended Preface'.

## NOTES FOR ALL EASTERTIDE

4 A **SOLEMNITY** falling on a Sunday in Eastertide is transferred to the Monday. (CW allows Dedications and Patronal Festivals.) A **Festum** falling on a Sunday in Eastertide is omitted (Roman rules) or *may* be transferred to the first available weekday (CW).

5 **According to the provisions of *The Liturgy of the Hours*, the Office Hymns for Eastertide begin on Easter Day. EH: MP 123 EP 125 (122 may be used optionally at MP on Ferias after Easter Week).**
***NEH: Sundays: MP 100 EP 101; Ferias: MP 124 EP 101.***

6 Prefaces: the CW provision is very austere. After Low Sunday (see note 3 above) your Compiler urges the use also of ASB 14 = R:4, and of ASB 15 and/or R: prefaces 2,3, and 5. (Unlike CW, R: draws upon Prefaces in the ancient Western Sacramentaries.)

7 The Paschal Candle is lit at Mass and Evening Prayer on Easter Day and daily during the octave; and thereafter on Sundays and greater feasts until the evening of Pentecost. It may be lit at other liturgical services according to custom.

8 *Regina Coeli* is recited instead of *Angelus* until the evening of Pentecost.

9 R: and CW provide *all three* Sunday Eucharistic readings from the New Testament throughout Eastertide.

10 On weekdays from Low Sunday until Pentecost, propers at mass are taken *either* from the Daily Eucharistic Lectionary (Weekday Missal) which is R: = CW, *or* from the previous Sunday (Friday and Saturday after Ascension, from the Ascension).

11 During the Easter Season it is particularly suitable to use the Asperges (Sprinkling) for the Penitential Rite, to remind us of our Baptism (Introduction Paragraph 12). See Introduction Paragraph 17 for the Creed.

12 The 'Julian' (Eastern) Easter this year is on the May 1.

| Day | | | | | |
|---|---|---|---|---|---|
| *MONDAY* | | | **MONDAY IN EASTER WEEK** | | |
| **28** | W | MP | Ps: 2, 110, 149 | Jonah 2:1–9<br>I Cor 15:1–11 | Exod 15:1–18<br>Lk 24:1–12 |
| R:Ps I | | Mass | *of the day; Gl; (Seq ad lib) Pref (I) of Easter*<br>*Acts 2:14 & 22–32; Ps: 16:1–2 & 5–end; Mt 28:8–15* | | |
| | | EP | Ps: 3, 135 | Exod 12:14–27<br>Jn 14:1–14 | Isa 12<br>Rev 7:9–end |
| *TUESDAY* | | | **TUESDAY IN EASTER WEEK** | | |
| **29** | W | MP | Ps: 63, 146 | Isa 30:18–21<br>I Cor 15:12–28 | Isa 25:1–9<br>I Pet 1:1–12 |
| | | Mass | *as Monday*<br>*Acts 2:36–41; Ps: 33:4–5 & 17–end; Jn 20:11–18* | | |
| | | EP | Ps: 118 | Exod 12:28–39<br>Jn 14:15–31 | Isa 26:1–19<br>Mt 28:1–15 |
| *WEDNESDAY* | | | **WEDNESDAY IN EASTER WEEK** | | |
| **30** | W | MP | Ps: 57, 147:12–end | Mic 7:7–15<br>I Cor 15:30–41 | Isa 61<br>I Pet 1:13–end |
| | | Mass | *as Monday*<br>*Acts 3:1–10; Ps: 105:1–9; Lk 24:13–35* | | |
| | | EP | Ps: 113, 117 | Exod 12:40–51<br>Jn 15:1–11 | Song of Sol 2:8–end<br>Mt 28:16–end |
| *THURSDAY* | | | **THURSDAY IN EASTER WEEK** | | |
| **31** | W | MP | Ps: 30, 148 | Ezel 37:1–14<br>I Cor 15:41–50 | Job 14:1–15<br>I Thess 4:13–end |
| | | Mass | *as Monday*<br>*Acts 3:11–26; Ps: 8; Lk 24:35–48* | | |
| | | EP | Ps: 111, 116 | Exod 13:1–16<br>Jn 15:12–27 | Dan 12<br>Mk 16 |

**A P R I L**

| Day | | | | | |
|---|---|---|---|---|---|
| *FRIDAY* | | | **FRIDAY IN EASTER WEEK** | | |
| **1** | W | MP | Ps: 29, 147:1–12 | Dan 12:1–4 & 13<br>I Cor 15:51–58 | Zeph 3:14–end<br>Acts 7:16–31 |
| | | Mass | *as Monday*<br>*Acts 4:1–12; Ps: 118:1–4 & 22–26; Jn 21:1–14* | | |
| | | EP | Ps: 114, 115 | Exod 13:17 – 14:4<br>Jn 16:1–15 | II Kgs 4:8–37<br>Jn 21:1–14 |
| *SATURDAY* | | | **SATURDAY IN EASTER WEEK** | | |
| **2** | W | MP | Ps: 103, 150 | Isa 25:1–9<br>II Cor 4:16–5:10 | Jer 31:1–14<br>Acts 26:1–23 |
| | | Mass | *as Monday*<br>*Acts 4:13–21; Ps: 118:1–4 & 14–21; Mk 16:9–15* | | |
| | W | 1 EP of foll | Ps: 136 | Exod 14:5–22<br>Jn 16:16–33 | Micah 7:7–end<br>Jn 21:15–end |

Low Sunday increasingly attracts in Western Christendom the title 'Divine Mercy Sunday'. In an Hour of Mercy before the End Time, the believer, even if perplexed by doubt, is drawn by the Risen Lord to reach out with trusting Faith to His Sacred Heart, pierced source (for all Christians as well as for the Paschal neophytes) of the Waters of Regeneration and the Blood of Redemption. (Acts 17:30–31; Mt 28:17; Jn 20:27–8 & 19:34; cf the Gallican collect now used in R: for this Sunday, and the Byzantine Festival, around this time of *Zoodochos Pege*, which also visits themes of Healing Streams but has a greater Marian bias). The old English title 'Mother of Mercy,' beloved of S Richard of Chichester and so many other saintly Anglicans, seems particularly suitable.

| | | | | | |
|---|---|---|---|---|---|
| ✠ *SUNDAY* | | | **2nd SUNDAY and WEEK within EASTERTIDE (BCP EASTER 1)** | | |
| | | | **DIVINE MERCY SUNDAY** | | |
| **3** | W | MP | Ps: 81:1–10 | Exod 12:1–17 | Isa 51:1–16 |
| | | | | I Cor 5:6b–8 | Lk 24:13–35 |
| R:Ps II | | Mass | *Gl; Cr; R: Pref I of Easter* | | |
| | | | *CW: Acts 2:14a & 22–32; Ps 16; I Pet 1:3–9; Jn 20:19–31* | | |
| | | | *R: Acts 2:42–47; Ps 118:2–4 & 13–15 & 22–24; I Pet 1:3–9; Jn 20:19–31 (Our East erJoy)* | | |
| | | 2 EP | | Dan 6:(1–5) 6–23 | Exod 15:1–8 |
| | | | Ps: 30:1–5 | Mk 15:46 – 16:8 | Jn 20:24–end |
| *MONDAY* | | | **ANNUNCIATION OF THE LORD** (Transferred) | | |
| **4** | W | MP | H: 214 (NEH 181) | I Sam 2:1–10 (R: I Chron 17:1–15) | Isa 52:7–12 |
| | | | Ps: 111 & 113 | Rom 5:12–21 | Heb 2:5–end |
| | | Mass | *Gl; Cr; (Kneel for Incarnatus); R: and CW Proper Prefaces* | | |
| | | | *CW: Isa 7:10–14; Ps 40:5–11; Heb 10:4–10; Lk 1:26–38* | | |
| | | | *R: Isa 7:10–14 & 8:10; Ps 40; Heb 10:4–10; Lk 1:26–38* | | |
| | | EP | | Isa 52:1–12 | I Sam 2:1–10 |
| | | | Ps: 131, 146 | Heb 2:5–18 | Mt 1–18–23 |
| *TUESDAY* | | | *Feria (☐ S Vincent Ferrer Pr)* | | |
| **5** | W | MP | Ps: 135, 146 | Dan 2:1–16 | Deut 2:1–25 |
| | | | | Jn 17:12–19 | Acts 2:1–21 |
| | | Mass | *No Gl or Cr; Pref of Easter (or of the Saint)* | | |
| | | | *Acts 4:32–end; Ps 93; Jn 3:7–15* | | |
| | | EP | | Job 28:1–6 & 12–end | Deut 2:26–3:5 |
| | | | Ps: 105:23–end | I Cor 2 | Acts 2:22–end |
| *WEDNESDAY* | | | *Feria* | | |
| **6** | W | MP | Ps: 139, 147:13–end | Dan 2:17–30 | Deut 3:18–end |
| | | | | Jn 17:20–end | Acts 3:1–4:4 |
| | | Mass | *As Tuesday* | | |
| | | | *Acts 5:17–26; Ps 34:1–8; Jn 3:16–21* | | |
| | | EP | | Job 5:8–16 | Deut 4:1–24 |
| | | | Ps: 103 | I Cor 3 | Acts 4:5–31 |
| *THURSDAY* | | | *☐ S John Baptist de la Salle Pr* | | |
| **7** | W | MP | Ps: 33, 148 | Dan 2:31–end | Deut 4:25–40 |
| | | | | II Jn | Acts 4:32–5:11 |
| | | Mass | *of the Saint* | | |
| | | | *Acts 5:27–33; Ps 34:1 & 15–end; Jn 3:31–end* | | |
| | | EP | | Lam 3:40–56 | Deut 5:1–21 |
| | | | Ps: 136 | I Cor 4 | Acts 5:12– end |
| *FRIDAY* | | | *Feria* | | |
| **8** | W | MP | Ps: 30, 147:1–12 | Dan 3:1–18 | Deut 5:22–end |
| | | | | III Jn | Acts 6:1 – 7:16 |
| | | Mass | *as Tuesday* | | |
| | | | *Acts 5:34–42; Ps 27:1–5 & 16–17; Jn 6:1–15* | | |
| | | EP | | Exod 18:13–26 | Deut 6 |
| | | | Ps: 107:33–43 | I Cor 6:1–11 | Acts 7:17–34 |
| *SATURDAY* | | | *Feria* | | |
| **9** | W | MP | Ps: 118, 149 | Dan 3:1–23 (& Benedicte) & 24 – 4:3 | Deut 7:1–11 |
| | | | | Col 1:1–14 | Acts 7:35–8:4 |
| | | Mass | *as Tuesday (**Dietrich Bonhoeffer M**)* | | |
| | | | *Acts 6:1–7; Ps 33:1–5 & 18–19; Jn 6:16–21* | | |
| | W | 1 EP of foll | | Deut 4:32–40 | Deut 7:12–end |
| | | | Ps: 116 | I Cor 8 | Acts 8:4–25 |

|  | |  | | | |
|---|---|---|---|---|---|
| ✠ *SUNDAY* | | | **3rd SUNDAY and WEEK within EASTERTIDE (BCP EASTER 2)** | | |
| **10** | W | MP | Ps: 23 | Isa 40:1–11 | Exod 16:2–15 |
| | | | | I Pet 5:1–11 | I Cor 15:1–26 |
| R:Ps III | | Mass | *Gl; Cr; Pref of Easter* | | |
| | | | *CW: Acts 2:14a & 36–41; Ps 116:1–3 & 10–17; I Pet 1:17–23; Lk 24:13–35* | | |
| | | | *R: Acts 2:14 & 22–33; Ps 16:1–2a & 5 & 7–11; I Pet 1:17–21; Lk 24:13–35 (Christ With Us On the Road)* | | |
| | | 2 EP | | Hag 1:13 – 2:9 | Exod 24 |
| | | | Ps: 48 | I Cor 3:10–17 | Jn 21:1–14 |
| *MONDAY* | | | *Feria (☐ S Stanislas B M) (The Annotine Easter)* | | |
| **11** | W (or R) | MP | Ps: 81, 150 | Dan 4:4–27 | Deut 8 |
| | | | | Col 1:15–23 | Acts 8:26–end |
| | | Mass | *no Gl or Cr; Pref of Easter (or of the Saint) (**George Augustus Selwyn B**)* | | |
| | | | *Acts 6:8–end; Ps 119:17–24; Jn 6:22–29* | | |
| | | EP | | Jer 1:4–10 | Deut 9:1–10 |
| | | | Ps: 113, 115 | I Cor 9:1–2 & 19–end | Acts 9:1–31 |
| *TUESDAY* | | | *Feria* | | |
| **12** | W | MP | Ps: 135, 146 | Dan 4:28–37 | Deut 9:11–end |
| | | | | Col 1:24 – 2:7 | Acts 9:32–end |
| | | Mass | *as Monday* | | |
| | | | *Acts 7:51 – 8:1; Ps 31:1–5 & 16; Jn 6:30–35* | | |
| | | EP | | Eccles 5:1–7 | Deut 10 |
| | | | Ps: 105:1–22 | I Cor 10:14 – 11:1 | Acts 10:1–23 |
| *WEDNESDAY* | | | *Feria (☐ S Martin I Pp M)* | | |
| **13** | W (or R) | MP | Ps: 139, 147:13–end | Dan 5:1–12 | Deut 11:1–12 |
| | | | | Col 2:8–end | Acts 10:24–end |
| | | Mass | *as Monday (or of the Saint)* | | |
| | | | *Acts 8:1b–8; Ps 66:1–6; Jn 6:35–40* | | |
| | | 1 EP | | Exod 12:1–14 | Deut 11:13–end |
| | | | Ps: 103 | I Cor 11:17–end | Acts 11:1–18 |
| *THURSDAY* | | | *Feria* | | |
| **14** | W | MP | Ps: 33, 148 | Dan 5:13–end | Deut 12:1–14 |
| | | | | Col 3:1–11 | Acts 11:19–end |
| | | Mass | *as Monday* | | |
| | | | *Acts 8:26–end; Ps 66:7–8 & 14–end; Jn 6:44–51* | | |
| | | EP | | Jer 10:1–10 | Deut 15:1–18 |
| | | | Ps: 136 | I Cor 12:1–11 | Acts 12:1–24 |
| *FRIDAY* | | | *Feria* | | |
| **15** | W | MP | Ps: 30, 147:1–12 | Dan 6:1–15 | Deut 16:1–20 |
| | | | | Col 3:12 – 4:1 | Acts 12:25 – 13:12 |
| | | Mass | *as Monday* | | |
| | | | *Acts 9:1–20; Ps 117; Jn 6:52–59* | | |
| | | EP | | Isa 44:6–11 | Deut 17:8–end |
| | | | Ps: 107:1–32 | I Cor 12:12–end | Acts 13:13–43 |
| *SATURDAY* | | | *Feria* | | |
| **16** | W | MP | Ps: 118, 149 | Dan 6:16–28 | Deut 18:9–end |
| | | | | Col 4:2–end | Acts 13:44 – 14:7 |
| | | Mass | *as Monday (**Isabella Gilmore**)* | | |
| | | | *Acts 9:31–42; Ps 116:10–15; Jn 6:60–69* | | |
| | W | 1 EP of foll | | Prov 10:1–12 | Deut 19 |
| | | | Ps: 116 | I Cor 13 | Acts 14:8–end |

| Day | Colour | Office | Psalms / Propers | Reading | Alternative |
|---|---|---|---|---|---|
| ✠ *SUNDAY* | | | **4th SUNDAY and WEEK within EASTERTIDE (BCP EASTER 3)** | | |
| **17** | W | MP | Ps: 106:6–24 | Neh 9:6–15 | Exod 32:1–14 & 30–end |
| | | | | I Cor 10:1–13 | 1 Cor 15:35–end |
| R:Ps IV | | Mass | *Gl; Cr; Pref of Easter* | | |
| | | | *CW: Acts 2:42–47; Ps 23; I Pet 2:19–25; Jn 10:1–10* | | |
| | | | *R: Acts 2:14a & 36–41; Ps 23; I Pet 2:20–25; Jn 10:1–10 (The Good Shepherd)* | | |
| | | 2 EP | | Ezra 3:1–13 | Exod 33:7–end |
| | | | Ps: 29 | Eph 2:11–22 | Jn 21:15–end |
| *MONDAY* | | | *Feria* | | |
| **18** | W | MP | Ps: 81, 150 | Wis 1:1 – 2:5 | Deut 21:22 – 22:8 |
| | | | | Phil 1:1–11 | Acts 15:1–21 |
| | | Mass | *no Gl or Cr; Pref of Easter* | | |
| | | | *Acts 11:1–18; Ps 42:1–2 & 43:1–4; Jn 10:1–10 or 10:11–18* | | |
| | | EP | | Num 11:24–30 | Deut 24:5–end |
| | | | Ps: 113, 115 | I Cor 14:1–17 | Acts 15:22–35 |
| *TUESDAY* | | | *Feria (S Alphege B M)* | | |
| **19** | W (or R) | MP | Ps: 135, 146 | Wis 2:21 – 3:9 | Deut 26 |
| | | | | Phil 1:12–end | Acts 15:36 – 16:5 |
| | | Mass | *as Monday (or of the Saint)* | | |
| | | | *Acts 11:19–26; Ps 87; Jn 10:22–30* | | |
| | | EP | | Isa 28:9–16 | Deut 28:58–end |
| | | | Ps: 105:23–45 | I Cor 14:18–33a & 37–end | Acts 16:6–end |
| *WEDNESDAY* | | | *Feria* | | |
| **20** | W | MP | Ps: 139, 147:13–end | Wis 4:16 – 5:8 | Deut 29:10–end |
| | | | | Phil 2:1–13 | Acts 17:1–15 |
| | | Mass | *as Monday* | | |
| | | | *Acts 12:24 – 13:5; Ps 67; Jn 12:44–end* | | |
| | | EP | | Wis 3:1–9 | Deut 30 |
| | | | Ps: 103 | I Cor 15:1–11 | Acts 17:16–end |
| *THURSDAY* | | | *Feria (S Anselm B Dr)* | | |
| **21** | W | MP | Ps: 33, 148 | Wis 5:9–end | Deut 31:1–13 |
| | | | | Phil 2:14–end | Acts 18:1–23 |
| | | Mass | *as Monday (or of the Saint) (**Our Lady of Good Counsel**)* | | |
| | | | *Acts 13:13–25; Ps 89:1–2 & 20–26; Jn 13:16–20* | | |
| | | EP | | Baruch 3:9–15 & 3:32 – 4:4 | Deut 31:14–29 |
| | | | Ps: 136 | I Cor 15:12–28 | Acts 18:24 – 19:7 |
| *FRIDAY* | | | *Feria* | | |
| **22** | W | MP | Ps: 30, 147:1–12 | Wis 6:12–23 | Deut 31:30 – 32:14 |
| | | | | Phil 3:1 – 4:1 | Acts 19:8–20 |
| | | Mass | *as Monday* | | |
| | | | *Acts 13:26–33; Ps 2; Jn 14:1–6* | | |
| | | | **S GEORGE, M, PATRON OF ENGLAND*** | | |
| | R | 1 EP | H: 185 | Jer 15:15–21 | ◁ |
| | | | Ps: 111, 116 | Heb 11:32 – 22:2 | ◁ |
| *SATURDAY* | | | | | |
| **23** | R | MP | H: 180 | Isa 43:1–7 | ◁ |
| | | | Ps: 5, 146 | Jn 15:1–8 | ◁ |
| | | Mass | *Gl; Cr; Pref of Martyrs (or Patrons) (CW of Saints)* | | |
| | | | *CW: Rev 12:7–12; Ps: 126; II Tim 2:3–13; Jn 15:18–21* | | |
| | | | *R: Acts 13:44–end; Ps 98:1–5; Jn 14:7–14* | | |
| | W | 1 EP of foll | | Josh 1:1–9 | Deut 32:48–end & 34 |
| | | | Ps: 116 | I Cor 16 | Acts 20:17–end |

* Sol in England, F in Wales, optional elsewhere.

| Day | | | | | |
|---|---|---|---|---|---|
| ✠ *SUNDAY* | | | **5th SUNDAY and WEEK within EASTERTIDE (BCP EASTER 4)** | | |
| **24** | W | MP | Ps: 30 | Ezek 37:1–12 | Exod 34:1–10 |
| | | | | Jn 5:19–29 | I Pet 3:8–end |
| R:Ps I | | Mass | *Gl; Cr; Pref of Easter* | | |
| | | | *CW: Acts 7:55–60; Ps 31:1–5 & 15–16; I Pet 2:2–10; Jn 14:1–14* | | |
| | | | *R: Acts 6:1–7; Ps 33; I Pet 2:4–9; Jn 14:1–12 (Our Royal Priesthood)* | | |
| | | 2 EP | | Zech 4:1–10 | Exod 35:30 – 36:1 |
| | | | Ps: 147:1–11 | Rev 21:1–14 | Lk 16:19–end |
| *MONDAY* | | | **S Mark Ev** | | |
| **25** | R | MP | Ps: 37:23–41, 148 | Isa 62:6–10 or ▷ | Ecclus 51:13–end |
| | | | | Acts 12:25 – 13:13 (R: Eph 4:1–16) | Acts 15:35–end |
| | | Mass | *Gl; R: Pref of Apostles (II); CW, Pref of Saints* | | |
| | | | *CW: Acts 15:35–41; Ps 119:9–16; Eph 4:7–16; Mk 13:5–13* | | |
| | | | *R: I Pet 5:5–14; Ps 89; Mk 16:15–20* | | |
| | | EP | | Ezek 1:4–14 | Isa 62:6–10 |
| | | | Ps: 45 | II Tim 4:1–11 | II Tim 4:1–11 |
| *TUESDAY* | | | *Feria* | | |
| **26** | W | MP | Ps: 135, 146 | Wis 10 | Josh 3 |
| | | | | I Pet 2 | Acts 21:37 – 22:22 |
| | | Mass | *no Gl or Cr: Pref of Easter* | | |
| | | | *Acts 14:19–end; Ps 145:10–end; Jn 14:27–end* | | |
| | | EP | | Prov 15:23–33 | Josh 4:1 – 5:1 |
| | | | Ps: 105:1–22 | II Cor 1:13 – 2:4 | Acts 22:23 – 23:11 |
| *WEDNESDAY* | | | *Feria* | | |
| **27** | W | MP | Ps: 139, 147:13–end | Wis 13:1–19 | Josh 5:13 – 6:20 |
| | | | | I Pet 3 | Acts 23:12–end |
| | | Mass | *as Tuesday (**Christina Rosetti**)* | | |
| | | | *Acts 15:1–6; Ps 122:1–5; Jn 15:1–8* | | |
| | | EP | | Dan 9:3–10 | Josh 7 |
| | | | Ps: 103 | II Cor 2:5–end | Acts 24:1–23 |
| *THURSDAY* | | | *Feria (S Peter Chanel Pr M; □ S Louis Marie Grignion de Montfort Pr)* | | |
| **28** | W (or R) | MP | Ps: 33, 148 | Wis 14:27 – 15:3 | Josh 9:3–end |
| | | | | I Pet 4:1–11 | Acts 24:24 – 25:12 |
| | | Mass | *as Tuesday (or of the Saint)* | | |
| | | | *Acts 15:7–21; Ps 96:1–3 & 7–10; Jn 15:9–11* | | |
| | | EP | | Exod 34:29–end | Josh 10:1–15 |
| | | | Ps: 136 | II Cor 3 | Acts 25:13–end |
| *FRIDAY* | | | **S Catharine of Sienna V & Dr Patron of Europe** | | |
| **29** | W | MP | [Ps: 30, 147:1–12] | [Wis 16:15 – 17:1] | [Josh 21:43 – 22:8] |
| | | | | [I Pet 4:12–end] | [Acts 26] |
| | | Mass | Office: Appendix 3 | | |
| | | | *Gl; no Cr; Pref of Patrons or Saints* | | |
| | | | *CW: Prov 8:1 & 6–11; Ps 34:11–17; Mt 25:1–13* | | |
| | | | *R: I Jn 1:5 – 2:2; Ps 45:10–11 & 13–16; Mt 25:1–13* | | |
| | | | *[Acts 15:22–31; Ps 57:8–end; Jn 15:12–17]* | | |
| | | EP | | [Job 10:2–9] | [Josh 22:9–end] |
| | | | [Ps: 107:1–32] | [II Cor 4] | [Acts 27] |
| *SATURDAY* | | | *Feria (□ S Pius V Pp)* | | |
| **30** | W | MP | Ps: 118, 149 | Wis 19 | Josh 23 |
| | | | | I Pet 5 | Acts 28:1–15 |
| | | Mass | *as Tuesday (or of the Saint) (**Pandita Mary Ramabai**)* | | |
| | | | *CW: Isa 43:1–7 or Ecclus 2:10–17; Ps 87; II cor 4:5–12; Jn 12:20–26* | | |
| | | | *Acts 16:1–10; Ps 100; Jn 15:18–21* | | |
| | W | 1 EP of foll | | Wis 9:1–11 | Josh 24:1–28 |
| | | | Ps: 116 | II Cor 5:1–16 | Acts 28:16–end |

## THE MAY DEVOTION TO OUR LADY,

so long traditional, suits well the Paschal celebration of Humanity, restored and deified. In the words of the great Russian Orthodox lay theologian Vladimir Lossky, 'freed from the limitations of time, Mary can be the cause of that which is before her; can preside over that which comes after her. She obtains eternal benefits. It is through her that men and angels receive grace. No gift is received in the Church without the assistance of the Mother of God, who is herself the first-fruits of the glorified Church. Thus, having attained to the limits of becoming, she necessarily watches over the destinies of the Church and of the Universe.' One of the greatest of the Greek fathers, S. Gregory Palamas, wrote that the All-Holy Mother of God 'is herself alone the boundary of created and uncreated nature, and nobody could come to God except through her . . . she is the Treasury and President of the Wealth of the Godhead . . . she stewards and encompasses God's graces . . .'. PPL comments that the May Devotion 'highlights the earthly role played by the glorified Queen of Heaven, here and now, in the celebration of Baptism, Confirmation, and Eucharist.'

Many priests begin the May Devotion with a (Class 2 – see p. xxi) votive of Our Lady on the first free day. **May 3**, in ancient 'Celtic' Calendars, was her Conception (in Poland, Solemnity of our Lady Queen of Poland, and in Russia the Feast of her Icon in the great Pechersk Monastery, fountainhead of the cenobitic monastic life in that country): which may suggest texts from December 8 appropriately adapted with Paschal Alleluias. On the Friday in Easter Week Byzantium emphasises the role of the Mother of God in pouring Christ's healing streams upon us (Zoodochos Pege: originally the Dedication of the ancient Sanctuary of the Mother of God of the Living Fountain beside its miraculous stream at Constantinople; the panorthodox chapel in the shrine church at Walsingham has this dedication). Collection of Masses (Int P 26b ii) mass 31 visits this theme; this Collection has a special section of Easter Votives of Our Lady. As well as the Rosary (especially on Saturdays), the Akathist hymn to Our Lady of Victories seems appropriate (see p. xxvi).

The **Visitation of Our Lady** was deliberately moved in 1969 to associate it with May 31, the day long connected with the celebration of Our Lady as Mediatrix of All Graces, as an appropriate conclusion to the May devotion.

Rome moved **Ss Philip and James** from May 1 to May 3 to accommodate S Joseph the Craftsmen on the Workers' festival. (EAD allows either date.) But he never caught on, least of all in England, and after Vatican II was reduced from a Solemnity to an Optional Memorial.

May 1 **S Joseph the Workman** (Optional Memorial) MP and EP as on March 19
*Mass: Gen 1:26–2:3; or Col 3:14–15 & 17 & 23–24; Ps 90; Mt 13: 54–58*

For those who care about such details, the following solution is in accordance with the Roman General Rubrics: May 1: Votive Mass and Office of Ss P and J; May 3: Votives of our Lady (since it is certainly episcopally permitted in the C of E to treat May 3 as a free day).

## ASCENSION AND PENTECOST

1. Modern liturgical reforms recovered the primitive concept of the fifty days of Eastertide as a unitary festival, a Week of Weeks, 'the One Day', 'the Great Sunday'. That is why the Paschal candle burns from Easter Night until Pentecost Evening, when it is removed (and placed near the font). **However**, recent Roman directions allow the BCP-style Whitmonday: Mass and Office 'as yesterday'.
2. *Rogations*, instituted in Gaul around 475 'to repel calamities', became spring processions to ask that God 'give and preserve to our use the kindly fruits of the earth.' They are Class 2 votives (page xxi); CLC pp 231 and 115. We have Synodical encouragement for processing the relics of Saints on these days; and Monday has been episcopally designated (EXETER) Feast of the Translation of the Relics.
3. Rome now provides a *Vigil* mass for Ascension (as well as Pentecost), the Collect of which is used at 1 EP (God, whose Son this day ascended into the heavens as his Apostles stood by; grant us we beseech/beg thee/you, that, according to his promise, he may ever be with us upon earth and that we may be worthy to live with him in heaven.) The Tridentine = BCP = CW collect for Ascension *day* is now restored by R: as an option!
4. ***Prefaces from Ascension to Pentecost (exclusively) (including Sunday)***
CW: 'From the day after Ascension Day until the Day of Pentecost'. R: Either of the Ascension or of Easter [even on Memorials]. CW *Short* Preface *for Ascension* is traditional.
5. ***Weekday Masses after Pentecost Sunday***
According to R:, any 'green' Sunday Collect may be used, and CW (p. 406) offers Roman Sunday Collect 10 (= BCP Easter 5) in its Cranmerian translation. Mass readings come from the Week of the Year.
6. ***Weekday Masses after Trinity Sunday***
CW expects the Trinity collect to be used; Rome both provides a collect and allows optionally any Sunday collect to be used. Mass readings come from the Week of the Year.
7. ***Hymns from Ascension to Pentecost (exclusively) (including Sunday)***
**MP 141 (NEH 128) EP 154 (NEH 138)** [or, optionally, on Memorials, of the Saint].

### SS PHILIP AND JAMES: MAY 2 (CW) OR MAY 3 (R:)?

Neither R: or CW allow them on a Sunday in Easter.

**Ss Philip and James Aps**

| | | | | |
|---|---|---|---|---|
| R | MP | Ps: 139, 146 | Prov 4:10–18 | Isa 30:15–21 |
| | | | James 1:1–12 | Jn 6:1–14 |
| | Mass | *Gl; R: Pref of Apostles (II); CW, Pref of Saints* | | |
| | | *CW: Isa 30:15–21; Ps 119:1–8; Eph 1:3–10; Jn 14:1–14* | | |
| | | *R: I Cor 15:1–8; Ps 19; Jn 14:6–14* | | |
| | EP | | Job 23:1–12 | Job 23:1–12 |
| | | Ps: 149 | Jn 1:43–51 | Jn 1:43–end |

| MAY | R: (Including the R: Calendar for England) | Common Worship |
|---|---|---|
| 24 Tues | Aldhelm† | (The Wesleys†) |
| 25 Wed | Bede* | Bede† Aldhelm† |
| 26 | CORPUS CHRISTI* | CORPUS CHRISTI |
| 27 Fri | Augustine* | |

In EAD Aldhelm (25th) is a FESTUM in Salisbury; and Augustine is a FESTUM throughout the Apostolic District (he landed at Ebbsfleet).

* Compulsory. † Optional.

| | | | | | |
|---|---|---|---|---|---|
| ✠ *SUNDAY* | | | **6th SUNDAY and WEEK within EASTERTIDE (BCP EASTER 5)*** | | |
| **1** | W | MP | Ps: 73:21–28 | Job 14:1–2 & 7–15 & 19:23–27a | Deut 34 |
| | | | | I Thess 4:13–18 | Acts 13:26–43 |
| R:Ps II | | Mass | *Gl; Cr; Pref of Easter; May Devotion to Our Lady, p. 32* | | |
| | | | *CW: Acts 17:22–31; Ps 66:7–18; I Pet 3:13–22; Jn 14:15–21* | | |
| | | | *R: Acts 8:5–8 & 14–17; Ps 66; I Pet 3:15–18; Jn 14:15–21 (The Spirit of Truth)* | | |
| | | 2 EP | | Zech 8:1–13 | Deut 6 |
| | | | Ps: 87, 36:5–10 | Rev 21:22 – 22:5 | Lk 10:38 – 11:13 |
| *MONDAY* | | | *S Athanasius B Dr (Rogation Day)** | | |
| **2** | W | MP | Ps: 81, 150 | Deut 8:1–10 | Deut 7:6–13 |
| | | | | Gal 1:1–17 | Mt 6:5–18 |
| | | Mass | *Rogations: see p. 33.* | | |
| | | | *Acts 16:11–15; Ps 149:1–5; Jn 15:26 – 16:4 (NOT Rogation readings)* | | |
| | | EP | | Ezra 1:1–8 & 11 | Deut 8 |
| | | | Ps: 113, 115 | II Cor 5:17 – 6:2 | Mt 6:19–end |
| *TUESDAY* | | | *Feria (Rogation Day)** | | |
| **3** | W | MP | Ps: 135, 146 | Deut 8:11–end | Deut 11:8–121 |
| | | | | Gal 1:18 – 2:10 | Lk 5:1–11 |
| | | Mass | *of Sunday; no Gl or Cr; Pref of Easter* | | |
| | | | *Acts 16:22–34; Ps 138; Jn 16:5– 11 (NOT Rogation readings)* | | |
| | | EP | | Ezra 3:8–end | I Kgs 8:22–43 |
| | | | Ps: 105:23–end | II Cor 6:3 – 7:1 | Jas 5:1–18 |
| *WEDNESDAY* | | | *The English Martyrs (CW: 'Of the Reformation Era') (Rogation Day)* | | |
| **4** | R | MP | Ps: 139, 147:13–end | Baruch 3:24–37 | Joel 2:21–27 |
| | | | | Gal 2:11–21 | Jn 6:22–40 |
| | | Mass | *of the Saints* | | |
| | | | *CW: Isa 43:1–7 or Ecclus 2:10–17; Ps 87; II Cor 4:5–12; Jn 12:20–26* | | |
| | | | *Acts 17:15 & 22–18:1; Ps 148:1–2 & 11–end; Jn 16:12–15 (NOT Rogation readings)* | | |
| ✠ | | | **ASCENSION OF THE LORD** | | |
| | W | 1 EP of foll | | II Sam 23:1–5 | Song of the Three 29–37 |
| | | | Ps: 15, 24 | Col 2:20–3:4 | Mt 28:16–end |
| *THURSDAY* | | | | | |
| **5** | W | MP | H: 141 (NEH 128) | Isa 52:7–15 | II Kgs 2:1–15 |
| | | | Ps: 110 | Heb 7: (11–25) 26–end (R:Eph 4:1–24) | Jn 17 |
| | | Mass | *Gl; Cr; Pref of the Ascension* | | |
| | | | *CW: Acts 1:1–11; Ps 47; Eph 1:15–23; Lk 24:44–53* | | |
| | | | *R: Acts 1:1–11; Ps 47:2–3 & 6–9; Eph 1:17–23; Mt 28:16–20* | | |
| | | 2 EP | H: 144 (NEH 129) | Song of the Three 29–37 | II Sam 23:1–5 |
| | | | Ps: 8 | Rev 5 | Heb 1 |
| *FRIDAY* | | | *Feria (Hymns, Preface, see p. 33)* | | |
| **6** | W | MP | Ps: 139, 149 | Ezek 1:28 – 3:3 | Judg 2:6–end |
| | | | | Gal 3:1–14 | Heb 2 |
| | | Mass | *no Gl or Cr; Pref see p. 32 (First Friday; Sacred Heart: see p. 39)* | | |
| | | | *Acts 18:9–18; Ps 47:1–6; Jn 16:20–23* | | |
| | | EP | | Exod 35:30 – 36:1 | Judg 4 |
| | | | Ps: 84, 138 | Gal 5:13–26 | Heb 3 |
| *SATURDAY* | | | *Feria* | | |
| **7** | W | MP | Ps: 92, 148 | Ezek 3:4–end | Judg 5 |
| | | | | Gal 3:15–22 | Heb 4:1–13 |
| | | Mass | *as Friday (First Saturday; Sacred Heart: see p. 39)* | | |
| | | | *Acts 18:23–end; Ps 47:1–2 & 7–end; Jn 16:23–28* | | |
| | W | 1 EP of foll | | Num 11:16–17 & 14–29 | Judg 6:1–24 |
| | | | Ps: 93, 97, 98 | I Cor 2 | Heb 4:14 – 5:10 |

* Ss Philip and James; see p. 33.

| | | | | | |
|---|---|---|---|---|---|
| ✠ *SUNDAY* | | | **7th SUNDAY and WEEK within EASTERTIDE (AFTER ASCENSION)** | | |
| **8** | W | MP | H: see p. 33 | Isa 65:17–25 | Isa 65:17–end |
| | | | Ps: 104:26–35 | Rev 21:1–8 | Lk 24:36–end |
| R:Ps III | | Mass | *Gl; Cr; Pref see p. 33* | | |
| | | | *CW: Acts 1:6–14; Ps 68:1–10 & 32–35; I Pet 4:12–14 & 5:6–11; Jn 17:1–11* | | |
| | | | *R: Acts 1:12–14; Ps 27:1 & 4 & 7–8a; I Pet 4:13–14 & 16; Jn 17:1–11 (The Spirit of Prayer)* | | |
| | | 2 EP | | II Sam 23:1–5 | Jer 31:1–13 |
| | | | Ps: 47 | Eph 1:15–23 | Jn 14:1–14 |
| *MONDAY* | | | *Feria [Hymns, Prefaces, see p. 33]* | | |
| **9** | W | MP | Ps: 18:1–32, 117 | Ezek 4 | Ezek 11:14–20 |
| | | | | Gal 3:23 – 4:11 | Acts 2:12–36 |
| | | Mass | *No Gl or Cr* | | |
| | | | *Acts 19:1–8; Ps 68:1–6; Jn 16:29–end* | | |
| | | EP | | Num 27:15–23 | Wisd 1:1–7 |
| | | | Ps: 122, 125, 126 | I Cor 3 | Acts 2:37–end |
| *TUESDAY* | | | *Feria* | | |
| **10** | W | MP | Ps: 66, 149 | Ezek 7:10–end | Ezek 37:1–14 |
| | | | | Gal 4:12–20 | I Cor 12:1–13 |
| | | Mass | *As Monday* | | |
| | | | *Acts 20:17–27; Ps 68:9–10 & 18–19; Jn 17:1–11* | | |
| | | EP | | I Sam 10:1–10 | Wisd 7:15 – 8:1 |
| | | | Ps: 120, 121, 133 | I Cor 12:1–13 | I Cor 12:27–13 end |
| *WEDNESDAY* | | | *Feria* | | |
| **11** | W | MP | Ps: 29, 148 | Ezek 11:14–end | I Kgs 19:1–18 |
| | | | | Gal 4:21–end | I Cor 2 |
| | | Mass | *As Monday* | | |
| | | | *Acts 20:28–end; Ps 68:27–28 & 32–end; Jn 17:11–19* | | |
| | | EP | | I Kgs 18:1–18 | Wisd 9 |
| | | | Ps: 123, 127, 128, 131 | Mt 3:13–end | I Cor 3 |
| *THURSDAY* | | | *Feria (☐ Ss Nereus & Achilleus Ms; ☐ S Pancras M)* | | |
| **12** | W (or R) | MP | Ps: 144, 146 | Ezek 18:1–4 & 19–end | II Sam 23:1–5 |
| | | | | Gal 5:1–15 | Eph 6:10–20 |
| | | Mass | *as Monday (or of the Saints)* | | |
| | | | *Acts 22:30 & 23:6–11; Ps 16:1 & 5–end; Jn 17:20–end* | | |
| | | EP | | Ezek 11:14–20 | Exod 35:30 – 36:1 |
| | | | Ps: 124, 129, 130 | Mt 9:35 – 10:20 | Gal 5:13–end |
| *FRIDAY* | | | *Feria (☐ Our Lady of Fatima)** | | |
| **13** | W | MP | Ps: 46, 76, 147:13–end | Ezek 34:17–end | Num 11:16–17 & 24–29 |
| | | | | Gal 5:16–end | II Cor 5:14 – 6:10 |
| | | Mass | *as Monday (or of Our Lady: Is 61:9–11; Ps 45:11–17; Lk 11:27–28)* | | |
| | | | *[Acts 25:13–21; Ps 103:1–2 & 11–12 & 19–20; Jn 21:15–19]* | | |
| | | EP | | Ezek 36:22–28 | Jer 31:31–34 |
| | | | Ps: 132, 134 | Mt 12:22–32 | II Cor 3 |
| *SATURDAY* | | | **S Matthias, Apostle** | | |
| **14** | R | MP | Ps: 16, 147:1–12 | I Sam 16:1–13a | Isa 22:15–22 |
| | | | | Mt 7:15–27 | Mt 7:15–27 |
| | | Mass | *Gl; R: Pref of Apostles (II); CW, Pref of Saints* | | |
| | | | *CW: Acts 1:15–26; Ps 15; I Cor 4:1–7; Jn 15:9–17* | | |
| | | | *R: Acts 1:15–17 & 20–26; Ps 113; Jn 15:9–17* | | |
| | R | 1 EP of Pentecost. | H: 154 (NEH 138) | Deut 16:9–15 | Gen 11:1–9 |
| | | | Ps: 48 | Jn 15:26 – 16:15 | Acts 18:24 – 19:7 |
| | | | *R: Vigil Mass: Gen 11:1–9 (or Exod 19:3–8a & 16–20b; or Ezek 37:1–14; or Joel 3:1–5)* | | |
| | | | *Ps: 104; Rom 8:22–27; Jn 7:37–39. The Vigil Collect is used at 1 EP.* | | |

* May 13, anciently *S. Maria ad Martyres*, is our Lady of Fatima. This devotion is particularly associated with the Biblical themes of the Immaculate Heart (p. 39). In recent years the prayer *sub tuum praesidium*, now identified on a Third Century papyrus, has increasingly been associated with our Lady of Fatima.

|  | |  | | | |
|---|---|---|---|---|---|
| ✠ *SUNDAY* | | | **PENTECOST** | | **(Whitsunday)** |
| **15** | R | MP | H: 151 (NEH 136) | Gen 11:1–9 | Joel 2:28–end |
| | | | Ps: 87 | Acts 10:34–48 | Rom 8:1–17 |
| | | Mass | *Gl; (R: Seq ad lib: EH 155 NEH 520) Cr; R: Proper Pref; CW, see From the Day after Ascension* | | |
| | | | *CW: Acts 2:1–21; Ps 104:26–36 & 37b; I Cor 12:3b–13; Jn 20:19–23* | | |
| | | | *R: Acts 2:1–11; Ps 104:1 & 24 & 29–31 & 34; I Cor 12:3b–7 & 12–13; Jn 20:19–23* | | |
| | | 2 EP | H: 154 (NEH 138) | Joel 2:21–32 | Isa 11:1–9 |
| | | | Ps: 67, 133 | Acts 2:14–21 (22–38) | Rom 8:18–end |
| | | | **'ORDINARY TIME' – 'PER ANNUM' – 'THE GREEN SEASON' – RESUMES** | | **7th WEEK OF YEAR** |
| *MONDAY* | | | *Feria* | | |
| **16** | G | MP | Ps: 119:1–16 | Ruth 1:1–18 | Judg 6:25–end |
| | | | | I Tim 1:1–17 | Heb 5:11–6 end |
| R:Ps III | | Mass | *no Gl or Cr; Common Pref (**Caroline Chisholm**) see p. 33* | | |
| | | | *Ecclus 1:1–10; Ps 93; Mk 9:14–29* | | |
| | | EP | | Prov 22:1–16 | Judg 7 |
| | | | Ps: 119:17–32 | James 1:16–25 | Heb 7 |
| *TUESDAY* | | | *Feria* | | |
| **17** | G | MP | Ps: 119:33–48 | Ruth 1:19 – 2:13 | Judg 10:17–11:28 |
| | | | | I Tim 1:18 – 2:8 | Heb 8 |
| | | Mass | *as Monday* | | |
| | | | *Ecclus 2:1–11; Ps 37:3–6 & 27–28; Mk 9:30–37* | | |
| | | EP | | Prov 30:1–9 | Judg 11:29–12:7 |
| | | | Ps: 119:49–64 | James 2:1–13 | Heb 9:1–14 |
| *WEDNESDAY* | | | *Feria (☐ S John I Pp M)* | | |
| **18** | G (or R) | MP | Ps: 119:65–80 | Ruth 2:14–end | Judg 13 |
| | | | | I Tim 3 | Heb 9:15–end |
| | | Mass | *as Monday (or of the Saint)* | | |
| | | | *Ecclus 4:11–19; Ps 119:161–168; Mk 9:38–40* | | |
| | | EP | | Eccles 1:1–11 | Judg 14 |
| | | | Ps: 119:81–96 | James 2:14–24 | Heb 10:1–18 |
| *THURSDAY* | | | *Feria (S Dunstan B)* | | |
| **19** | G (or W) | MP | Ps: 119:97–12 | Ruth 3 | Judg 16:4–end |
| | | | | I Tim 4 | Heb 10:19–end |
| | | Mass | *as Monday (or of the Saint) (**Mary Mediatrix of Grace [30]; or Mother of Fairest Love [36]**)* | | |
| | | | *Ecclus 5:1–8; Ps 1; Mk 9:41–end* | | |
| | | EP | | Eccles 2:1–11 | Ruth 1 |
| | | | Ps: 119:113–128 | James 4:1–12 | Heb 11 |
| *FRIDAY* | | | *Feria (☐ S Bernardine of Sienna Pr)* | | |
| **20** | G (or W) | MP | Ps: 119:129–144 | Ruth 4:1–17 | Ruth 2 |
| | | | | I Tim 5:(1–16) & 17–end | Heb 12:1–13 |
| | | Mass | *as Monday (or of the Saint) (**Alcuin Dcn**)* | | |
| | | | *Ecclus 6:5–17; Ps 119:19–24; Mk 10:1–12* | | |
| | | EP | | Eccles 2:12–17 | Ruth 3 |
| | | | Ps: 119:145–160 | James 5:1–12 | Heb 12:14–end |
| *SATURDAY* | | | *Our Lady on Saturday or the Feria (☐ Ss Christopher Magallanes Pr Comp Ms; S Helena)* | | |
| **21** | W (or G or R) | MP | Ps: 119:161–end | Deut 1:1–8 | Ruth 4:1–17 |
| | | | | I Tim 6 | Heb 13 |
| | | Mass | *(Intro para 26(b))* | | |
| | | | *Ecclus 17:1–15; Ps 103:13–18; Mk 10:13–16* | | |
| | W | 1 EP of Trinity Sun; | | Exod 34:1–10 | Isa 61 |
| | | | Ps: 97, 98 | Mk 1:1–13 | II Tim 1:3–14 |

1. **CORPUS CHRISTI** is now officially known in the Roman Church as The Body and Blood of Christ, and, where it is not regarded as a Day of Obligation, is to be observed on the following Sunday. (See Introduction Para 5C4.) CW says that 'the Thursday after Trinity Sunday may be observed as a day of Thanksgiving for the Holy Communion (sometimes known as Corpus Christi), and may be kept as a festival'; readings were authorised by CW. The CW **short** preface for Maundy Thursday is suitable. R: Preface of the Eucharist.

   The Collect given in CW interferes less with S Thomas Aquinas' original than does its R: (ICEL) rendering.

   The traditional procession, in which the priest carries the vessel containing the Blessed Sacrament, follows the post-communion collect of the Eucharist and concludes with EH 326 (NEH 268) (or at least part 2); and the Corpus Christi collect (or another suitable hymn and collect); and the priest blessing the congregation with the Sacrament in Its vessel (saying nothing) before replacing It in the aumbry or tabernacle.

2. **BENEDICTION PROCESSIONS AND EXPOSITION OF THE BLESSED SACRAMENT** are services clearly lawful under Canon B.5.2 if 'the minister having the cure of souls' considers them 'suitable' and uses, or 'permits another minister, to use' them. (The requirement of Canon B.5.3 that such services shall be 'neither contrary to, nor indicative of any departure from, the doctrine of the Church of England in any *essential* matter' need create no anxiety since ARCIC 1979 endorsed by Lambeth 1988 held that 'differences of practice' in this area can 'coexist with real consensus on the *essentials*'. A form is offered in Celebrating Common Prayer commended by the Archbishop of Canterbury.) If a reading and the Our Father are incorporated, Benediction etc come within the umbrella of CW pp 21–24 A Service Of The Word.

   The *Assistant Curates Society* publishes a small, cheap *Rite of Eucharistic Exposition and Benediction* giving many alternatives for these most flexible of services. The traditional '**V** Thou gavest/You gave them Bread from Heaven **R** Containing in itself all sweetness' no longer appears in Roman texts but (Elliot) 'is still widely used.'

   An Anglican variant called 'Devotions' (Exposition and prayers, but no physical act of Blessing) is now authorised by Rome for *laypeople* to perform; but is unsuitable if a priest is available. 'In the full rite of Benediction the blessing of the people with the Sacred Host as the climax of the service reminds them inescapably of the fact that, in our relation with God, it is He, and not we, who is the primary agent and who takes the initiative' (Eric Mascall).

| JUNE/JULY | R: Calendar including the R: Calendar for England | Common Worship |
|---|---|---|
| June 20 | Alban† | |
| June 22 | John and Thomas FESTUM | Alban† |
| July 6 | Mary Goretti† | John and Thomas† |

† Optional.

## S THOMAS APOSTLE

S Thomas, only a Festum, disappears according to Roman rules, unless he is a Patron, when he displaces the Sunday. CW: Sunday, Monday, or a convenient weekday. We print him here, leaving him a local decision

| | | **S Thomas, Apostle** | | |
|---|---|---|---|---|
| R | MP | Ps: 92, 146 | II Sam 15:17–21 or Ecclus 2 | II Sam 15:17–21 |
| | | | Jn 11:1–16 | Jn 11:1–16 |
| | Mass | *Gl; R: Pref of the Apostles; CW, of the Saint* | | |
| | | *CW: Hab 2:1–4; Ps 31:1–6; Eph 2:19–22; Jn 20:24–29* | | |
| | | *R: Eph 2:19–22; Ps 117; Jn 20:24–29* | | |
| | EP | | Job 42:1–6 | Gen 12:1–5a |
| | | Ps: 139 | I Pet 1:3–12 | I Pet 1:3–9 |

|  | |  |  | | |
|---|---|---|---|---|---|
| ✠ *SUNDAY* | | | **TRINITY SUNDAY** | | |
| **22** | W | MP | Ps: 86:8–13 | Exod 3:1–6 & 13–15 | Isa 6:1–8 |
| | | | | Jn 17:1–11 | Mk 1:1–13 |
| R:Ps IV | | Mass | *Gl; Cr; Pref of the Trinity* | | |
| | | | *CW: Isa 40:12–17 & 27–31; Ps 8; II Cor 13:11–13; Mt 28:16–20* | | |
| | | | *R: Exod 34:4–6 & 8–9; Song of Three 29–34; II Cor 13:11–13; Jn 3:16–18* | | |
| | | 2 EP | H: 159 | Isa 6:1–8 | Isa 40:12–end |
| | | | Ps: 93, 150 | Jn 16:5–15 | I Pet 1:3–12 |
| *MONDAY* | | | *Feria* | | **8th WEEK of YEAR** |
| **23** | G | MP | Ps: 1, 2 | Deut 4:1–14 | I Sam 1 |
| | | | | II Tim 1:1–14 | Jas 1 |
| | | Mass | *no Gl or Cr; Common Pref* | | |
| | | | *Ecclus 17:24–29; Ps 32:1–8; Mk 10:17–27* | | |
| | | EP | | Eccles 3:1–15 | I Sam 2:1–21 |
| | | | Ps: 3 [4] | I Jn 1 | Mk 1:14–31 |
| *TUESDAY* | | | *Feria (S Aldhelm see p. 33)* | | |
| **24** | G (or W) | MP | Ps: 5 | Deut 4:15–24 | I Sam 2:22–end |
| | | | | II Tim 1:15 – 2:13 | Jas 2:1–13 |
| | | Mass | *as Monday (**John and Charles Wesley Prs**)* | | |
| | | | *(**Our Lady Help of Christians [42]**)* | | |
| | | | *Ecclus 35:1–12; Ps 50:1–6; Mk 10:28–31* | | |
| | | EP | | Song of Solomon 1:12 – 2:7 | I Sam 3 |
| | | | Ps: 6 | I Jn 2:1–11 | Mk 1:32–end |
| *WEDNESDAY* | | | *S Bede the Venerable Pr (see p. 33)* | | |
| **25** | W | MP | Ps: 7 | Deut 4:25–31 | I Sam 4 |
| | | | | II Tim 2:14–end | Jas 2:14–end |
| | | Mass | *of the Saint* | | |
| | | | *Ecclus 36:1 & 4–5 & 10–17; Ps 79:8–9 & 12 & 14; Mk 10:32–45* | | |
| ✠ | | | **CORPUS CHRISTI** | | |
| | W | 1 EP of foll | H:326 (NEH 268) | Exod 16:2–15 | Exod 16:2–15 |
| | | | Ps: 110, 111 | Jn 6:22–35 | Jn 6:22–35 |
| *THURSDAY* | | | | | |
| **26** | W | MP | H: 330 (NEH 269) | Deut 8:2–16 | Exod 24:1–11 (=R:) |
| | | | Ps: 147 | I Cor 10:1–17 | Mk 14:12–25 |
| | | Mass | *Gl; Seq ad lib (EH 317 NEH 521); Cr; Pref: see p. 36* | | |
| | | | *CW: Gen 14:18–20; Ps 116:10–17; I Cor 11:23–26; Jn 6:51–58* | | |
| | | | *R: Deut 8:2–3 & 14b–16a; Ps 147; I Cor 10:16–17; Jn 6:51–8* | | |
| | | 2 EP | H:326 (NEH 268) | Prov 9:1–5 | Prov 9:1–5 |
| | | | Ps: 23, 42, 43 | Lk 9:11–17 | I Cor 10:1–17 |
| *FRIDAY* | | | *S Augustine B (EAD Festum) (see p. 33)* | | |
| **27** | W | MP | [Ps: 13, 14] | [Deut 5:1–22] | [I Sam 9:26 – 10:16] |
| | | | | [II Tim 4:1–18] | [Jas 4] |
| | | Mass | *of the Saint* | | |
| | | | *[Ecclus 4:1 & 9–13; Ps 149:1–5; Mk 11:11–26]* | | |
| | | EP | | [Song of Solomon 5:4 – 6:3] | [I Sam 10:17–end] |
| | | | [Ps: 15, 16] | [I Jn 5:1–5 & 10–12] | [Mk 3:13–end] |
| *SATURDAY* | | | *Our Lady on Saturday or the Feria* | | |
| **28** | W (or G) | MP | Ps: 19 | Deut 5:22–30 | I Sam 11 |
| | | | | II Tim 4:9–end | Jas 5 |
| | | Mass | *see Intro Para 26(b) (**Lanfranc B**)* | | |
| | | | *Ecclus 51:12b–20a; Ps 19:7–end; Mk 11:27–end* | | |
| | G | 1 EP of foll | | Song of Solomon 8:5–7 | I Sam 12 |
| | | | Ps: 17 | Philemon | Mk 4:1–34 |

**SACRED HEART.** One of the most popular English devotions before 1559 and one of the most commonly used votive masses was the Five Wounds. This devotion to the Suffering Humanity of our loving Saviour received a broader Biblical and doctrinal form in the Western Church as the Sacred Heart of Jesus came to be celebrated on the second Friday after Trinity Sunday. (It is also common to say a public Class 2 votive of the Sacred Heart [as long as there is no solemnity or festum] on the first Friday of each month, except during Lent. White vestments.) (EAD: the Solemnity 'may be celebrated on the nearest Sunday': see Introd Para 5D. But this year the Apostles occupy next Sunday.)

EAD follows the Tridentine custom of allowing Mass and Office of the Sacred Heart on Trinity 2.

In Biblical language, the Heart (Leb) indicates the centre of human life, the point where reason, will, temperament and sensitivity converge, where the person finds his unity and his interior orientation. It is because the loving Heart of Jesus the consubstantial Word is intimately at one with His Father that He feels our transgressions as a wound.

The following lectionary provision, to supplement CW, draws upon Roman materials. Other hymns: see especially NEH 89; EH 71 & 413 (=NEH 63 & 382); AMR 211.

| THE SACRED HEART of JESUS | *Mass: Gl; Cr; Proper Pref. WHITE.* YEAR A (2005) | YEAR B (2006) | YEAR C (2007) |
|---|---|---|---|
| 1 EP (Thursday) | H: 419 pt 1 (NEH 385) Ps: 113; 146 | ◁ | ◁ |
| | Hos 11:1–9 | Ezek 34:11–16 | Deut 7:6–11 |
| | Lk 15:3–7 | Jn 7:37–39 | Mt 11:25–30 |
| MP (Friday) | H: 419 pt 2 (NEH 386) Ps: 36; 61 | ◁ | ◁ |
| | Jer 31:1–11 & 31–4 | ◁ | ◁ |
| | Rom 8:28–end (=R:) | ◁ | ◁ |
| Mass | Deut 7:6–11 | Hos 11:1 & 3–4 & 8c–9 | Ezek 34:11–16 |
| | Ps 103:1–2 & 3–4 & 6–7 & 8 & 10 | Ps Isa 12:2–3 & 4bcd & 5–6 | Ps 22:1–3a & 3b–4 & 5–6 |
| | I Jn 4:7–16 | Eph 3:8–12 & 14–19 | Rom 5:5b–11 |
| | Mt 11:25–30 | Jn 19:31–37 | Lk 15:3–7 |
| 2 EP (Friday) | H: 419 pt 3 (NEH 385) Ps: 110; 111 | ◁ | ◁ |
| | Ezek 34:11–16 | Deut 7:6–11 | Hos 11:1–9 |
| | Rom 5:5b–11 | Jn 20:26–29 | Eph 3:8–19 |

**The Immaculate Heart of Mary** is kept on the Saturday after the Sacred Heart. Mary kept and pondered in her heart all the great deeds of God. According to Mt 5:8, the Immaculate Heart is a heart which, with God's grace, has come to a perfect interior unity and therefore sees God. Because her Immaculate (Ps 119: 80: *Tamin, amomos*: perfectly fitted to be a sacrifice to the Lord) Heart is attuned to Him (Luke 1:49, 2:19, 2:51) and to the needs of others (John 2:3), even before the Hour of the Lord's Glory (John 2:4) the intercession of her heart mediates through shared obedience (John 2:5) the first Sign of the fullness of His Kingdom (John 2:11). To be 'devoted' to the Immaculate Heart of Mary means to make Saying Yes to God – may His will be done – the defining centre of one's whole life, that the Kingdom may come.

There is a custom of saying a public Class 2 votive of the Immaculate Heart of Mary [as long as there is no solemnity or festum] on the first Saturday of each month, except during Lent (and MP may be a votive of the observance). The Fatima visionaries believed that our Lady called for communions of reparation on first Saturdays.

CW (p.307, Presentation, Extended Preface) is suitable.

The Roman Collection of Masses (Int Para 26b ii) gives variety for the celebration (Mass 26).

**THE IMMACULATE HEART OF MARY** *Mass: no Gl or Cr; Pref of our Lady*
*Mass readings: Isa 61:9–11; Ps I Sam 2:1 & 4–8; Lk 2:41–51*
*MP readings of the feria. EP of the Apostles.*

✠ *SUNDAY* **29** G — R:Ps I

**9th SUNDAY and WEEK of YEAR** — **TRINITY 1**

| | | | | |
|---|---|---|---|---|
| MP | Ps: 37:1–18 | Deut 5:1–21 | Josh 1:1–9 |
| | | Acts 21:17–39a | Mk 1:21–34 |
| Mass | *Gl; Cr; Sunday Pref [PROPER 4]* | | |
| | *CW: Deut 11:18–21 & 26–28; Ps 31:1–5 & 19–24;* | | |
| | *Rom 1:16–17 & 3:22b–28 (29–31); Mt 7:21–29* | | |
| | *R: Deut 11:18 & 26–28; Ps 31; Rom 3:21–25 & 28; Mt 7:21–27 (Keep My Words)* | | |
| 2 EP | | Ruth 2:1–20a | Hos 6:1–6 |
| | Ps: 33 | Lk 8:4–15 | Acts 1:1–14 |

*MONDAY* **30** G (or W)

*Feria (S Joan of Arc)*

| | | | |
|---|---|---|---|
| MP | Ps: 22 | Deut 11:1–21 | I Sam 13 |
| | | Acts 1:1–14 | I Pet 1:1–21 |
| Mass | *of Sunday; no Gl or Cr; Common Pref (**Josephine Butler; Apolo Kivebulaya Pr**)* | | |
| | *Tobit 1:1–2 & 2:1–8; Ps 15; Mk 12:1–12* | | |
| EP | | II Kgs 1:1–8 | I Sam 14:1–23 |
| | Ps: 23 [24] | Lk 3:1–6 | Mk 4:35–5:20 |

*TUESDAY* **31** W

**Visitation of the BVM**

| | | | |
|---|---|---|---|
| MP | H: 229 | I Sam 2:1–10 [R: Song of S 2:8–14 & 8:6–7] | ◁ |
| | Ps: 85, 150 | Mk 3:31–35 | ◁ |
| Mass | *of the Festival; Gl; R: Pref of the BVM; CW , of the Annunciation; or ASB 6* | | |
| | *CW: Zeph 3:14–18; Ps 113; Rom 12:9–16; Lk 1:39–49 (50–56)* | | |
| | *R: Zeph 3:14–18 or Rom 12:9–16b; Ps = Isa 12:2–6; Lk 1:39–56* | | |
| EP | | Zech 2:10–13 | ◁ |
| | Ps: 122, 127, 128 | Jn 3:25–30 | ◁ |

**JUNE**

*WEDNESDAY* **1** R

*S Justin M*

| | | | |
|---|---|---|---|
| MP | Ps: 28, 29 | Deut 13:1–11 | I Sam 16 |
| | | Acts 2:1–21 | I Pet 2:11–3:7 |
| Mass | *of the Saint* | | |
| | *Tobit 3:1–11 & 16–end; Ps 25:1–7; Mk 12:18–27* | | |
| EP | | Deut 8:1–10 | I Sam 17:1–30 |
| | Ps: 30 | Lk 4:1–13 | Mk 6:1–29 |

*THURSDAY* **2** G (or R)

*Feria (□ Ss Marcellinus and Peter Ms)*

| | | | |
|---|---|---|---|
| MP | Ps: 31 (1–6) 7–end | Deut 17:14–end | I Sam 17:31–54 |
| | | Acts 2:22–36 | I Pet 3:8–4:6 |
| Mass | *as Monday (or of the Saints)* | | |
| | *Tobit 6:10–11 & 7:1–15 & 8:4–8; Ps 128; Mk 12:28–34* | | |

**HEARTS OF JESUS AND MARY:** **see p. 39**.

If they are not observed, the following ***FERIAL*** *readings are used.*

| | | | |
|---|---|---|---|
| EP | | Isa 64 | I Sam 17:55–18:16 |
| | Ps: 32 | Lk 4:14–30 | Mk 6:30–end |

*FRIDAY* **3**

*(The Ugandan Martyrs)*

| | | | |
|---|---|---|---|
| MP | Ps: 33 | Deut 26:1–11 | I Sam 19 |
| | | Acts 2:37–end | I Pet 4:7–end |
| Mass | | | |
| | *Tobit 11:5–15; Ps 146; Mk 12:35–37* | | |
| EP | | Num 6:22–end | I Sam 20:1–17 |
| | Ps: 34 | Lk 4:31–end | Mk 7:1–23 |

*SATURDAY* **4**

*(S Petroc, Patron of Cornwall)*

| | | | |
|---|---|---|---|
| MP | Ps: 35 | Deut 29:1–15 | I Sam 20:18–end |
| | | Acts 3:1–11 | I Pet 5 |
| Mass | | | |
| | *Tobit 12:1 & 5–15 & 20a; Ps 103:1 & 8–13; Mk 12:38–end* | | |
| G — 1 EP of foll | | Isa 6:1–8 | I Sam 21:1–22:5 |
| | Ps: 36 | Lk 5:1–11 | Mk 7:24–8:10 |

| Day | Colour | Office | Psalms / Mass | Readings | |
|---|---|---|---|---|---|
| ✠ *SUNDAY* | | | **10th SUNDAY and WEEK of YEAR*** | | **TRINITY 2** |
| **5** | G | MP | Ps: 38 | Deut 6:10–25 | Josh 2 |
| | | | | Acts 22:22 – 23:11 | Mk 2:23 – 3:19 |
| R:Ps II | | Mass | *Gl; Cr; Sunday. [PROPER 5]* | | |
| | | | *CW: Hos 5:15 – 6:6; Ps 50:7–15; Rom 4:13–25; Mt 9:9–13 & 18–26* | | |
| | | | *R: Hos 6:3–6; Ps 50:7–15; Rom 4:18–25; Mt 9:9–13* | | |
| | | | *(The Lord Demands Love And Mercy, Not Sacrifice)* | | |
| | | 2 EP | | I Sam 18:1–16 | Hos 11:1–9a |
| | | | Ps: 39, 41 | Lk 8:41–56 | Acts 2:1–21 |
| *MONDAY* | | | *Feria (□ S Norbert B)* | | |
| **6** | G (or W) | MP | Ps: 37:1–22 | Deut 29:1 & 16–end | I Sam 22:6–end |
| | | | | Acts 3:12–end | II Pet 1 |
| | | Mass | *of Sunday; no Gl or Cr; Common Pref (**Ini Kopuria Rel**)* | | |
| | | | *II Cor 1:1–7; Ps 34:1–8; Mt 5:1–12* | | |
| | | EP | | II Kgs 5:1–14 | I Sam 23 |
| | | | Ps: 37:23–end | Lk 5:12–26 | Mk 8:11 – 9:1 |
| *TUESDAY* | | | *Feria* | | |
| **7** | G | MP | Ps: 38 | Deut 30 | I Sam 24 |
| | | | | Acts 4:1–12 | II Pet 2 |
| | | Mass | *as Monday* | | |
| | | | *II Cor 1:18–22; Ps 119:129–136; Mt 5:13–16* | | |
| | | EP | | Hos 14:1–7 | I Sam 25:2–42 |
| | | | Ps: 39 | Lk 5:27–end | Mk 9:2–29 |
| *WEDNESDAY* | | | *Feria* | | |
| **8** | G | MP | Ps: 40 | Deut 31:30 – 32:14 | I Sam 26 |
| | | | | Acts 4:13–31 | II Pet 3 |
| | | Mass | *as Monday (**Thomas Ken B**)* | | |
| | | | *II Cor 3:4–11; Ps 78:1–4; Mt 5:17–19* | | |
| | | 1 EP | | I Sam 21:1–6 | I Sam 28:3–end |
| | | | Ps: 41 | Lk 6:1–11 | Mk 9:30–end |
| *THURSDAY* | | | *Feria (S Columba Ab; IRELAND FESTUM; S Ephraem Dcn Dr)* | | |
| **9** | G (or W) | MP | Ps: 42, 43 | Ecclus 44:19 – 45:5 | I Sam 31 |
| | | | | Acts 4:32–5:11 | Jude |
| | | Mass | *as Monday (or of the Saint)* | | |
| | | | *II Cor 3:15 – 4:1 & 3–6; Ps 78:36–40; Mt 5:20–26* | | |
| | | EP | | Exod 24:3–11 | II Sam 1 |
| | | | Ps: 44 | Lk 6:12–19 | Mk 10:1–31 |
| *FRIDAY* | | | *Feria* | | |
| **10** | G | MP | Ps: 45 | Ecclus 45:6–16 | II Sam 2:1 – 3:1 |
| | | | | Acts 5:12–26 | I Jn 1:1 – 2:6 |
| | | Mass | *as Wednesday* | | |
| | | | *II Cor 4:7–15; Ps 99; Mt 5:27–32* | | |
| | | EP | | Isa 30:15–21 | II Sam 3:17–end |
| | | | Ps: 46, 47 | Lk 6:20–26 | Mk 10:32–end |
| *SATURDAY* | | | **S Barnabas Apt†** | | |
| **11** | R | MP | Ps: 100, 101, 117 | Tobit 4:5–11 | ◁ |
| | | | | Acts 9:26–31 | ◁ |
| | | Mass | *Gl; R: Pref of Apostles, CW, of Saints* | | |
| | | | *CW: Job 29:11–16; Ps 112; Acts 11:19–30; Jn 15:12–17* | | |
| | | | *R: Acts 11:21–26 & 13:1–3; Ps 98; Mt 10:7–13* | | |
| | G | 1 EP of foll | | Deut 10:12 – 11:1 | II Sam 6 |
| | | | Ps: 49 | Lk 6:27–38 | Mk 11:1–26 |

* S Boniface B M Solemnity in Cornwall, Devon, Dorset.
† In R: and EAD, only a Memorial (no Gloria)

| Day | | | | | |
|---|---|---|---|---|---|
| ✠ *SUNDAY* | | | **11th SUNDAY and WEEK of YEAR** | | **TRINITY 3** |
| **12** | G | MP | Ps: 45 | Deut 10:12–11:1 | Josh 3 |
| | | | | Acts 23:12–35 | Mk 3:20–end |
| R:Ps III | | Mass | *Gl; Cr; Sunday Pref [PROPER 6]* | | |
| | | | *CW: Exod 19:2–8a; Ps 100; Rom 5:1–8; Mt 9:35 – 10:8 (9–23)* | | |
| | | | *R: Exod 19:2–6a; Ps 100; Rom 5:6–11; Mt 9:36 – 10:8 (The Lord's Call)* | | |
| | | 2 EP | | I Sam 21:1–15 | Hos 14 |
| | | | Ps: 42, 43 | Lk 11:14–28 | Acts 2:22–42 (43–end) |
| *MONDAY* | | | □ *S Antony of Padua Pr Dr* | | |
| **13** | W | MP | Ps: 50 | I Sam 1:1–20 | II Sam 7 |
| | | | | Acts 6 | I Jn 3:1–12 |
| | | Mass | *of the Saint* | | |
| | | | *II Cor 6:1–10; Ps 98; Mt 5:38–42* | | |
| | | EP | | Haba 2:1–4 | II Sam 9 |
| | | | Ps: 51 | Lk 6:39–end | Mk 11:27 – 12:12 |
| *TUESDAY* | | | *Feria* | | |
| **14** | G | MP | Ps: 52, 53 | I Sam 1:21 – 2:11 | II Sam 11 |
| | | | | Acts 7:1–16 | I Jn 3:13 – 4:6 |
| | | Mass | *of Sunday; no Gl or Cr; Common Pref (**Richard Baxter**)* | | |
| | | | *II Cor 8:1–9; Ps 146; Mt 5:43–end* | | |
| | | EP | | Job 29:11–16 | II Sam 12:1–23 |
| | | | Ps: 54, 55 | Lk 7:1–17 | Mk 12:13–34 |
| *WEDNESDAY* | | | *Feria* | | |
| **15** | G | MP | Ps: 56 | I Sam 2:12–26 | II Sam 13:38 – 14:24 |
| | | | | Acts 7:17–29 | I Jn 4:7–end |
| | | Mass | *as Tuesday (**Evelyn Underhill**)* | | |
| | | | *II Cor 9:6–11; Ps 112; Mt 6:1–6 & 16–18* | | |
| | | EP | | Deut 34 | II Sam 14:25 – 15:12 |
| | | | Ps:57 | Lk 7:18–35 | Mk 12:35 – 13:13 |
| *THURSDAY* | | | *Feria (S Richard B*)* | | |
| **16** | G (or W) | MP | Ps: [58] 59 | I Sam 2:27–end | II Sam 15:13–end |
| | | | | Acts 7:30–43 | I Jn 5 |
| | | Mass | *as Tuesday (or of the Saint) (**Joseph Butler B**)* | | |
| | | | *II Cor 11:1–11; Ps 111; Mt 6:7–15* | | |
| | | EP | | Isa 65:17–end | II Sam 16:1–19 |
| | | | Ps: 60 | Lk 7:36–50 | Mk 13:14–end |
| *FRIDAY* | | | *Feria* | | |
| **17** | G | MP | Ps: 61 | I Sam 3:1 – 4:1a | II Sam 17:1–23 |
| | | | | Acts 7:44 – 8:1a | II Jn |
| | | Mass | *as Tuesday (**Samuel and Henrietta Barnett**)* | | |
| | | | *II Cor 11:18 & 21a–30; Ps 34:1–6; Mt 6:19–23* | | |
| | | EP | | Deut 8:11–end | II Sam 17:24 – 18:18 |
| | | | Ps: 62 | Lk 8:1–15 | Mk 14:1–26 |
| *SATURDAY* | | | *Our Lady on Saturday or the Feria* | | |
| **18** | W (or G) | MP | Ps: [63] 64 | I Sam 4:1b–end | II Sam 18:19–end |
| | | | | Acts 8:1b–13 | III Jn |
| | | Mass | *Introduction Paragraph 26(b); (**Bernard Mizeki M**)* | | |
| | | | *II Cor 12:1–10; Ps 89:20–33; Mt 6:24–end* | | |
| | G | 1 EP of foll | | II Sam 12:1–10 | II Sam 19:1–23 |
| | | | Ps: 65 | Lk 8:16–25 | Mk 14:27–52 |

* **S RICHARD, B, SOLEMNITY, COPRINCIPAL PATRON** in the Diocese of Chichester.

| Day | | | | | |
|---|---|---|---|---|---|
| ✠ *SUNDAY* | | **12th SUNDAY and WEEK of YEAR** | | | **TRINITY 4** |
| **19** G | MP | Ps: 49 | Deut 11:1–15 | | Josh 5:13 – 6:20 |
| | | | Acts 27:1–12 | | Mk 4:21–end |
| R:Ps IV | Mass | *Gl; Cr; Sunday Pref [PROPER 7]* | | | |
| | | *CW: Jer 20:7–13; Ps 69:8–11 (12–17) 18–20; Rom 6:1b–11; Mt 10:24–39* | | | |
| | | *R: Jer 20:10–13; Ps 69:7–10 & 16–18; Rom 5:12–15;* | | | |
| | | *Mt 10:26–33 (He protects us from our attackers)* | | | |
| | 2 EP | | I Sam 24:1–17 | | Joel 2:1–14) |
| | | Ps: 46, 48 | Lk 14:12–24 | | Acts 3:1–16 (17–end) |
| *MONDAY* | | *(see p. 37)* | | | |
| **20** | MP | Ps: 66 | I Sam 5 | | 2 Sam 19:24–end |
| | | | Acts 8:14–25 | | Rom 1 |
| | Mass | *of Sunday; no Gl; no Cr; Common Pref* | | | |
| | | *Gen 12:1–9; Ps 33:12–end; Mt 7:1–5* | | | |
| | EP | | Dan 4:28–end | | 2 Sam 23:1–17 |
| | | Ps: [67], 68 | Lk 8:26–39 | | Mk 14:53–end |
| *TUESDAY* | | ☐ *S Aloisius Gonzaga Rel* | | | |
| **21** W | MP | Ps: 69 | I Sam 6:1–16 | | II Sam 24 |
| | | | Acts 8:26–end | | Rom 2:1–16 |
| | Mass | *of the Saint* | | | |
| | | *Gen 13:2 & 5–end; Ps 15; Mt 7:6 & 12–14* | | | |
| | EP | | I Kgs 17:17–end | | I Kgs 1:5–31 |
| | | Ps: 70, 71 | Lk 8:40–end | | Mk 15:1–41 |
| *WEDNESDAY* | | *Feria (Ember Day)* (see p. 37)* | | | |
| **22** | MP | Ps: 72 | I Sam 7:2–17 | | I Kgs 1:32–end |
| | | | Acts 9:1–9 | | Rom 2:17–end |
| | Mass | | | | |
| | | *Gen 15:1–12 & 17–18; Ps 105:1–9; Mt 7:15–20* | | | |
| | EP | | Isa 55:1–11 | | I Chron 22:2–end |
| | | Ps: 73 | Lk 9:1–17 | | Mk 15:42–16 end |
| *THURSDAY* | | *Feria (S Etheldreda Ab)* | | | |
| **23** G (or W) | MP | Ps: 74 | I Sam 8 | | I Chron 28:1–10 |
| | | | Acts 9:10–19a | | Rom 3 |
| | Mass | *as Monday (or of the Saint)* | | | |
| | | *Gen 16:1–12 & 15–16; Ps 106:1–5; Mt 7:21–end* | | | |
| W | | **BIRTH OF S JOHN BAPTIST** | | | |
| | | *R: Vigil Mass: Jer 1:4–10; Ps 71; I Pet 1:8–12; Lk 1:5–17 (Vigil Collect; GL; Cr)* | | | |
| | 1 EP | H: 223 (NEH 168) | Judg 13:2–7 & 24–25 | | Mal 3:1–6 |
| | | Ps: 71 | Lk 1:5–25 (Vigil Collect) | | Lk 3:1–20 |
| *FRIDAY* | | | | | |
| **24** | MP | H: 224 | Mal 3:1–6 or Ecclus 48:1–10 | | Judg 13:1–7 |
| | | Ps: 50, 149 | Lk 3:1–17 | | Lk 1:5–25 |
| W | Mass | *Gl; Cr; R: Proper Pref; CW, of Saints* | | | |
| | | *CW: Isa 40:1–11; Ps 85:7–13; Acts 13:14b–26; Lk 1:57–66 & 80* | | | |
| | | *R: Isa 49:1–6; Ps 138; Acts 13:22–26; Lk 1:57–66 & 80* | | | |
| | 2 EP | H: 223 (NEH 168) | Mal 4 (R: Jer 1:4–10 & 17–19) | | Mal 4 |
| | | Ps: 80, 82 | Mt 11:2–19 | | Mt 11:2–19 |
| *SATURDAY* | | *Our Lady on Saturday or the Feria or Ember** | | | |
| **25** W (or G) | MP | Ps: 78:21–55 | I Sam 9:15 – 10:1 | | I Kgs 4:21–end |
| | | | Acts 9:32–end | | Rom 5 |
| | Mass | *Introduction Paragraph 26(b)* | | | |
| | | *Gen 18:1–15; Canticle: Lk 1:46b–55; Mt 8:5–17* | | | |
| | EP | | Ecclus 5:1–13 | | I Kgs 5 |
| | | Ps: 78:56–end | Lk 9:37–50 | | Lk 1:57–end |

* For Ember Masses see Introduction para 25.

# JUNE

R: CW Year A. Weekday Lectionaries Year 1

| | | | | | |
|---|---|---|---|---|---|
| ✠ *SUNDAY* | | | **13th SUNDAY and WEEK of YEAR** | | **TRINITY 5** |
| **26** | G | MP | Ps: 52, 53 | Deut 15:1–11 | Josh 24:1–5 & 13–25 |
| | | | | Acts 27:(13–32) 33–44 | Mk 6:7–32 |
| R:Ps I | | Mass | *Gl; Cr; Sunday Pref [PROPER 8]* | | |
| | | | *CW: Jer 28:5–9; Ps 89:1–4 & 15–18; Rom 6:12–23; Mt 10:40–42* | | |
| | | | *R: II Kgs 4:8–11 & 14–16a; Ps 89:2–3 & 16–19; Rom 6:3–4 & 8–11; Mt 10:37–42* | | |
| | | | *(Giving him room)* | | |
| | | 2 EP | | I Sam 28:3–19 | Joel 2:15–27 |
| | | | Ps: 50 | Lk 17:20–37 | Acts 4:1–22 (23–31) |
| *MONDAY* | | | *Feria (S Cyril of Alexandria B Dr)* | | |
| **27** | G (or W) | MP | Ps: 79 | I Sam 10:1–24 | I Kgs 6:1–14 |
| | | | | Acts 10:1–16 | Rom 6 |
| | | Mass | *of Sunday; no Gl or Cr; Common Pref (or of the Saint)* (***Our Lady of Perpetual Succour***) | | |
| | | | *Gen 18:16–end; Ps 103:6–17; Mt 8:18–22* | | |
| | | EP | | Ecclus 24:1–12 | I Kgs 8:1–21 |
| | | | Ps: 80 | Lk 9:51–end | Lk 2:1–21 |
| *TUESDAY* | | | *S Irenaeus B M Dr* | | |
| **28** | R | MP | Ps: 81 | I Sam 10:25–end of 11 | I Kgs 8:22–53 |
| | | | | Acts 10:17–33 | Rom 7 |
| | | Mass | *of the Saint* | | |
| | | | *Gen 19:15–29; Ps 26; Mt 8:23–27* | | |
| | | | **SS PETER & PAUL, APOSTLES** | | |
| | R | 1 EP of foll; H: 226 (NEH 171) | | Ezek 3:4–11 | ◁ |
| | | | Ps: 66, 67 | Gal 1:13–2:8 (=R:) (Vigil Collect) | ◁ |
| | | Mass | *R: Vigil Mass; Acts 3:1–10; Ps 19; Gal 1:11–20; Jn 21:15–19 (Vigil Collect; Gl; Cr)* | | |
| *WEDNESDAY* | | | | | |
| **29** | R | MP | Ps: 71, 113 | Isa 49:1–6 | ◁ |
| | | | | Acts 11:1–18 | ◁ |
| | | Mass | *Gl; Cr; R: Pref of Ss Peter and Paul; CW, of Saints* | | |
| | | | *CW: = R: Acts 12:1–11; Ps 125 (R: 34:2–9); II Tim 4:6–8 & 17–18; Mt 16:13–19* | | |
| | | 2 EP | H:226 (NEH 171) | Ezek 34:11–16 | ◁ |
| | | | Ps: 124, 138 | Jn 21:15–22 | ◁ |
| *THURSDAY* | | | *Feria (□ The Holy Protomartyrs of the Holy Roman Church)* | | |
| **30** | G (or R) | MP | Ps: 87, 88 | I Sam 13:5–18 | I Kgs 11:26–end |
| | | | | Acts 11:1–18 | Rom 8:18–end |
| | | Mass | *of Monday (or of the Saints)* | | |
| | | | *Gen 22:1–19; Ps 116:1–7; Mt 9:1–8* | | |
| | | EP | | Deut 10:12 – 11:1 | I Kgs 12:1–24 |
| | | | Ps: 89:1–18 | Lk 10:25–37 | Lk 4:1–30 |

# JULY

| | | | | | |
|---|---|---|---|---|---|
| *FRIDAY* | | | *Feria (□ S Oliver Plunket B M: IRELAND FESTUM)* | | |
| **1** | G (or R) | MP | Ps: 89:19–37 | I Sam 13:19 – 14:15 | I Kgs 12:25 – 13:10 |
| | | | | Acts 11:19–end | Rom 9 |
| | | Mass | *as Monday (or of the Saints) (First Friday: Sacred Heart: see p. 39)* | | |
| | | | (***John and Henry Venn Prs***) | | |
| | | | *Gen 23:1–14 & 19 & 24:1–8 & 62–end; Ps 106:1–5; Mt 9:9–13* | | |
| | | EP | | Job 5:8–end | I Kgs 13:11–end |
| | | | Ps: 89:38–end | Lk 10:38–end | Lk 4:31–end |
| *SATURDAY* | | | *Our Lady on Saturday or the Feria* | | |
| **2** | W (or G) | MP | Ps: 90 | I Sam 14:16–30 | I Kgs 14:1–20 |
| | | | | Acts 12:1–17 | Rom 10 |
| | | Mass | *Introduction Paragraph 26(b) (First Saturday: Immaculate Heart: see p. 39)* | | |
| | | | *Gen 27:1–5a & 15–29; Ps 135:1–6; Mt 9:14–17* | | |
| | G | 1 EP of foll | | Prov 30:1–9 | II Chron 12 |
| | | | Ps: [91] 92 | Lk 11:1–13 | Lk 5:1–16 |

| Day | Colour | Office | | | |
|---|---|---|---|---|---|
| ✠ *SUNDAY* | | | **14th SUNDAY and WEEK of YEAR** | | |
| | | | | | **TRINITY 6 (S Thomas, see p. 37)** |
| **3** | G | MP | Ps: 55:1–15 & 18–22 | Deut 24:10–22 | Judg 5 |
| | | | | Acts 28:1–16 | Mk 6:53 – 7:23 |
| R:Ps II | | Mass | *Gl; Cr; Sunday Pref [PROPER 9]* | | |
| | | | *CW: Zech 9:9–12; Ps 145:8–15; Rom 7:15–25a; Mt 11:16–19 & 25–30* | | |
| | | | *R: Zech 9:9–10; Ps 145; Rom 8:9 & 11–13; Mt 11:25–30 (He Comes in Humility)* | | |
| | | 2 EP | | II Sam 2:1–11 & 3:1 | Zech 2 |
| | | | Ps: 56, 57 | Lk 18:31 – 19:10 | Acts 6 |
| *MONDAY* | | | *Feria (see p. 37) (□ S Elizabeth of Portugal)** | | |
| **4** | G (or W) | MP | Ps: 93, 94 | I Sam 14:36–45 | II Chron 13 |
| | | | | Acts 12:18–end | Rom 11:1–24 |
| | | Mass | *of Sunday; no Gl or Cr; Common Pref (or of the Saint)* | | |
| | | | *Gen 28:10–end; Ps 91:1–10; Mt 9:18–26* | | |
| | | EP | | Deut 18:9–18 | II Chron 14 |
| | | | Ps: [96] 97 | Lk 11:14–26 | Lk 5:17–end |
| *TUESDAY* | | | *Feria (□ S Antony Mary Zaccaria Pr)* | | |
| **5** | G (or W) | MP | Ps: [95] 98 | I Sam 15 | II Chron 15 |
| | | | | Acts 13:1–12 | Rom 11:25–end |
| | | Mass | *as Monday* | | |
| | | | *Gen 32:22–end; Ps 17:1–8; Mt 9:32–end* | | |
| | | EP | | Ecclus 2:1–11 | II Chron 16 |
| | | | Ps: 99 | Lk 11:27–36 | Lk 6:1–9 |
| *WEDNESDAY* | | | *See p. 37* | | |
| **6** | | MP | Ps: [100] 101 | I Sam 16:1–13 | I Kgs 16:15–end |
| | | | | Acts 13:13–25 | Rom 12 |
| | | Mass | | | |
| | | | *Gen 41:55–end & 42:5–7 & 17–end; Ps 33:1–4 & 18–end; Mt 10:1–7* | | |
| | | EP | | Exod 34:1–9 & 27–29 | I Kgs 17 |
| | | | Ps: 102 | Lk 11:37 – 12:1 | Lk 6:20–38 |
| *THURSDAY* | | | *Feria* | | |
| **7** | G | MP | Ps: [103] or 105:1–22 | I Sam 16:14 – 17:11 | I Kgs 18:1–16 |
| | | | | Acts 13:26–43 | Rom 13 |
| | | Mass | *as Monday* | | |
| | | | *Gen 44:18–21 & 23–29 & 45:1–5; Ps 105:11–17; Mt 10:7–15* | | |
| | | EP | | Josh 23:1–8 | I Kgs 18:17–end |
| | | | Ps: [104] or 105:23–end | Lk 12:2–12 | Lk 6:39 – 7:10 |
| *FRIDAY* | | | *Feria* | | |
| **8** | G | MP | Ps: 106:1–23 | I Sam 17:17–49 | I Kgs 19 |
| | | | | Acts 13:44end | Rom 14 |
| | | Mass | *as Monday* | | |
| | | | *Gen 46:1–7 & 28–30; Ps 37:3–6 & 27–28; Mt 10:16–23* | | |
| | | EP | | Hos 8:11–14 & 10:1–2 | I Kgs 21 |
| | | | Ps: 106:24–end | Lk 12:13–21 | Lk 7:11–35 |
| *SATURDAY* | | | *Our Lady on Saturday or the Feria (or □ Ss Augustine Zhao Rong Pr Comp Ms)* | | |
| **9** | W (or G or R) | MP | Ps: 107:1–22 | I Sam 17:50 – 18:4 | I Kgs 22:1–40 |
| | | | | Acts 14:1–18 | Rom 15:1–13 |
| | | Mass | *Introduction Para 26(b) (**Our Lady, Mother of Divine Hope [37]**)* | | |
| | | | *Gen 49:29– end & 50:15–25; Ps 105:1–7; Mt 10:24–33* | | |
| | G | 1 EP of foll | | Deut 26:1–11 | II Chron 20:1–30 |
| | | | Ps: 107:23–end | Lk 12:22–48 | Lk 7:36–end |

✠ *SUNDAY* **15th SUNDAY and WEEK of YEAR.** **TRINITY 7**

**10** G

| | | | | |
|---|---|---|---|---|
| R:Ps III | MP | Ps: 64, 65 | Deut 28:1–14<br>Acts 28:17–31 | Judg 7:1–23<br>Mk 9:14–29 |
| | Mass | *Gl; Cr; Sunday Pref [PROPER 10]*<br>*CW: Isa 55:10–13; Ps 65: (1–7) 8–13; Rom 8:11; Mt 13:1–9 & 18–23*<br>*R: Isa 55:10–11; Ps 65: (1–8) 9–13; Rom 8:18–23;*<br>*Mt 13:1–9 (10–23) (The fruitful Word goes forth)* | | |
| | 2 EP | Ps: 60, 63 | II Sam 7:18–29<br>Lk 19:41 – 20:8 | Zech 8:1–17<br>Acts 8:4–17 |

*MONDAY* **S Benedict Abbot Patron of Europe**

**11** W

| | | | |
|---|---|---|---|
| MP | [Ps: 108 [109]] | [I Sam 18:5–end]<br>[Acts 14:19–end] | [II Kgs 1]<br>[Rom 15:14–end] |
| Mass | *Office Readings from Appendix 3: Religious*<br>*of the Saint; Gl; no Cr; Pref (R:) or Patrons, (CW) of Saints*<br>*R: Prov 2:1–9; Ps 34:1–10; Mt 19:27–29*<br>*[Exod 1:8–14 & 22; Ps 124; Mt 10:34 – 11:1]* | | |
| EP | [Ps: 110, 111] | [Lev 19:9–18]<br>[Lk 12:49–end] | [II Kgs 2:1–22]<br>[Lk 8:1–21] |

*TUESDAY* *Feria*

**12** G

| | | | |
|---|---|---|---|
| MP | Ps: 112 | I Sam 19:1–19<br>Acts 15:1–11 | II Kgs 4:1–37<br>Rom 16 |
| Mass | *of Sunday; no Gl or Cr; Common Pref*<br>*Exod 2:1–15; Ps 69:1–2 & 31–end; Mt 11:20–24* | | |
| EP | Ps: 113 | Jer 8:4–12<br>Lk 13:1–9 | II Kgs 5<br>Lk 8:22–end |

*WEDNESDAY* *Feria (□ S Henry)*

**13** G (or W)

| | | | |
|---|---|---|---|
| MP | Ps: 114 | I Sam 20:1–23<br>Acts 15:12–21 | II Kgs 6:1–23<br>I Cor 1:1–25 |
| Mass | *as Tuesday (or of the Saint)*<br>*Exod 3:1–6 & 9–12; Ps 103:1–7; Mt 11:25–27* | | |
| EP | Ps: 115 | Isa 29:17–end<br>Lk 13:10–17 | II Kgs 6:24 – 7:2<br>Lk 9:1–17 |

*THURSDAY* *Feria (□ S Camillus de Lellis Pr)*

**14** G (or W)

| | | | |
|---|---|---|---|
| MP | Ps: 116, 117 | I Sam 20:24–end<br>Acts 15:22–35 | II Kgs 7:3–end<br>I Cor 1:26–2 end |
| Mass | *as Tuesday (or of the Saint)* (***John Keble Pr***)<br>*Exod 3:13–20; Ps 105:1–2 & 23; Mt 11:28–end* | | |
| EP | Ps: 118 | Isa 49:8–16a<br>Lk 13:18–end | II Kgs 8:1–15<br>Lk 9:18–50 |

*FRIDAY* *S Bonaventure B Dr*

**15** W

| | | | |
|---|---|---|---|
| MP | Ps: 119:1–16 | I Sam 21:1 – 22:5<br>Acts 15:36 – 16:5 | II Kgs 9<br>I Cor 3 |
| Mass | *of the Saint* (***S Swithun B***)<br>*Exod 11:10 – 12:14; Ps 116:10–end; Mt 12:1–8* | | |
| EP | Ps: 119:17–32 | II Kgs 20:1–11<br>Lk 14:1–14 | II Kgs 11:1–20<br>Lk 9:51–end |

*SATURDAY* *Our Lady of Mount Carmel or the Feria (S Osmund B: EAD Compulsory and FESTUM in Salisbury)*

**16** W (or G)

| | | | | |
|---|---|---|---|---|
| | MP | Ps: 119:33–48 | I Sam 22:6–end & 23:(1–6) & 7–18<br>Acts 16:6–15 | II Kgs 11:21–12 end<br>I Cor 4:1–17 |
| | Mass | *Readings of Our Lady: Zec 2:10–13; Ps = Lk 1:46–55; Mt 12:46–50*<br>*Exod 12:37–42; Ps 136:1–4 & 10:15; Mt 12:14–21* | | |
| G | 1 EP of foll | Ps: 119:49–64 | Isa 57:14–end<br>Lk 14:15–24 | II Kgs 13<br>Lk 10:1–24 |

✠ *SUNDAY* **16th SUNDAY and WEEK of YEAR** **TRINITY 8**

**17** G MP Ps: 71 Deut 30:1–10 Judg 16:4–end
I Pet 3:8–18 Mk 9:30–end

R:Ps IV Mass *Gl; Cr; Sunday Pref [PROPER 11]*
*CW: Wisd 12:13 & 16–19; Ps 86:11–17; Rom 8:12–25; Mt 13:24–30 & 36–43*
*R: Wisd 12:13 & 16–19; Ps 86:11–17; Rom 8:26–27; Mt 13:24–30 (31–43) (The Judge)*

2 EP I Kgs 2:10–12 & 3:16–28 Jonah 1 & 2
Ps: 67, 70 Acts 4:1–22 Acts 8:26–39

*MONDAY* *Feria*

**18** G MP Ps: 119:65–80 I Sam 24 II Kgs 14
Acts 16:16–24 I Cor 4:18–5 end

Mass *of Sunday; no Gl or Cr; Common Pref (**Elizabeth Ferard)***
*Exod 14:5–18; Ps 136:1–4 & 10–15 or Exod 15:1–6; Mt 12:38–42*

EP Num 27:15–end II Chron 26
Ps: 119:81–96 Lk 14:25–end Lk 10:25–end

*TUESDAY* *Feria (Ss Gregory of Nyssa B Dr and his sister Macrina)**

**19** G (or W) MP Ps: 119:97–112 I Sam 25:1–22 II Kgs 15:17–end
Acts 16:25–end I Cor 6

Mass *as Monday (or of the Saint)*
*Exod 14:21 – 15:1; Ps 105:37–44 or Exod 15:8–10& 12 & 17; Mt 12:46–end*

EP Joel 2:12–17 II Kgs 16
Ps: 119:113–128 Lk 15:1–10 Lk 11:1–28

*WEDNESDAY* *Feria (S Margaret M)*

**20** G (or R) MP Ps: 119:129–144 I Sam 25:23–end Isa 7:1–17
Acts 17:1–15 I Cor 7

Mass *as Monday (**Bartolomé de las Casas**)*
*Exod 16:1–5 & 9–15; Ps 78:17–31; Mt 13:1–9*

EP Song of the Three vv 1–14 Is 8:1–18
Ps: 119:145–160 Lk 15:11–end Lk 11:29–end

*THURSDAY* *Feria (□ S Lawrence of Brindisi Pr Dr)*

**21** G (or W) MP Ps: 119:161–176 I Sam 28:3–20 II Kgs 17:1–23
Acts 17:16–end I Cor 8

Mass *as Monday (or of the Saint)*
*Exod 19:1–2 & 9–11 & 16–20; Canticle: Benedicite; Mt 13:10–17*

EP Micah 6:1–8 II Kgs 17:24–end
Ps: 120, 121 Lk 16:1–13 Lk 12:1–34

*FRIDAY* **S Mary Magdalene†**

**22** W MP H: 231 (NEH 174)† I Sam 16:14–23 ◁
Ps: 30, 32, 150 Lk 8:1–3 ◁

Mass *Gl†; no Cr; Pref of Saints*
*CW = R: Song S 3:1–4; Ps 42:1–7 (R: 63); II Cor 5:14–17; Jn 20:1–2 & 11–18*

2 EP Zeph 3:14–20 Isa 25:1–9
Ps: 63 Mk 15:40–16:7 ◁

*SATURDAY* **S Bridget, Religious, Patron of Europe**

**23** W MP [Ps: 126, 127] [II Sam 1] [II Kgs 18:13–end]
[Acts 18:12–end] [I Cor 10:1 – 11:1]

Mass *Office Reading from Appendix 3 Religious*
*of the Saint; Gl no Cr; Pref (R:) of Patrons (CW) of Saints*
*R: Judith 8:2–8 or I Tim 5:3–10; Ps 10:1–2 & 10–15; Lk 2:36–38 or Mt 5:13–16*
*[Exod 24:3–8; Ps 50:1–6 & 14–15; Mt 13:24–30]*

G 1 EP of foll Dan 12:1–9 II Kgs 19
Ps: 128, 129 Lk 16:19–31 Lk 12:54 – 13:9

* In Byzantium, her memorial. CW united her brother with her on this day, presumably so as to give Archbishop Laud a free run on January 10, S Gregory's Byzantine date.

† Like Byzantium, Rome , CW now disentangles S Mary M from Mary of Bethany and the Sinful Woman. In the Hymn, verse 5, correct 'feet' to 'limbs'. (In R: she is only a Memorial; no Gl).

| | | | | | |
|---|---|---|---|---|---|
| ✠ *SUNDAY* | | | **17th SUNDAY and WEEK of YEAR** | | **TRINITY 9** |
| **24** | G | MP | Ps: 77 | I Macc 2: (1–14) 15–22 | I Sam 1–20 |
| | | | | I Pet 4:7–14 | Mk 10:17–31 |
| R:Ps I | | Mass | *Gl; Cr; Sunday Pref [PROPER 12]*<br>*CW: I Kgs 3:5–12; Ps 119:129–136; Rom 8:26–39; Mt 13:31–33 & 44–52*<br>*R: I Kgs 3:5 & 7–12; Ps 119:129–136; Rom 8:28–30*<br>*Mt 13:44–52 (or 44–46) (Seeking God's Treasure)* | | |
| | | 2 EP | | I Kgs 6:11–14 & 23–28 | Jonah 3 & 4 |
| | | | Ps: 75, 76 | Acts 12:1–17 | Acts 11:1–18 |
| *MONDAY* | | | **S James Apostle** | | |
| **25** | R | MP | Ps: 7, 29, 117 | II Kgs 1:9–15 | Jer 26:1–15 |
| | | | | Lk 9:46–56 | Lk 9:46–56 |
| | | Mass | *Gl; R: Pref of Apostles; CW, of Saints*<br>*CW: Jer 45:1–5 or Acts 11:27–12:2; II Cor 4:7–15; Ps 126; Mt 20:20–28*<br>*R: II Cor 4:7–15; Ps 126; Mt 20:20–28* | | |
| | | EP | | Jer 26:1–15 | Jer 45 |
| | | | Ps: 94 | Mk 1:14–20 | Mk 14:32–42 |
| *TUESDAY* | | | *Ss Joachim & Anne, Parents of the BVM* | | |
| **26** | W | MP | Ps: 133, [134], 147:1–12 | II Sam 3:6–21 | II Kgs 22 |
| | | | | Acts 19:11–20 | I Cor 12:1–27 |
| | | Mass | *of the Saints*<br>*CW: Zeph 3:14–17; Ps 127; Rom 8:28–30; Mt 13:16–17*<br>*R: Ecclus 44:1 & 10–15; Mt 13:16–17*<br>*[Exod 33:7–11 & 34:5–9 & 28; Ps 103:8–12; Mt 13:36–43]* | | |
| | | EP | | Song of the Three vv 29–34 | II Kgs 23:1–20 |
| | | | Ps: 135 | Lk 17:11–19 | Lk 14:1–24 |
| *WEDNESDAY* | | | *Feria* | | |
| **27** | G | MP | Ps: 136, 147:13–end | II Sam 3:22–end | II Kgs 23:21–35 |
| | | | | Acts 19:21–end | I Cor 12:27–13 end |
| | | Mass | *as Sunday; no Gl or Cr; Common Pref (**Brooke Foss Westcott B**)*<br>*Exod 34:29–end; Ps 99; Mt 13:44–46* | | |
| | | EP | | Isa 33:17–22 | II Kgs 23:36 – 24:17 |
| | | | Ps: 137, 138 | Lk 17:20–end | Lk 14:25 – 15:10 |
| *THURSDAY* | | | *Feria* | | |
| **28** | G | MP | Ps: 139, 148 | II Sam 4 | II Kgs 24:18 – 25:7 |
| | | | | Acts 20:1–16 | I Cor 14:1–19 |
| | | Mass | *as Wednesday*<br>*Exod 40:16–21 & 34–end; Ps 84:1–6; Mt 13:47–53* | | |
| | | EP | | Ezek 12:21–end | II Kgs 25:8–end |
| | | | Ps: 140 | Lk 18:1–8 | Lk 15:11–end |
| *FRIDAY* | | | *S Martha (CW adds: Mary and Lazarus)* | | |
| **29** | W | MP | Ps: 141, 149 | II Sam 5:1–12 | Jer 19 |
| | | | | Acts 20:17–end | I Cor 14:20–end |
| | | Mass | *of the Saint(s)*<br>*CW: Isa 25:6–9; Ps 49:5–10 & 16; Heb 2:10–15; Jn 12:1–8*<br>*R: I Jn 4:7–16; Jn 11:19–27 or Lk 10:38–42*<br>*[Lev 23:1 & 4–11 & 15–16 & 27 & 34–37; Ps 81:1–8; Mt 13:54–end]* | | |
| | | EP | | Amos 5:6–15 | Jer 21:1–10 |
| | | | Ps: 142, 143 | Lk 18:9–14 | Lk 16 |
| *SATURDAY* | | | *Our Lady on Saturday or the Feria (□ S Peter Chrysologus B Dr)* | | |
| **30** | W (or G) | MP | Ps: 144, 150 | II Sam 5:22–end of 6 | Jer 22:20 – 23:8 |
| | | | | Acts 21:1–14 | I Cor 15:1–34 |
| | | Mass | *Introduction Paragraph 26(b) (**William Wilberforce**)*<br>*Lev 25:1 & 8–17; Ps 67; Mt 14:1–12* | | |
| | G | 1EP of foll | | Exod 20:1–17 | Jer 24 |
| | | | Ps: 145 | Lk 18:15–30 | Lk 17:1–19 |

| Day | Colour | Service | | | |
|---|---|---|---|---|---|
| ✠ *SUNDAY* | | | **18th SUNDAY and WEEK of YEAR** | | **TRINITY 10** |
| **31** | G | MP | Ps: 85 | I Macc 3:1–12 | I Sam 3:1 – 4:1a |
| | | | | II Pet 1:1–15 | Mk 12:18–end |
| R:Ps II | | Mass | *Gl; Cr; Sunday Pref. [PROPER 13] [TRANSFIGURATION? Int P.5])* | | |
| | | | *CW: Isa 55:1–5; Ps 145:8–9 & 15–22; Rom 9:1–5; Mt 14:13–21* | | |
| | | | *R: Isa 55:1–3; Ps 145; Rom 8:35 & 37–39; Mt 14:13–21 (Rich Rood, Freely Given)* | | |
| | | 2 EP | | I Kgs 10:1–13 | Prov 1:20–end |
| | | | Ps: 80 | Acts 13:1–13 | Acts 15:1–31 |
| **AUGUST** | | | | | |
| *MONDAY* | | | *☐ S Alfonso Maria de' Liguori B Dr* | | |
| **1** | W | MP | Ps: 1, 2 | II Sam 7:1– 17 | Jer 25:1–14 |
| | | | | Acts 21:15–26 | I Cor 15:35–end |
| | | Mass | *of the Saint* | | |
| | | | *Num 11:4–15; Ps 81:11–end; Mt 14:22–end* | | |
| | | EP | | Isa 53:7–end | Jer 27:2–end |
| | | | Ps: 3 [4] | Lk 18.31–end | Lk 17:20–end |
| *TUESDAY* | | | *Feria (☐ S Eusebius of Vercelli B; ☐ S Peter Julian Eymard Pr)* | | |
| **2** | G (or W) | MP | Ps: 5 | II Sam 7:18–end | Jer 28 |
| | | | | Acts 21:27–36 | I Cor 16 |
| | | Mass | *of Sunday; no Gl or Cr; Common Pref (or of the Saint)* | | |
| | | | *Num 12:1–13; Ps 51:1–8; Mt 15:1–2 & 10–14* | | |
| | | EP | | Ecclus 15:15–end | Jer 29:1–20 |
| | | | Ps: 6 | Lk 19:1–10 | Lk 18:1–30 |
| *WEDNESDAY* | | | *Feria* | | |
| **3** | G | MP | Ps: 7 | II Sam 9 | Jer 32:1–25 |
| | | | | Acts 21:37 – 22:16 | II Cor 1:1–22 |
| | | Mass | *as Tuesday* | | |
| | | | *Num 13:1–2 & 25 – 14:1 & 26–35; Ps 106:14–24; Mt 15:21–28* | | |
| | | EP | | Prov 4:1–13 | Jer 32:26–end |
| | | | Ps: 8, 9 | Lk 19:11–27 | Lk 18:31 – 19:10 |
| *THURSDAY* | | | *S John Mary Vianney Pr* | | |
| **4** | W | MP | Ps: 10 | II Sam 11 | Jer 33 |
| | | | | Acts 22:17–19 | II Cor 1:23–2 end |
| | | Mass | *of the Saint* | | |
| | | | *Num 20:1–13; Ps 95:1 & 8–end; Mt 16:13–23* | | |
| | | EP | | Zech 9:9–12 | Jer 34:8–end |
| | | | Ps: 11, 12 | Lk 19:28–38 | Lk 19:11–28 |
| *FRIDAY* | | | *Feria (☐ Dedication of the Basilica of Great S Mary's; S Oswald K and M) (Assumption Novenas may start)* | | |
| **5** | G (or W or R) | MP | Ps: 13, 14 | II Sam 12:1–25 | Jer 37 |
| | | | | Acts 22:30 – 23:11 | II Cor 3 |
| | | Mass | *as Tuesday (or of our Lady or the Saint) (First Friday; Sacred Heart: see p. 38)* | | |
| | | | *Deut 4:32–40; Ps 77:11–end; Mt 16:24–end* | | |
| | | EP | | Jer 7:1–11 | Jer 38:1–13 |
| | | | Ps: 15, 16 | Lk 19:39–end | Lk 19:29–end |
| *SATURDAY* | | | **Transfiguration of the Lord** | | |
| **6** | W | MP | H: 233 or 238:1, 2, 4, 7, 8 | Ecclus 48:1–10 | Exod 34:29–end |
| | | | Ps: 27, 150 | I Jn 3:1–3 | II Cor 3(=R:) |
| | | Mass | *Gl; R: Pref of Transfiguration; CW, Common Pref.* | | |
| | | | *CW = R: Dan 7:9–10 & 13–14; Ps 97; II Pet 1:16–19; Lk 9:28–36 (R: Mt 17:1–9)* | | |
| | W | EP | H: 234 (NEH 176) | Exod 34:29–35 | I Kgs 19:1–16 |
| | | | Ps: 72 | II Cor 3 | II Pet 1:12–end |

## ASSUMPTION OF THE BVM

1. August 15 was the Festival of Our Lady in Jerusalem by the fourth Century. (The word 'Assumption' in early Christian Latin antedates by many centuries the definition of 1950.) PPL: "In many places the feast is synonymous with the person of our Lady. It is simply referred to as 'Lady Day' or as 'The Immacolada' in Spain and Latin America." CW follows this Hispanic baroque instinct.
2. 'Anglicans and Roman Catholics can agree in much of the truth that [the dogma of the Assumption is] designed to affirm; . . . the affirmation that her glory in heaven involves full participation in the fruits of salvation expresses and reinforces our faith that the life of the world to come has already broken into the life of our world.' (ARCIC 1981).

2a When August 15 is a Monday, Rome orders it, in England, to be transferred to Sunday. CW also permits this when S Mary is the Patron.

3. The EVE: the Assumption has been called the Easter of the Mother of God (and preceded, in the Byzantine rite, by a Lent of fourteen days; in the west Novenas are kept). R: provides a separate collect for 1 EP and the Vigil mass. In some places the Eve is marked with some solemnity – texts from the compiler:–

- the lit Paschal Candle may be processed to our Lady's statue or icon, and incense offered to both;
- a form of *Exsultet;* then the Vigil mass *or* 1 EP *or* a Liturgy of the Word, including:
- Gospel (Ceremonies as at mass; Lk 10:38–42 & 11:27b–28 – cf Byzantium and Rome before 1950);
- Te Deum;
- Collect from the Vigil mass;
- Blessing or Benediction.

4. The *Office Hymns*, Eleventh Century and later, now used are not in EH or NEH but may be obtained from the Compiler. The Common Hymns are 213, 214, 215 (NEH 180, 181, 183). The Assumption is mentioned in EH215 and 217, and NEH 182, 183, 184, and 185. For the Akathist Hymn see p. xxvi.

   EH 218 (NEH 188) – Fr V.S.S. Coles' hymn *Ye Who Own The Faith Of Jesus* – contains verses omitted in the hymnbooks. Since the hymn thus (except as a Processional) becomes rather long, it could be divided and treated as two separate hymns: (A) 1, 2, 3, 4, 5, 7; (B) 1, 2a, 2b, 2c, 6, 7.

2a Thus prepared, and thus exalted,
Lowly still, and still unknown,
Mary waited till the fullness
Of her destiny was shown,
Till the maid became God's Mother,
And her nursing arms his throne: *Hail Mary . . .*

2b For the King of men and angels
Chose her out of all He made,
And in robes of grace and glory
Her humility arrayed,
With the radiant sun He clothed her,
At her feet the moon He laid: *Hail Mary . . .*

2c As we sing, her prayer is rising,
For her Heart with us is one;
We with confidence will ask it
That the Mother from her Son
May obtain the full perfection
Of His work in us begun: *Hail Mary . . .*

5. *Readings* prefixed * are those customarily offered in this ORDO, based upon Western Catholic tradition. Their use is covered by CLC p. 36 paragraph 6. Those prefixed † are now offered by CW.

| Day | | Office | Psalms / Notes | Readings | Alternative |
|---|---|---|---|---|---|
| ✠ *SUNDAY* **7** | G | | **19th SUNDAY and WEEK of YEAR.** | | **TRINITY 11** |
| | | MP | Ps: 88 | I Macc 14:4–15<br>II Pet 3:8–13 | I Sam 9:1 – 10:1<br>Rom 1:1–25 (26 end) |
| R: Ps III | | Mass | *Gl; Cr; Sunday Pref [PROPER 14]*<br>*CW: I Kgs 19:9–18; Ps 85:8–13; Rom 10:5–15; Mt 14:22–33*<br>*R: I Kgs 19:9a; 11–13a; Ps 85; Rom 9:1–5; Mt 14:22–33 (His Voice Speaks of Peace)* | | |
| | | 2 EP | Ps: 86 | I Kgs 11:41 – 12:20<br>Acts 14:8–20 | Prov 8:1–17<br>Mk 4:23 – 5.20 |
| *MONDAY* **8** | W | | *S Dominic Pr* | | |
| | | MP | Ps: 18:1–25 | II Sam 13:23–end<br>Acts 23:23–35 | Jer 40<br>II Cor 5:1–19 |
| | | Mass | *of the Saint*<br>*Deut 10:12–end; Ps 147:13–end; Mt 17:22–end* | | |
| | | EP | Ps: 18:26–end | Gen 22:1–18<br>Lk 20:9–19 | Jer 41<br>Lk 20:27 – 21:4 |
| *TUESDAY* **9** | R | | **□ S Teresa Benedicta of the Cross V & M Patron of Europe** | | |
| | | MP | Ps: [20] | [II Sam 14:1–20]<br>[Acts 24:1–23] | [Jer 42]<br>[II Cor 5:20 – 7:1] |
| | | Mass | *Office Readings from Appendix 3, Martyrs*<br>*of the Saint; Gl; no Cr; Pref (R:) of Patrons (CW) of Saints (**Mary Sumner**)*<br>*[Deut 31:1–8; Ps 107:1–3 & 42–end; Mt 18:1–5 & 10 & 12–14]* | | |
| | | EP | Ps: [21] | [Isa 45:1–7]<br>[Lk 20:20–26] | [Jer 43]<br>[Lk 21:5–end] |
| *WEDNESDAY* **10** | R | | **S Laurence Dcn M** | | |
| | | MP | Ps: [22] | [II Sam 14:21–end]<br>[Acts 24:24 – 25:12] | [Jer 44:1–14]<br>[II Cor 7:2–end] |
| | | Mass | *Office Readings from Appendix 3, Martyrs*<br>*of the Saint; Gl; no Cr; R: Pref of Ms; CW, of Saints*<br>*R: II Cor 9–6–10; Ps 111; Jn 12:24–26*<br>*[Deut 34; Ps 66:14–end; Mt 18:15–20]* | | |
| | | EP | Ps: [23 [24]] | [II Kgs 4:18–37]<br>[Lk 20:27–40] | [Jer 44:15–end]<br>[Lk 22:1–38] |
| *THURSDAY* **11** | W | | *S Clare V* | | |
| | | MP | Ps: 25 | II Sam 15:1–18<br>Acts 25:13–end | Ezek 1:1–14<br>II Cor 8 |
| | | Mass | *of the Saint (**John Henry Newman Pr**)*<br>*Josh 3:7–11 & 13–17; Ps 114; Mt 18:21 – 19:1* | | |
| | | 2 EP | Ps: 26, 27 | I Kgs 17:8–16<br>Lk 20:41 – 21:4 | Ezek 2:1 – 3:3<br>Lk 22:39–53 |
| *FRIDAY* **12** | G (or W) | | *Feria (□ S Jane Frances de Chantal Rel)* | | |
| | | MP | Ps: 28, 29 | II Sam 15:19–end<br>Acts 26:1–23 | Ezek 3:4–end<br>II Cor 9 |
| | | Mass | *of Sunday; no Gl or Cr; Common Pref (as of the Saint)*<br>*Josh 24:1–13; Ps 136:1–3 & 16–22; Mt 19:3–12* | | |
| | | EP | Ps: 30 | Mal 3:1–5<br>Lk 21:5–28 | Ezek 8<br>Lk 22:54–end |
| *SATURDAY* **13** | W (or G or R) | | *Our Lady on Saturday or the Feria (□ Ss Pontianus Pp and Hippolytus M)* | | |
| | | MP | Ps: 31:(1–6) 7–end | II Sam 16<br>Acts 26:24 – 27–8 | Ezek 11:14–end<br>II Cor 10 |
| | | Mass | *Introduction Paragraph 26(b) (**Jeremy Taylor B; Florence Nightingale; Octavia Hill**)*<br>*Josh 24:14–29; Ps 16:1 & 5–end; Mt 19:13–15* | | |
| ✠ | W | | ***ASSUMPTION OF THE BVM** (see p. 50)*<br>*R: Vigil Mass: I Chron 15:3–4 & 15–16 & 16:1–2; Ps 132; I Cor 15:54–57*<br>*Lk 11:27–28 (Collect of Vigil; Gl; Cr)* | | |
| | | 1 EP of foll | Ps: 72 | *Song of S 4:7–12<br>* Lk 1:26–38 } or from the Vigil Mass | †Prov 8:22–31<br>†Jn 19:23–27 |

*† See p. 50 note 5.

| Day | Colour | Service | Psalms / Propers | Readings | |
|---|---|---|---|---|---|
| ✠ *SUNDAY* | | | ***ASSUMPTION OF* THE BVM** | | |
| **14** | W | MP | Ps: 98, 138, 147:1–12 | *Gen 3:1–15 | †Isa 7:10–15 |
| | | | | *Eph 1:16–2:10 (=R:) | †Lk 11:27–28 |
| | | Mass | *Gl; Cr; R: Proper Pref; CW, of the Annunciation; or ASB 6* | | |
| | | | *R: Rev 11:19a & 12:1 & 3–6a & 10ab; Ps 45; I Cor 15:20–27a; Lk 1:39–56* | | |
| | | | *CW: Rev 11:19–12:6 & 10; Ps 45:10–17; Gal 4:4–7; Lk 1:46–55* | | |
| | | 2 EP | | *Song of S 6:3–10 | †Song of S 2:1–7 |
| | | | Ps: 132 | * I Cor 15:37–44 & 49–54 (55–7) | †Acts 1:6–14 |
| *MONDAY* | | | *Feria* | | **20th WEEK of YEAR** |
| **15** | G | MP | Ps: 33 | II Sam 17 | Ezek 13:1–16 |
| | | | | Acts 27:9–26 | Ii Cor 11 |
| R: Ps IV | | Mass | *of Sunday (Trinity 12); no Gl or Cr; Common Pref* | | |
| | | | *Judg 2:11–19; Ps 106:34–42; Mt 19:16–22* | | |
| | | EP | | Lev 16:1–10 & 20–22 | Ezek 14:1–11 |
| | | | Ps: 34 | Heb 1 | Lk 23:26–49 |
| *TUESDAY* | | | *Feria (☐ S Stephen of Hungary)* | | |
| **16** | G (or W) | MP | Ps: 35 | II Sam 18:1–18 | Ezek 14:12–end |
| | | | | Acts 27:27–end | II Cor 12:1–13 |
| | | Mass | *as Monday (or of the Saint)* | | |
| | | | *Judg 6:11–24; Ps 85:8–end; Mt 19:23–end* | | |
| | | EP | | Lev 23:1–14 | Ezek 20:12–20 |
| | | | Ps: 36 | Heb 2:5–18 | Lk 23:50 – 24:12 |
| *WEDNESDAY* | | | *Feria* | | |
| **17** | G | MP | Ps: 37:1–22 | II Sam 18:19–end | Ezek 20:27–44 |
| | | | | Acts 28:1–10 | II Cor 12:14–13 end |
| | | Mass | *as Monday* | | |
| | | | *Judg 9:6–15; Ps 21:1–6; Mt 20:1–16* | | |
| | | EP | | Lev 25:1–17 | Ezek 33:21–end |
| | | | Ps: 37:23–end | Heb 4:12 – 5:10 | Lk 24:13–end |
| *THURSDAY* | | | *Feria* | | |
| **18** | G | MP | Ps: 38 | II Sam 19:1–23 | Ezek 34:1–16 |
| | | | | Acts 28:11–22 | Gal 1 |
| | | Mass | *as Monday* | | |
| | | | *Judg 11:29–end; Ps 40:4–11; Mt 22:1–14* | | |
| | | EP | | Deut 4:15–24 | Ezek 34:1 – 17–end |
| | | | Ps: 39 | Heb 6:13–end | Jn 1:1–28 |
| *FRIDAY* | | | *Feria (☐ S John Eudes Pr)* | | |
| **19** | G (or W) | MP | Ps: 40 | II Sam 19:24–end | Ezek 36:22–36 |
| | | | | Acts 28:23–end | Gal 2 |
| | | Mass | *as Monday (or of the Saint) (**Our Lady of the Don**)* | | |
| | | | *Ruth 1:1 & 3–6 & 14–16 & 22; Ps 146; Mt 22:34–40* | | |
| | | EP | | Deut 4:32–40 | Ezek 37:1–14 |
| | | | Ps: 41 | Heb 7:11–end | Jn 1:29–end |
| *SATURDAY* | | | *S Bernard Ab Dr* | | |
| **20** | W | MP | Ps: 42, 43 | II Sam 24 | Ezek 37:15–end |
| | | | | II Tim 3:10 – 4:8 | Gal 3 |
| | | Mass | *of the Saint (**William and Catherine Booth**)* | | |
| | | | *Ruth 2:1–3 & 8–11 & 4:13–17; Ps 128; Mt 23:1–12* | | |
| | G | 1 EP of foll | | Deut 6:1–12 | Ezek 47:1–12 |
| | | | Ps: 44 | Heb 9:11–end | Jn 2 |

| | | | | | |
|---|---|---|---|---|---|
| ✠ *SUNDAY* | | | **21st SUNDAY and WEEK of YEAR** | | **TRINITY 13** |
| **21** | G | MP | Ps: 104:1–25 | Ecclus 3:17–29 | I Sam 17:1–11 & 32–51 |
| | | | | Rev 1 | Rom 12 |
| R: Ps I | | Mass | *Gl; Cr; Sunday Pref [PROPER 16]* | | |
| | | | *CW: Isa 51:1–6; Ps 138; Rom 12:1–8; Mt 16:13–20* | | |
| | | | *R: Isa 22:19–23; Ps 138:1–3 & 6 & 8bc; Rom 11:33–36; Mt 16:13–20 (Peter Bears the Keys)* | | |
| | | 2 EP | | 2 Kgs 6:8–23 | Rev 14:31 – 15:17 |
| | | | Ps: 95 | Acts 17:15–34 | Mt 6:1–18 |
| *MONDAY* | | | *□ Our Lady, Queen** | | |
| **22** | W | MP | Ps: 45 | I Kgs 1:5–31 | Ezra 1 |
| | | | | Mt 1:1–17 | Gal 4:1 – 5:1 |
| | | Mass | *of Our Lady* | | |
| | | | *R: Isa 9:2–4 & 6–7; Ps 113; Lk 1:26–38* | | |
| | | | *[I Thess 1:2–5 & 8–10; Ps 149:1–5; Mt 23:13–22]* | | |
| | | EP | | Deut 15:1–11 | Ezra 3 |
| | | | Ps: 46, 47 | Heb 10:1–18 | Jn 3:1–21 |
| *TUESDAY* | | | *Feria (S Rose of Lima V)* | | |
| **23** | G (or W) | MP | Ps: 48 | I Kgs 1:38 – 2:4 | Ezra 4 |
| | | | | Mt 1:18–end | Gal 5:2–end |
| | | Mass | *of Sunday; no Gl or Cr; Common Pref (or of the Saint)* | | |
| | | | *I Thess 2:1–8; Ps 139:1–9; Mt 23:23–26* | | |
| | | EP | | Deut 34 | Hag 1:1–29 |
| | | | Ps: 49 | Heb 10:19–25 & 35–end | Jn 3:22–end |
| *WEDNESDAY* | | | **S Bartholomew, Apostle** | | |
| **24** | R | MP | Ps: 86, 117 | Gen 28:10–17 | Deut 18:15–19 |
| | | | | Jn 1:43–51 | Mt 10:1–15 |
| | | Mass | *Gl; R: Pref of Apostles; CW; of Saints* | | |
| | | | *CW: Isa 43:8–13; Ps 145:1–7; Acts 5:12–16; Lk 22:24–30* | | |
| | | | *R: Rev 21:9–14; Ps 145; Jn 1:45–51* | | |
| | | EP | | Ecclus 39:1–10 | Is 49:1–13 |
| | | | Ps: 91, 116 | Mt 10:1–22 | Mt 10:16–22 |
| *THURSDAY* | | | *Feria (□ S Louis; □ S Joseph de Calasanz Pr)* | | |
| **25** | G (or W) | MP | Ps: 52, 53 | I Kgs 3:16–end | Zech 3 |
| | | | | Mt 2:13–end | Eph 1:1–14 |
| | | Mass | *as Tuesday (or of the Saint)* | | |
| | | | *I Thess 3:7–end; Ps 90:13–end; Mt 24:42–end* | | |
| | | EP | | Hos 6:1–16 | Zech 4 |
| | | | Ps: 54, 55 | Heb 11:23–end | Jn 4:27–end |
| *FRIDAY* | | | *Feria (p. 54, note 9) (□ Bl Dominic Barberi of the Mother of God Pr)* | | |
| **26** | G (or W) | MP | Ps: 56 | I Kgs 5:1 – 6:1 &7 | Zech 6:9–end |
| | | | | Mt 3:1–12 | Eph 1:15–end |
| | | Mass | *as Monday* | | |
| | | | *I Thess 4:1–8; Ps 97; Mt 25:1–13* | | |
| | | EP | | Hos 11:1–9 | Hag 2:10–end |
| | | | Ps: 57 | Heb 12:1–13 | Jn 5:1–23 |
| *SATURDAY* | | | *S Monica* | | |
| **27** | W | MP | Ps: [58] 59 | I Kgs 7:51 – 8:30 | Ezra 5 |
| | | | | Mt 3:13–end | Eph 2:1–10 |
| | | Mass | *of the Saint* | | |
| | | | *I Thess 4:9–12; Ps 98:1–2 & 8–end; Mt 25:14–30* | | |
| | G | 1 EP of foll | | Hos 14 | Ezra 6 |
| | | | Ps: 60 | Heb 12:14–end | Jn 5:24–end |

* EXETER: ordered to be kept as a FESTUM.

SEPTEMBER FESTIVALS

1. On **September 2** the Ebbsfleet Apostolic District observes an optional Memorial of Blessed Vivian Redlich Pr and his Companions Martyrs (of Papua New Guinea); which is not in any Roman Calendar. But a Votive of Martyrs is always permitted. Use Commons (p. xxx).
2. On **September 3** (or on the Sunday) the Ebbsfleet Apostolic District celebrates S Gregory, who sent S Augustine (Ebbsfleet his landing place), as its Patron with the rank of Solemnity. Gl and Cr at mass; 1 EP on Friday; 2 EP displaces 1 EP of the Sunday; Office from the Commons (p. xxx; a R: reading is Titus 1:7–11 & 2:1–8). Ebbsfleet propers: *Ecclus 47:8–11; Ps 36:1–3 & 7–8 & 10; Response verse 3; I Thess 2:2–8; Alleluia, Alleluia! The Lord sent me to bring the good news to the poor, and liberty to captives. Alleluia! Mt 16:13–19.*
3. **September 8** began in Jerusalem as a festival of the (5th Century) Basilica of Holy Mary's Birthplace; such tend to be the origins of early feasts of those who left no bodily relics (cf. September 29 and November 21). September 14 also began in Jerusalem when, on the day after the Dedication of the Basilica of the Resurrection, the Wood of the Holy Cross was exposed for veneration.
4. Since CW provides no Office for **September 8**, we offer: *middle column* the ASB provision; *right hand column* a typological provision based upon Orthodox provisions, which your Compiler owes to Bishop Wilkinson of the Canadian TAC.
5. In Churches where August 15 is not observed, CW suggests **September 8** as the principal solemnity of our Lady. In such churches it will have a 1 EP. The Propers of August 14–15 are used.
6. The memorial of the Holy Name of Mary, which originally occupied the Sunday after her Nativity, has now been restored, as an optional memorial, to **September 12**. The mass propers may be had from your Compiler (see p. a) and remind us that, as well, as 'Mary', the Lord's Mother is 'named' Mother of God and Ever-Virgin. Rome urges those compiling local calendars who need a place for 'Our Lady of N' to consider September 12.
7. If the Holy Cross is a Solemnity (e.g., SSC), it has a first EP (p. xxx) and the Creed is said.
8. The old Octave day of the Nativity, **September 15**, which is also the day after Holy Cross Day, is, very neatly, the memorial of our Lady *Perdolentis*. (It was David Silk who had the happy notion of Englishing this as *Mary at the Cross*.) But when CW put S John Chrysostom back onto its R: date of September 13, S Cyprian was evicted onto September 15, leaving our Lady out in the cold. This ORDO lets her back in and follows the significant tradition of associating S Cyprian with S Cornelius on their R: date of the 16th.
9. In R: **September 16** is 'Ss Cornelius Pp and Cyprian B, Ms'. CW and other Anglican calendars keep S Ninian B on September 16; his usual R: date is August 26. He is a Festum in the Scotch Episcopal Church.
10. Our Lady of Walsingham (Solemnity in Walsingham, Festum in the Diocese) is, outside England, Our Lady of Ransom.
11. **September 29** (originally the Dedication of the Roman Basilica of S Michael) had 'And All Angels' added by Dr Cranmer; 'And Ss Gabriel and Raphael' by the Roman revisers of 1969.

OCTOBER has traditionally been marked by the saying of the Rosary, followed by the Litany of our Lady. October 1, among Byzantines, commemorates the Protecting Veil of his Mother of God – ie., Our Lady, Mother of Mercy.

| Day | Col | Service | Psalms / Mass | Readings | |
|---|---|---|---|---|---|
| ✠ *SUNDAY* | | | **22nd SUNDAY and WEEK of YEAR** | | **TRINITY 14** |
| **28** | G | MP | Ps: 107:1–32 | Ecclus 11:(7–18) 19–28 | I Sam 18:1–16 |
| | | | | Rev 3:14–22 | Rom 14:1 – 15:3 |
| R: Ps II | | Mass | *Gl; Cr; Sunday Pref [PROPER 17]* | | |
| | | | *CW: Jer 15:15–21; Ps 26:1–8; Rom 12:9–21; Mt 16:21–28* | | |
| | | | *R: Jer 20:7–9; Ps 63:2 & 8–9; Rom 12:1–2; Mt 16:21–27 (Bearing The Cross)* | | |
| | | 2 EP | | II Kgs 6:24–25 & 7:3–20 | Prov 31:10–end |
| | | | Ps: 105:1–15 | Acts 18:1–16 | Mt 6:19–end |
| *MONDAY* | | | *The Passion of S John Baptist M* | | |
| **29** | R | MP | Ps: 61 | II Chron 6:32 – 7:7 | Zech 7 |
| | | | | Mt 4:1–11 | Eph 2:11–end |
| | | Mass | *of the Saint* | | |
| | | | *CW: Jer 1:4–10; Ps 11; Heb 11:32 – 12:2; Mt 14:1–12* | | |
| | | | *R: Jer 1:17–19; Ps 71; Mk 6:17–29* | | |
| | | | *[I Thess 4:13–end; Ps 96; Lk 4:16–30]* | | |
| | | EP | | Gen 1:1–28 or Gen 1:1–5 & 26–28 | Zech 8 |
| | | | Ps: 62 | Jn 1:1–18 | Jn 6:1–21 |
| *TUESDAY* | | | *Feria (□ Ss Margaret Clitherow, Anne Line, & Margaret Ward V Ms)* | | |
| **30** | G (or R) | MP | Ps: [63] 64 | I Kgs 8:65 – 9:9 | Ezra 7 |
| | | | | Mt 4:12–17 | Eph 3 |
| | | Mass | *of Sunday; no Gl or Cr; Common Pref (or of the Saints) (**John Bunyan**)* | | |
| | | | *I Thess 5:1–6 & 9–11; Ps 27:1–8; Lk 4:31–37* | | |
| | | EP | | Isa 40:1–5 | Ezra 8:15 end |
| | | | Ps: 65 | Jn 1:19–28 | Jn 6:22–40 |
| *WEDNESDAY* | | | *Feria (S Aidan B and Saints of Lindisfarne)* | | |
| **31** | G (or W) | MP | Ps: 66 | I Kgs 9:24 – 10:13 | Ezra 9 |
| | | | | Mt 4:18–end | Eph 4:1–16 |
| | | Mass | *as Tuesday (or of the Saint)* | | |
| | | | *Col 1:1–8; Ps 34:11–18; Lk 4:38–end* | | |
| | | EP | | Isa 53:1–9 | Ezra 10:1–19 |
| | | | Ps: [67] 68 | Jn 1:29–34 | Jn 6:41–end |
| **S E P T E M B E R** | | | | | |
| *THURSDAY* | | | *Feria (S Giles Rel)* | | |
| **1** | G (or W) | MP | Ps: 69 | I Kgs 11:1–13 | Neh 1 |
| | | | | Mt 5:1–10 | Eph 4:17–30 |
| | | Mass | *as Tuesday (or of the Saint)* | | |
| | | | *Col 1:9–14; Ps 98:1–5; Lk 5:1–11* | | |
| | | EP | | I Sam 3:1–10 | Neh 2 |
| | | | Ps: 70, 71 | Jn 1:35–42 | Jn 7:1–24 |
| *FRIDAY* | | | *Feria** | | |
| **2** | G | MP | Ps: 72 | I Kgs 11:26–end | Neh 4 |
| | | | | Mt 5:11–16 | Eph 4:31 – 5:21 |
| | | Mass | *as Monday (First Friday: Sacred Heart: see p. 39)* | | |
| | | | *Col 1:15–20; Ps 89:19b–28; Lk 5:33–end* | | |
| | | EP* | | Gen 28:10–17 | Neh 5 |
| | | | Ps: 73 | Jn 1:43–end | Jn 7:25–end |
| *SATURDAY* | | | *S Gregory the Great Pp Dr†* | | |
| **3** | W | MP | Ps: 74 | I Kgs 12:1–24 | Neh 6:1 – 7:4 |
| | | | | Mt 5:17–20 | Eph 5:22–end |
| | | Mass | *(First Saturday; Immaculate Heart: see p. 39)* | | |
| | | | *Col 1:21–23; Ps 117; Lk 6:1–5* | | |
| | G | 1 EP of foll* | | Exod 33:12–end | Neh 8 |
| | | | Ps: 75, 76 | Jn 2:1–11 | Jn 8:1–30 |

* Ebbsfleet Apostolic District, p. 54, note 1. † Ebbsfleet Apostolic District, p. 54, note 2.

|  | |  | | | |
|---|---|---|---|---|---|
| ✠ *SUNDAY* | | | **23th SUNDAY and WEEK of YEAR** | | **TRINITY 15** |
| **4** G | | MP | Ps: 119:17–32 | Ecclus 27:30 – 28:9 | I Sam 26 |
| | | | | Rev 8:1–5 | I Pet 1:13–end |
| R: Ps III | | Mass | *Gl; Cr; Sunday Pref [PROPER 18] (Our Ldy: p. 54)* | | |
| | | | *CW: Ezek 33:7–11; Ps 119:33–40; Rom 13:8–14; Mt 18:15–20* | | |
| | | | *R: Ezek 33:7–9; Ps 95; Rom 13:8–10; Mt 18:15–20 (Winning Back The Sinful Brother)* | | |
| | | 2 EP | | Ezek 12:21 – 13:16 | Job 1 |
| | | | Ps: 108, 115 | Acts 19:1–20 | Mt 7:1–14 |
| *MONDAY* | | | *Feria (☐ Bl Teresa of Calcutta, Rel: EAD)* | | |
| **5** G | (or W) | MP | Ps: 77 | I Kgs 12:25 – 13:10 | Neh 9:1–23 |
| | | | | Mt 5:21–26 | Eph 6:1–9 |
| | | Mass | *as Sunday; no Gl or Cr; Common Pref (or of the Beata)* | | |
| | | | *Col 1:24 – 2:3; Ps 62:1–7; Lk 6:6–11* | | |
| | | EP | | Deut 16:1–6 | Neh 9:24–end |
| | | | Ps: 78:1–20 | Jn 2:12–22 | Jn 8:31–end |
| *TUESDAY* | | | *Feria* | | |
| **6** G | | MP | Ps: 78:21–55 | I Kgs 16:23–end | Neh 13 |
| | | | | Mt 5:27–37 | Eph 6:10–end |
| | | Mass | *as Monday (**Allen Gardener**)* | | |
| | | | *Col 2:6–15; Ps 8; Lk 6:12–19* | | |
| | | EP | | Ezek 36:24–28 | Dan 1 |
| | | | Ps: 78:56–end | Jn 3:1–10 | Jn 9 |
| *WEDNESDAY* | | | *Feria* | | |
| **7** G | | MP | Ps: 79 | I Kgs 17 | Dan 2:1–24 |
| | | | | Mt 5:38–end | Phil 1:1–11 |
| | | Mass | *as Monday* | | |
| | | | *Col 3:1–11; Ps 15; Lk 6:20–26* | | |
| | | EP | | Num 21:4–9 | Dan 2:25–end |
| | | | Ps: 80 | Jn 3:11–21 | Jn 10:1–21 |
| *THURSDAY* | | | **Birth of the BVM** *(see p. 54)* | | |
| **8** W | | MP | H: 214 or 215 | Is 61:10–62:3 (R: Gen 3:9–20) | Gen 28:10–17 |
| | | | (NEH 181 or 183) | | |
| | | | Ps: 72 | Jn 2:1–12 | Rev 12:1–6 |
| | | Mass | *Gl; Pref of BVM(R:); Annunciation (CW); or ASB (6)* | | |
| | | | *CW: Micah 5:1–4; Ps 45:10–17; Rom 8:18–30; Lk 1:39–47* | | |
| | | | *R: Micah 5:1–4 or Rom 8:28–30; Ps 13; Mt 1:(1–16) 18–23* | | |
| | | EP | H: 213 (NEH 180) | Prov 8:22–31 | Ezek 44:1–4 |
| | | | Ps: 98, 138 | Jn 19:23–27 | Rev 7:9–12 |
| *FRIDAY* | | | *Feria (☐ S Peter Claver Pr)* | | |
| **9** G | (or W) | MP | Ps: 84 | I Kgs 18:20–end | Dan 7:9–end |
| | | | | Mt 6:7–15 | Phil 2:1–11 |
| | | Mass | *as Monday (or of the Saint) (**Charles Fuge Lowder Founder Pr**)* | | |
| | | | *I Tim 1:1–2 & 12–14; Ps 16; Lk 6:39–42* | | |
| | | EP | | II Kgs 17:29 & 34–39 | Dan 9 |
| | | | Ps: [85], 86 | Jn 4:1–26 | Jn 11:1–44 |
| *SATURDAY* | | | *Our Lady on Saturday or the Feria* | | |
| **10** W | (or G) | MP | Ps: 87, 88 | I Kgs 19 | Dan 10 |
| | | | | Mt 6:19–24 | Phil 12:12–end |
| | | Mass | *Introduction Paragraph 26(b)* | | |
| | | | *I Tim 1:15–17; Ps 113; Lk 6:43–end* | | |
| W | | 1 EP | | Micah 6:9–end | Dan 12 |
| | | | Ps: 89:1–18 | Jn 4:27–42 | Jn 11:45–end |

| | | | | | |
|---|---|---|---|---|---|
| ✠ *SUNDAY* | | | **24th SUNDAY and WEEK of YEAR** | | **TRINITY 16** |
| **11** | G | MP | Ps: 119:65–88 | Isa 44:24 – 45:8 | I Sam 28:3–end |
| | | | | Rev 12:1–12 | I Pet 2:1–17 |
| R: Ps IV | | Mass | *Gl; Cr; Sunday Pref [PROPER 19]* | | |
| | | | *CW: Gen 50:15–21; Ps 103:(1–7) 8–13; Rom 14:1–12; Mt 18:21–35* | | |
| | | | *R: Ecclus 27:30 – 28:7; Ps 103; Rom 14:7–9; Mt 18:21–35* | | |
| | | | *(The Lord Will Exact As We Exact)* | | |
| | | 2 EP | | Ezek 20.1–8 & 33–34 | Job 2 |
| | | | Ps: 119:41–48 (49–64) | Acts 20:17–38 | Mt 7:15–end |
| *MONDAY* | | | *Feria (□ Most Holy Name of Mary; p. 54)* | | |
| **12** | G (or W) | MP | Ps: 89:19–37 | I Kgs 21:1–16 | Esther 1 |
| | | | | Mt 6:25–end | Phil 3 |
| | | Mass | *of Sunday; no Gl or Cr; Common Pref (or of our Lady)* | | |
| | | | *Our Lady: Gal 4:4–7; Ps Magnificat; Lk 1:39–47* | | |
| | | | *[I Tim2:1–8; Ps 28; Lk 7:1–10]* | | |
| | | EP | | Prov 16:1–20 | Esther 2:5–11 & 15–end |
| | | | Ps: 89.38–end | Jn 4:43–end | Jn 12:1–19 |
| *TUESDAY* | | | *S John Chrysostom B Dr* | | |
| **13** | W | MP | Ps: 90 | I Kgs 21:17–end | Esther 3 |
| | | | | Mt 7:1–12 | Phil 4 |
| | | Mass | *of the Saint* | | |
| | | | *I Tim 3:1–13; Ps 101; Lk 7:11–17* | | |
| | | EP | | Neh 3:1–2 & 4:1–6 | Esther 4 |
| | | | Ps: [91] 92 | Jn 5:2–18 | Jn 12:20–end |
| *WEDNESDAY* | | | **The Exaltation of the Holy Cross (see p. 54)** | | |
| **14** | R | MP | H: 96 (NEH 78) | Gen 3:1–15 | ◁ |
| | | | Ps: 2, 8, 146 | Jn 12:27–36a | ◁ |
| | | Mass | *of the Feast; Gl; Pref of Cross (R:) or (CW) the Short Pref 'From the Fifth Sunday of Lent . . .'* | | |
| | | | *CW=R: Num 21:4–9; Ps 22:23–28 (R: 78); Phil 2:6–11; Jn 3:13–17* | | |
| | | EP | H: 94 (NEH 79) | Isa 63:1–16 | ◁ |
| | | | Ps: 110, 150 | I Cor 1:18–25 | ◁ |
| *THURSDAY* | | | *□ Our Lady at the Cross (see p. 54)* | | |
| **15** | W | MP | Ps: [95], 98 | I Kgs 22:29–45 & 50 | I Macc 1:1–19 |
| | | | | Mt 7:22–29 | Col 1:21 – 2:7 |
| | | Mass | *of our Lady (Heb 5:7–9; Ps 31; Jn 19:25–7 or Lk 2:33–5)* | | |
| | | | *[I Tim 4:12–end; Ps 111:6–end; Lk 7:36–end]* | | |
| | | EP | | Exod 16:1–16 | I Macc 1:20–40 |
| | | | Ps: 99 | Jn 6:1–21 | Jn 14 |
| *FRIDAY* | | | *Ss Cornelius Pp and Cyprian B Ms (see p. 54)* | | |
| **16** | R | MP | Ps: [100] 101 | II Kgs 1:2–17 | I Macc 1:41–end |
| | | | | Mt 8:1–17 | Col 2:8–19 |
| | | Mass | *of the Saints (**Edward Bouverie Pusey Pr**)* | | |
| | | | *I Tim 6:2–12; Ps 49:1–9; Lk 8:1–3* | | |
| | | EP | | Exod 16:17–35 | I Macc 2:1–28 |
| | | | Ps: 102 | Jn 6:25–40 | Jn 15 |
| *SATURDAY* | | | *Our Lady on Saturday or the Feria (□ S Robert Bellarmine B & Dr; S Hildegard Ab)* | | |
| **17** | W (or G) | MP | Ps: [103] or 105:1–22 | II Kings 2 | I Macc 2:29–48 |
| | | | | Mt 8:18–27 | Col 2:20 – 3:11 |
| | | Mass | *Introduction Paragraph 26(b)* | | |
| | | | *I Tim 6:13–16; Ps 100; Lk 8:4–15* | | |
| | G | 1 EP of foll | | Exod 17:1–7 | I Macc 2:49–end |
| | | | Ps: [104] or 105:23–end | Jn 6:41–58 | Jn 16 |

| Day | Colour | Office | Psalms / Mass | Lessons | Alternative |
|---|---|---|---|---|---|
| ✠ *SUNDAY* | | | **25th SUNDAY and WEEK of YEAR** | | **TRINITY 17** |
| **18** | G | MP | Ps: 119:153–176 | Isa 45:9–22 | II Sam 1 |
| | | | | Rev 14:1–5 | I Pet 4 |
| R: Ps I | | Mass | *Gl; Cr; Sunday Pref [PROPER 20]* | | |
| | | | *CW: Jonah 3:10 – 4:11; Ps 145:1–8; Phil 1:21–30; Mt 20:1–16* | | |
| | | | *R: Isa 55:6–9; Ps 145; Phil 1:20–24 & 27; Mt 20:1–16 (God's More Generous Way)* | | |
| | | 2 EP | | Ezek 33:23 & 30 – 34:10 | Job 4:1 & 5:6–end |
| | | | Ps: 119:113–136 | Acts 26:1 & 9–25 | Mt 11:2–19 |
| *MONDAY* | | | *Feria (☐ S Januarius B M; S Theodore B)* | | |
| **19** | G (or R or W) | MP | Ps: 106:1–23 | II Kgs 4:8–37 | I Macc 3:1–26 |
| | | | | Mt 8:28–end | Col 3:12 – 4:1 |
| | | Mass | *of Sunday; no Gl or Cr; Common Pref (or of the Saint)* | | |
| | | | *Ezra 1:1–6; Ps 126; Lk 8:16–18* | | |
| | | EP | | I Sam 24:1–17 | I Macc 3:27–41 |
| | | | Ps: 106:24–end | Jn 7:53 – 8:11 | Jn 17 |
| *TUESDAY* | | | *S Andrew Kim Taegon and All Martyrs of Korea and the Pacific** | | |
| **20** | R | MP | Ps: 107:1–22 | II Kgs 5 | I Macc 3:42–end |
| | | | | Mt 9:1–8 | Col 4:2–end |
| | | Mass | *of the Saints* | | |
| | | | *Ezra 6:7–8 & 12 & 14–20; Ps 124; Lk 8:19–21* | | |
| | | EP | | Isa 58:1–8 | I Macc 4:1–25 |
| | | | Ps: 107:23–end | Jn 8:12–20 | Jn 18:1–27 |
| *WEDNESDAY* | | | **S Matthew Ap** | | |
| **21** | R | MP | Ps: 49, 117 | I Kgs 19:15–21 | Prov 3:1–17 |
| | | | | II Tim 3:14–17 | Mt 19:16–end |
| | | Mass | *Gl; R: Pref of Apostles; CW, of Saints CRP* | | |
| | | | *CW: Prov 3:13–18; Ps 119:65–72; II Cor 4:1–6; Mt 9:9–13* | | |
| | | | *R: Eph 4:1–7 & 11–13; Ps 19; Mt 9:9–13* | | |
| | | EP | | Eccles 5:4–12 | I Chron 29:9–18 |
| | | | Ps: 119:33–40 & 89–96 | Mt 19:16–30 | I Tim 6:6–19 |
| *THURSDAY* | | | *Feria* | | |
| **22** | G | MP | Ps: 112 | II Kgs 9:1–16 | I Macc 6:1–17 |
| | | | | Mt 9:18–26 | I Thess 1 |
| | | Mass | *of Monday (or of the Saints)* | | |
| | | | *Haggai 1:1–8; Ps 149:1–5; Lk 9:7–9* | | |
| | | EP | | Gen 15:1–15 | I Macc 6:18–47 |
| | | | Ps: 113 | Jn 8:48–end | Jn 19:1–30 |
| *FRIDAY* | | | *☐ S Pius of Pietrelcina Pr Rel†* | | |
| **23** | W | MP | Ps: 114 | II Kgs 9:17–end | I Macc 7:1–20 |
| | | | | Mt 9:27–34 | I Thess 2:1–16 |
| | | Mass | *of the Saint (**'Padre Pio'**)* | | |
| | | | *Haggai 1:15b – 2:9; Ps 43; Lk 9:18–22* | | |
| | | EP | | Ezek 18:1–4 & 19–23 | I Macc 7:21–end |
| | | | Ps: 115 | Jn 9:1–12 | Jn 19:31–end |
| *SATURDAY* | | | *Our Lady of Walsingham (p. 54)* | | |
| **24** | W | MP | Ps: 116, 117 | II Kgs 11:1–20a | I Macc 9:1–22 |
| | | | | Mt 9:35 – 10:4 | I Thess 2:17–3 end |
| | | Mass | *of our Lady* | | |
| | | | *Zech 2:1–5 & 10 & 11; Ps 125; Lk 9:43–45* | | |
| | G | 1 EP of foll | | Wis 7:22–30 | I Macc 13:41–end & 14:4–15 |
| | | | Ps: 118 | Jn 9:13–17 & 24–41 | Jn 20 |

* The R: memorial of Ss Andrew Kim Taegon, pr, Paul Chong Hasang, and their Companions, Martyrs (of Korea, where both Anglicans and Roman Catholics died for their Faith) coincides with CW: John Coleridge Patteson. The Compiler suggests a convenient combination as above.

† Anniversary of the Episcopal Ordination in 1996 of John, Tenth Bishop of Fulham.

✠ *SUNDAY* **26th SUNDAY and WEEK of YEAR** **TRINITY 18**

**25** G MP Ps: 125, 126, 127 Isa 48:12–21 II Sam 7
Lk 11:37–54 I Pet 5:1–11

R: Ps II Mass *Gl; Cr; Common Pref ([PROPER 21]*
*CW: Ezek 18:1–4 & 25–32; Ps 25:1–8; Phil 2:1–13; Mt 21:23–32*
*R: Ezek 18:25–28; Ps 25; Phil 2:1–5 (6–11); Mt 21:28–32*
*(Who is Upright, Who The Sinner?)*

2 EP Ezek 37:15–28 Job 19:1–27a
Ps: 120, 123, 124 I Jn 2:22–29 Mt 11:20–end

*MONDAY* *Feria (□ Ss Cosmos and Damian Ms)*

**26** G (or R) MP Ps: 119:1–16 II Kgs 17:1–8 (9–33) 34–end Job 1
Mt 10:5–15 I Thess 4:1–12

Mass *of Sunday; no Gl or Cr; Common Pref (or of the Saint)* ***(Wilson Carlile)***
*Zech 8:1–8; Ps 102:12–22; Lk 9:46–50*

EP Zech 10:6–end Job 2
Ps: 119:17–32 Jn 10:1–10 Jn 21

*TUESDAY* *S Vincent de Paul Pr*

**27** W MP Ps: 119:33–48 II Chron 30 Job 3
Mt 10:16–23 I Thess 4:13 – 5:11

Mass *of the Saint*
*Zech 8:20–end; Ps 87; Lk 9:51–56*

EP Ezek 34:11–16 Job 4
Ps: 119:49–64 Jn 10:11–18 Heb 1

*WEDNESDAY* *Feria (□ S Wenceslas M; □ Ss Laurence Ruiz Comp Ms) (Ember Day)**

**28** G (or R) MP Ps: 119:65–80 II Kgs 18:9–25 Job 5
Mt 10:24–33 I Thess 5:12–end

Mass *of Monday (or of the Saints)*
*Neh 2:1–8; Ps 137:1–6; Lk 9:57–end*

EP Job 17 Job 6
Ps: 119:81–96 Jn 11:1–16 Heb 2

*THURSDAY* **S Michael and** *(see p. 54)*

**29** W MP H: 241 Tobit 12:6–22 or Dan 12:1–4 II Kgs 6:8–17
Ps: 34, 150 Acts 12:1–11 Acts 12:1–11

Mass *Gl; R: Pref of Angels; ASB 21; CW Common Pref*
*CW: Gen 28:10–17; Ps 103:19–22; Rev 12:7–12; Jn 1:47–51*
*R: Dan 7:7–9 & 13–14 or Rev 12:7–12; Ps 138; Jn 1:47–51*

EP Dan 10:4–21 Dan 12:1–4
Ps: 138, 148 Rev 5 Rev 5

*FRIDAY* *S Jerome Pr Dr (Ember Day)**

**30** W MP Ps: 119:129–144 II Kgs 19:1–19 Job 9
Mt 11:1–6 Ii Thess 2

Mass *of the Saint*
*Baruch 1:15–end; Ps 79:1–9; Lk 10:13–16*

EP Ezek 37:1–14 Job 10
Ps: 119:145–160 Jn 11:28–44 Heb 4:1–13

**OCTOBER**

*SATURDAY* *S Teresa of the Child Jesus V Dr (Ember Day)**

**1** W MP Ps: 119:161–end II Kgs 19:20–36 Job 11
Mt 11:7–15 II Thess 3

Mass *(First Saturday: Immaculate Heart see p. 39)* ***(S Remigius B; Anthony Ashley Cooper)***
***(The Protecting Veil of Our Lady)***
*Baruch 4:5–12 & 27–29; Ps 69:33–37; Lk 10:17–24*

G 1 EP of foll Isa 28:9–16 Job 12
Ps: 120, 121 Jn 11:45–end Heb 4:14 – 5:10

* Ember Masses see Introduction para 25.

## OCTOBER *R: CW Year A. Weekday Lectionaries Year 1*

| Day | Colour | Service | Psalms / Mass | Readings | Readings |
|---|---|---|---|---|---|
| ✠ *SUNDAY* | | | **27th SUNDAY and WEEK of YEAR** | | **TRINITY 19*** |
| **2** | G | MP | Ps: 128, 129, 134 | Isa 49:13–23 | II Sam 12:1–23 |
| | | | | Lk 12:1–12 | Col 1:21 – 2:7 |
| R: Ps III | | Mass | *Gl; Cr; Sunday Pref [PROPER 22]* | | |
| | | | *CW: Isa 5:1–7; Ps 80:9–17; Phil 3:4b–14; Mt 21:33–46* | | |
| | | | *R: Isa 5:1–7; Ps 80; Phil 4:6–9; Mt 21:33–43 (The Lord's Vineyard)* | | |
| | | 2 EP | | Prov 2:1–11 | Job 28 |
| | | | Ps: 136 | I Jn 2:1–17 | Mt 12:22–45 |
| *MONDAY* | | | *Feria* | | |
| **3** | G | MP | Ps: 122, 123 | II Kgs 20 | Job 13 |
| | | | | Mt 11:16–24 | I Tim 1:1–17 |
| | | Mass | *of Sunday; no Gl or Cr; Common Pref* | | |
| | | | *Jonah 1:1 – 2:2 & 10; Canticle: Jonah 2:3 – 5 & 8; Lk 10:25–37* | | |
| | | EP | | Deut 15:1–11 | Job 14 |
| | | | Ps: 124, 125 | Jn 12:1–8 | Heb 5:11–6 end |
| *TUESDAY* | | | *S Francis of Assisi* | | |
| **4** | W | MP | Ps: 126, 127 | II Kgs 21:1–18 | Job 15:1–16 |
| | | | | Mt 11:25–end | I Tim 1:18–2 end |
| | | Mass | *of the Saint* | | |
| | | | *Jonah 3; Ps 130; Lk 10:38–end* | | |
| | | EP | | Zech 9:9–12 | Job 16:1 – 17:2 |
| | | | Ps: 128, 129 | Jn 12:12–19 | Heb 7 |
| *WEDNESDAY* | | | *Feria* | | |
| **5** | G | MP | Ps: 130, 131, 146 | II Kgs 22:1 – 22:3 | Job 17:3–end |
| | | | | Mt 12:1–14 | I Tim 3 |
| | | Mass | *of Monday* | | |
| | | | *Jonah 4; Ps 86:1–9; Lk 11:1–4* | | |
| | | EP | | Zech 8:14–end | Job 18 |
| | | | Ps: 132 | Jn 12:20–26 | Heb 8 |
| *THURSDAY* | | | *Feria (☐ S Bruno Pr)* | | |
| **6** | G (or W) | MP | Ps: 133 [134], 147:1–12 | II Kgs 23:4–25 | Job 19 |
| | | | | Mt 12:15–21 | I Tim 4 |
| | | Mass | *as Monday Wednesday (or of the Saint)* ***(William Tyndale Ref M)*** | | |
| | | | *Malachi 3:13 – 4:2a; Ps 1; Lk 11:5–13* | | |
| | | EP | | Ezek 37:24–end | Job 21 |
| | | | Ps: 135 | Jn 12:27–36a | Heb 9:1–24 |
| *FRIDAY* | | | *☐ Our Lady of the Rosary* | | |
| **7** | W | MP | Ps: 136, 147:13–end | II Kgs 23:36 – 24:17 | Job 22 |
| | | | | Mt 12:22–32 | I Tim 5 |
| | | Mass | *of our Lady (R: Acts 1:12–14; Ps Magnificat; Lk 1:26–38)* | | |
| | | | *(First Friday; Sacred Heart: see p. 39)* | | |
| | | | *[Joel 1:13–15 & 2:1–2; Ps 9:1–7; Lk 11:15–26]* | | |
| | | EP | | Ecclus 32:14–20 & 24 | Job 23 |
| | | | Ps: 137, 138 | Jn 12:37–end | Heb 9:15–end |
| *SATURDAY* | | | *Our Lady on Saturday or the Feria* | | |
| **8** | W (or G) | MP | Ps: 139, 148 | II Kgs 25:8–26 | Job 24 |
| | | | | Mt 12:33–42 | I Tim 6 |
| | | Mass | *Introduction Paragraph 26(b)* | | |
| | | | *Joel 3:12–21; Ps 97:1 & 8–end; Lk 11:27–28* | | |
| | G | 1 EP of foll | | Lam 3:1–6 & 19–26 | Job 25 & 26 |
| | | | Ps: 145 | Jn 13:1–20 | Heb 10:1–18 |

* See Introduction Appendix 2 for Dedication.

| Day | Colour | Service | Psalms / Mass | Lessons | Alternative lessons |
|---|---|---|---|---|---|
| ✠ *SUNDAY* **9** | G | | **28th SUNDAY and WEEK of YEAR** | | **TRINITY 20** |
| | | MP | Ps: 138, 141 | Isa 50:4–10 | II Sam 18 |
| | | | | Lk 13:22–30 | Col 3:12 – 4:6 |
| R: Ps IV | | Mass | *Gl; Cr; Sunday Pref [PROPER 23]* | | |
| | | | *CW: Isa 25:1–9; Ps 23; Phil 4:1–9; Mt 22:1–14* | | |
| | | | *R: Isa 25:6–10a; Ps 23; Phil 4:12–14 & 19–20; Mt 22:1–10 (11–14)* | | |
| | | | *(The Lord's Great Banquet)* | | |
| | | 2 EP | | Prov 3:1–18 | Job 38 & 42:1–6 |
| | | | Ps: 139:1–18 | I Jn 3:1–15 | Mt 13:44–end |
| *MONDAY* **10** | G (or W) | | *Feria (S Paulinus B)* | | |
| | | MP | Ps: 141, 149 | Jer 29:1 & 4–14 | Job 27 |
| | | | | Mt 12:43–end | Titus 1:1 – 2:8 |
| | | Mass | *of Sunday; no Gl or Cr; Common Pref (or of the Saint)* (***Thomas Traherne***) | | |
| | | | *Rom 1:1–7; Ps 98; Lk 11:29–32* | | |
| | | EP | | Lev 19:1 & 17–18 | Job 28 |
| | | | Ps: 142, 143 | Jn 13:21–end | Heb 10:19–end |
| *TUESDAY* **11** | G (or W) | | *Feria (S Ethelburga Ab; S James Dcn; □ Bl John XXIII Pp)** | | |
| | | MP | Ps: 144, 150 | Jer 35 | Job 29:1 – 30:1 |
| | | | | Mt 13:1–9 | Titus 2:9–3 end |
| | | Mass | *of Monday (or of the Saint)†* | | |
| | | | *Rom 1:16–25; Ps 19:1–4; Lk 11:37–41* | | |
| | | EP | | Deut 31:1–13 | Job 31:13–end |
| | | | Ps: 145 | Jn 14:1–7 | Heb 11:1–16 |
| *WEDNESDAY* **12** | G (or W) | | *Feria (S Wilfrid B: CHICHESTER Co-Principal Patron)* | | |
| | | MP | Ps: 1, 2 | Jer 36:1–26 | Job 32 |
| | | | | Mt 13:10–17 | II Tim 1 |
| | | Mass | *as Monday (or of the Saint)* (***Elizabeth Fry; Edith Cavell***) | | |
| | | | *Rom 2:1–11; Ps 62:1–8; Lk 11:42–46* | | |
| | | EP | | Wisd 6:12–20 | Job 33 |
| | | | Ps: 3 [4] | Jn 14:8–24 | Heb 11:17–end |
| *THURSDAY* **13** | G (or W) | | *Feria (S Edward the Confessor)* | | |
| | | MP | Ps: 5 | Jer 36:27 – 37:10 | Job 38:1–21 |
| | | | | Mt 13:18–23 | II Tim 2 |
| | | Mass | *as Monday (or of the Saint)* | | |
| | | | *Rom 3:21–30; Ps 130; Lk 11:47–end* | | |
| | | EP | | Exod 19:1–6 | Job 38:22–end |
| | | | Ps: 6 | Jn 14:25–end | Heb 12:1–13 |
| *FRIDAY* **14** | G (or R) | | *Feria (□ S Callistus I Pp M)* | | |
| | | MP | Ps: 7 | Jer 37:11 – 38:13 | Job 39 |
| | | | | Mt 13:24–30 | II Tim 3 |
| | | Mass | *as Monday (or of a Saint)* | | |
| | | | *Rom 4:1–8; Ps 32; Lk 12:1–7* | | |
| | | EP | | Isa 5:1–10 | Job 40 |
| | | | Ps: 8, 9 | Jn 15:1–11 | Heb 12:14–end |
| *SATURDAY* **15** | W | | *S Teresa of Jesus V Dr* | | |
| | | MP | Ps: 10 | Jer 38:14–end | Job 41 |
| | | | | Mt 13:31–35 | II Tim 4 |
| | | Mass | *of the Saint* | | |
| | | | *Rom 4:13 & 16–18; Ps 105:6–10 & 41–44; Lk 12:8–12* | | |
| | G | 1 EP of foll | | Deut 7:6–11 | Job 42 |
| | | | Ps: 11, 12 | Jn 15:12–17 | Heb 13 |

* In the Church of Ireland, S Philip the Deacon enters the Calendar as a FESTUM.

† Feast of the Miraculous IKON of our Lady called the Iverian. A copy is venerated in the Shrine Church at Walsingham.

✠ *SUNDAY* **29th SUNDAY and WEEK of YEAR** **TRINITY 21**

**16** G MP Ps: 145, 149 Isa 54:1–14 Wisd 2
Lk 13:31–35 Philemon

R: Ps I Mass *Gl; Cr; Sunday Pref [PROPER 24]*
*CW: Isa 45:1–7; Ps 96:1–9 (10–13); I Thess 1:1–10; Mt 22:15–22*
*R: Isa 45:1 & 4–6; Ps 96; I Thess 1:1–5b; Mt 22:15–21 (God and Caesar*

2 EP Prov 4:1–18 Baruch 3:1–14
Ps: 142, 143:1–11 I Jn 3:16 – 4:6 Mt 14:13–33

*MONDAY* *S Ignatius of Antioch B M*

**17** R MP Ps: 13, 14 Jer 44:1–14 Prov 1:1–19
Mt 13:46–43 Jas 1:1–11

Mass *of the Saint*
*Rom 4:20–end; Canticle: Benedictus vv 1–6; Lk 12:13–21*

EP Wisd 8:2–9 Prov 1:20–end
Ps: 15, 16 Jn 15:26 – 16:15 Jas 1:12–end

*TUESDAY* **S Luke, Evangelist**

**18** R MP Ps: 145, 146 Isa 55 Isa 61:1–6
Lk 1:1–4 II Tim 3:10–end

Mass *Gl; R: Pref of the Apostles; CW, of Saints*
*CW: Isa 35:3–6 or Acts 16:6–12a; Ps 147:1–7; II Tim 4:5–17; Lk 10:1–9*
*R: II Tim 4:10–17b; Ps 145; Lk 10:1–9*

EP Ecclus 38:1–14 or Isa 61:1–6 Isa 55
Ps: 103 Col 4:7–18 Col 4:7–end

*WEDNESDAY* *Feria (☐ Ss John de Brebeuf & Isaac Jogues Prs Comp Ms;*
*☐ S Paul of the Cross Pr; S Frideswide V SOL in Oxford)*

**19** G (orR or W) MP Ps: 18:1–25 Lamentations 2:8–15 Prov 3:27 – 4:19
Mt 13:53–58 Jas 3

Mass *of Sunday; no Gl or Cr; Common Pref (or of the Saints)* (***Henry Martyn***)
*Rom 6:12–18; Ps 124; Lk 12:39–48*

EP Isa 63:7–14 Prov 4:20 – 5:14
Ps: 18:26–end Jn 16:25–end Jas 4

*THURSDAY* *Feria*

**20** G MP Ps: 20 Ezra 1 Prov 6:1–19
Mt 14:1–12 Jas 5

Mass *as Wednesday*
*Rom 6:19–end; Ps 1; Lk 12:49–53*

EP Ezek 37:15–23 Prov 8
Ps: 21 Jn 17:1–19 I Pet 1:1–12

*FRIDAY* *Feria*

**21** G MP Ps: 22 Ezra 3:1–13 Prov 9
Mt 14:13–21 I Pet 1:13–end

Mass *as Wednesday*
*Rom 7:18–end; Ps 119:33–40; Lk 12:54–end*

EP Isa 56:1–8 Prov 10:1–22
Ps: 23 [24] Jn 17:20–26 I Pet 2:1–10

*SATURDAY* *Our Lady on Saturday or the Feria*

**22** W (or G) MP Ps: 25 Ezra 4:7–end Prov 11:1–25
Mt 14:22–end I Pet 2:11 – 3:7

Mass *Introduction Paragraph 26(b)* (***Our Lady of Kazan***)
*Rom 8:1–11; Ps 24:1–6; Lk 13:1–9*

G 1 EP of foll Eccles 5:1–7 Prov 12:10–end
Ps: 26, 27 II Tim 1:1–7 I Pet 3:8–end

| Day | Colour | Office | Psalms / Notes | Readings | BCP |
|---|---|---|---|---|---|
| ✠ *SUNDAY* | | | **30th SUNDAY and WEEK of YEAR; CW: LAST after TRINITY BCP TRINITY 22*** | | |
| **23** | G | MP | Ps: 119:137–152 | Isa 59:9–20<br>Lk 14:1–14 | Wisd 4:7–17<br>James 1:1–18 (19–end) |
| R: Ps II | | Mass | *Gl; Cr; Sunday Pref [PROPER 25]*<br>*CW: Lev 19:1–2 & 15–18; Ps 1; I Thess 2:1–8; Mt 22:34–46*<br>*R: Exod 22:21–26; Ps: 18; I Thess 1:5c–10; Mt 22:34–40*<br>*(The Commandment of Love)* | | |
| | | 2 EP | Ps: 119:89–104 | Eccles 11 & 12<br>II Tim 2:1–7 | Baruch 4:36 – 5:end<br>Mt 16:13–end |
| *MONDAY* | | | *Feria (☐ S Antony Mary Claret B)* | | |
| **24** | G (or W) | MP | Ps: 28, 29 | Zech 1:7–17<br>Mt 15:1–20 | Prov 14:9–27<br>I Pet 4:1–11 |
| | | Mass | *Sunday; no Gl or Cr; Common Pref (or of the Saint)*<br>*Rom 8:12–17; Ps 68:1–6 & 19; Lk 13:10–17* | | |
| | | EP | Ps: 30 | Eccles 5:10–end<br>II Tim 1:8–end | Prov 15:18–end<br>I Pet 4:12–end |
| *TUESDAY* | | | *Feria (Ss Crispin and Crispinian Ms)* | | |
| **25** | G (or R) | MP | Ps: 31:(1–6) 7–end | Haggai 1<br>Mt 15:21–28 | Prov 16:31 – 17:17<br>I Pet 5 |
| | | Mass | *as Monday (or of the Saints)*<br>*Rom 8:18–25; Ps 126; Lk 13:18–21* | | |
| | | EP | Ps: 32 | Eccles 7:1–13<br>II Tim 2:1–13 | Prov 18:10–end<br>I Jn 1:1 – 2:6 |
| *WEDNESDAY* | | | *Feria (Ss Chad and Cedd)* | | |
| **26** | G (or W) | MP | Ps: 33 | Haggai 2<br>Mt 15:29–end | Prov 20:1–22<br>I Jn 2:7–17 |
| | | Mass | *as Monday (or of the Saint)*<br>*Rom 8:26–30; Ps 13; Lk 13:22–30* | | |
| | | EP | Ps: 34 | Eccles 11<br>II Tim 2:14–26 | Prov 22:1–16<br>I Jn 2:18–end |
| *THURSDAY* | | | *Feria* | | |
| **27** | G | MP | Ps: 35 | Ezra 5<br>Mt 16:1–12 | Prov 24:23–end<br>I Jn 3:1–18 |
| | | Mass | *as Monday*<br>*Rom 8:31–end; Ps 109:20–21; Lk 13:31–end* | | |
| | | EP | Ps: 36 | Eccles 12<br>II Tim 3 | Prov 25<br>I Jn 3:19 – 4:6 |
| *FRIDAY* | | | **Ss Simon & Jude, Apostles** | | |
| **28** | R | MP | Ps: 116, 117 | Wisd 5:1–16 or Isa 45:18–26<br>Lk 6:12–16 | Isa 45:18–end<br>Lk 6:12–19 |
| | | Mass | *Gl; R: Pref of Apostles; CW, of Saints*<br>*CW: Isa 28:14–16; Ps 119:89–96; Eph 2:19–22; Jn 15:17–27*<br>*R: Eph 2:19–22; Ps 19; Lk 6:12–16 (17–19)* | | |
| | | EP | Ps: 119:1–16 | I Macc 2:42–66<br>or Jer 3:11–18<br>Jude 1–4 & 17–25 | Jer 3:11–18<br>Eph 2:11–end |
| *SATURDAY* | | | *Our Lady on Saturday or the Feria* | | |
| **29** | W (or G) | MP | Ps: 38 | Neh 1<br>Mt 16:21–end | Prov 30:1–16<br>II Jn |
| | | Mass | *Introduction Paragraph 26(b) (**James Hannington BM**)*<br>*Rom 11:1–2 & 11–12 & 25–29; Ps 94:14–19; Lk 14:1 & 7:11* | | |
| | G | 1 EP of foll† | Ps: 39 | Job 38:19–end & 42:1–6<br>II Pet 1:1–11 | Prov 31:10–end<br>III Jn |

* Dedication: See Introduction Appendix 2. In the new Church of Ireland Calendar, S James, Brother of the Lord, enters the Calendar as a FESTUM. He appears to be borrowed from the Byzantine Calendar, where he is described as Brother of God.

† All Saints: see p. 64.

NOVEMBER FESTIVALS

1. Rome leaves All Saints on Tuesday November 1, while allowing **also** an External Solemity (Introduction Paragraph 5A) on Sunday October 30. CW allows All Saints on EITHER November 1 OR Sunday October 30 OR both.

2. ALL SOULS DAY. Rome retains the custom that arose (1915) during the carnage of the First World War, of allowing every priest to say three masses, for these intentions: (1) the priest's own; (2) for all the Departed; (3) to make up for testamentary masses neglected or forgotten, and for the souls of all, especially youth, who fall victim to the appalling carnage of war. The Missal provides three sets of texts; CW 'Pastoral Services' could be drawn upon. (The three masses should be said at different times.) PHG provides the Office.

3. **November 8**: CW 'Ss and Ms of England'; Scotland 'Ss Ms Drs of Scotland, England, Wales and Ireland'; Wales R: 'All Saints of Wales'; Church in Wales 'The Saints of Wales'. 'Saints and Martyrs (etc etc)' seems to pile up pleonasm. Your Compiler suggests the traditional Western 'All Saints of N' and continues to offer Office readings from PHG. (Mass propers: National Appendix to Weekday Missal under November 6.) Some religious orders have traditionally kept, around this season, a Festival of All their Saints. All the Saints whose Relics were preserved in a Church or Diocese used to be commemorated in many places with the Mass which the English Missal, National Supplement, preserves on November 5 (EXETER: Monday after the Ascension).

4. **November 9**: Dedication of the Lateran Basilica, the papal Cathedral in Rome, dedicated to Christ (replicated by S Augustine in the dedication of Canterbury Cathedral), is a Festum of the Lord. Office and Mass readings from Appendix 2. *Gl but not Cr; Dedication Pref.* In creating a 'Little Rome' at Canterbury, the Augustinian Mission there also perpetuated the Roman dedications to Ss Peter and Paul and S Mary (see August 5).

5. Where the great patriarch of Western Monasticism, S Martin of Tours, is Patron, PHG suggests:1EP Isa 58:6–12 & Acts 20:28–35 MP Ezek 34:11–16 & 11 Cor 4:1–10 2EP Mal 2:5–7 & Phil 4:4–9 (Psalms 1, 15, 112). Forward in Faith celebrates this day as its foundation day.

6. November 17, 18, and 19:

| | R: | CW |
|---|---|---|
| November 17 | Ss Hilda†, Hugh†, or Elizabeth† | S Hugh† |
| 18 | Dedication of the Basilicas of Ss Peter and Paul†* | S Elizabeth† |
| 19 | Our Lady on Saturday† | S Hilda† or S Mechtild† |

† Optional – all of them, in both Calendars.
* Mass: Acts 28:11–16 & 30–31; Ps 98; Mt 14:22–33. Propers of Apostles NOT of Dedication; the mass theme is Rome as the place of their linked martyrdoms.

7. November 21: Presentation of our Lady: *not* a mistaken duplication of February 2! Originally (543) the Dedication of New S Mary's By The Temple in Jerusalem, it is one of the year's Twelve Great Festivals among the Orthodox, from whom it reached Saxon England (it was not grudgingly accepted by Rome until 1585).

   The *mythos* that, aged three, Mary was lodged as a contemplative in the Temple and fed by angels with fruit as from the Tree of Life in Eden highlights her immaculate sanctity and anticipates her bodily Assumption.

| Day | Col. | Office | | Lesson I | Lesson II |
|---|---|---|---|---|---|
| ✠ *SUNDAY* | | | **31st SUNDAY and WEEK of YEAR; CW: 4th BEFORE ADVENT or ALL SAINTS (p. 64). BCP TRINITY 23** | | |
| **30** | G | MP | Ps: 33 | Isa 66:20–23 | Wisd 6:1–21 |
| | | | | Eph 1:11–23 | James 2:1–13 (14–end) |
| R: Ps III | | Mass | *Gl; Cr; Sunday Pref* | | |
| | | | *CW: Mic 3:5–12; Ps 43; I Thess 2:9–13; Mt 24:1–14* | | |
| | | | *R: Mal 1:14 – 2:2 & 8–10; Ps 131; I Thess 2:7–9 & 13; Mt 23:1–12* | | |
| | | | *(The Leaders have strayed)* | | |
| | | 2 EP | | Dan 7:1–18 | Jer 11:1–14 |
| | | | Ps: 111, 117 | Lk 6:17–31 | Mt 18:1–20 |
| *MONDAY* | | | *Feria* | | |
| **31** | G | MP | Ps: 139, 150) | Neh 2 | Ecclus 1:1–10 |
| | | | | Mt 17:1–13 | Acts 1 |
| | | Mass | *Sunday; no Gl r Cr; Common Pref (**Martin Luther Pr Rel**)* | | |
| | | | *Rom 11:29–end; Ps 69:31–37; Lk 14:12–14* | | |
| | | | **ALL SAINTS (see p. 64)** | | |
| | W | 1 EP of foll; | H: 249 (NEH 196) | Ecclus 44:1–15 or Isa 40:27–31 | Isa 65:17–end |
| | | | Ps: 1, 5 | Rev 19:6–10 (R: 5:1–14) | Heb 11:32 – 12:2 |

**N O V E M B E R : YOU NEED THE 2005/6 ORDO**

| Day | Col. | Office | | Lesson I | Lesson II |
|---|---|---|---|---|---|
| *TUESDAY* | | | | | |
| **1** | W | MP | Ps: 15, 84, 149 | Isa 35:1–9 | Wisd 3:1–9 |
| | | | | Lk 9:18–27 | Rev 19:6–10 |
| | | Mass | *Gl; Cr; R: and CW: Proper Pref* | | |
| | | | *CW: Rev 7:9–17; Ps 34:1–10; I Jn 3:1–3; Mt 5:1–12* | | |
| | | | *R: Rev 7:2–4 & 9–14; Ps 24:1–6; I Jn 3:1–3; Mt 5:1–12* | | |
| | | 2 EP* | H: 249 (NEH 196) | Isa 65:17–25 | Ecclus 44:1–15 |
| | | | Ps: 148, 150 | Heb 11–32 – 12:2 | Heb 12:18–24 |
| *WEDNESDAY* | | | **ALL SOULS DAY** | | |
| **2** | B or P | MP | Ps: 90 | Job 19:21–27a | ◁ |
| | | | | II Cor 4:16 – 5:10 | ◁ |
| | | Mass | *of the day; no Gl or Cr; Seq ad lib (EH 351 NEH 524); ASB Pref (16) is the traditional Pref for the Departed. R: additionally offers four more Prefaces of Christian Death.* | | |
| | | | *CW: Lam 3:17–26 & 31–33 or Wisd 3:1–9; Ps 23 or 27:1–6 & 16–17; Rom 5:5–11 or I Pet 1:3–9; Jn 5:19–25 or Jn 6:37–40* | | |
| | | | *R: (others allowed) Isa 25:6–9; Ps 23; Rom 5:5–11; Jn 6:37–40 (three Masses may be said)* | | |
| | B or P | EP of the day: | H: 350 (NEH 327) | Dan 12:1–3 | ◁ |
| | | | Ps: 121, 130 | I Thess 4:13–end | ◁ |
| *THURSDAY* | | | *Feria (S Martin de Porres Rel; □ S Winefride V)* | | |
| **3** | G (or W) | MP | Ps: 145, 148 | Neh 6:1 – 7:4 | Ecclus 6:14–31 |
| | | | | Mt 18:1–9 | Acts 5:12–end |
| | | Mass | *as Monday (or of the Saint) (**Richard Hooker Pr**)* | | |
| | | | *Rom 14:7–12; Ps 27:14–end; Lk 15:1–10* | | |
| | | EP | | Dan 3:13–18 | Ecclus 7:27–end |
| | | | Ps: 34 | Rev 2:8–11 | Acts 6:1–7 – 7:16 |
| *FRIDAY* | | | *□ S Charles Borromeo B* | | |
| **4** | W | MP | Ps: 23, 125, 147:1–12 | Neh 7:73b–end of 8 | Ecclus 10:6–8 & 12–24 |
| | | | | Mt 18:10–20 | Acts 7:17–34 |
| | | Mass | *of the Saint (First Friday: Sacred Heart: see p. 39)* | | |
| | | | *Rom 15:14–21; Ps 98; Lk 16:1–8* | | |
| | | EP | | Dan 5:1–8 | Ecclus 11:7–28 |
| | | | Ps: 142, 143 | Rev 2:12–17 | Acts 7:35 – 8:4 |
| *SATURDAY* | | | *Our Lady on Saturday or the Feria* | | |
| **5** | W (or G) | MP | Ps: 92, 97, 149 | Lev 1:1–9 | Ecclus 14:20 – 15:10 |
| | | | | Mt 18:21–end | Acts 8:4–25 |
| | | Mass | *Introduction Paragraph 26(b) (First Saturday: Immaculate Heart: see p. 39)* | | |
| | | | *Rom 16:3–9 & 16 & 22–end; Ps 145:1–7; Lk 16:9–15* | | |
| | W | EP of the day | | Dan 5:13–30 | Ecclus 15:11–end |
| | | | Ps: 84 | Rev 2:18–29 | Acts 8:26–end |

* May be followed by an EP for the Departed.

| Day | Colour | Office | Psalms / Mass | Lessons | |
|---|---|---|---|---|---|
| ✠ *SUNDAY* | | | **32nd SUNDAY and WEEK of YEAR; CW: 3rd before ADVENT BCP TRINITY 24** | | |
| **6** | G | MP | Ps: 91 | Deut 17:14–20 | Wisd 7:15 – 8:1 |
| | | | | I Tim 2:1–7 | James 3 |
| R: Ps IV | | Mass | *Gl; Cr; Sunday Pref* | | |
| | | | *CW: Wisd 6:12–16; Ps: Wisd 6:17–20; I Thess 4:13–18; Mt 25:1–13* | | |
| | | | *R: Wisd 6:12–16; Ps 63; I Thess 4:13–14 (15–18); Mt 25:1–13 (Be awake)* | | |
| | | 2 EP | | Judg 7:2–22 | Jer 22:1–9 |
| | | | Ps: 20, 82 | Jn 15:9–17 | Mt 21:12–32 |
| *MONDAY* | | | *Feria (S Willibrord B)* | | |
| **7** | G (or W) | MP | Ps: 139, 150 | Lev 16:1–16 | Ecclus 16:17–end |
| | | | | Mat 19:1–12 | Acts 9:1–31 |
| | | Mass | *of Sunday; no Gl or Cr; Common Pref (or of the Saint)* | | |
| | | | *Wisd 1:1–7; Ps 139:1–9 or 24:1–6; Lk 17:1–6* | | |
| | | EP | | Dan 6:1–23 | Ecclus 17:1–24 |
| | | | Ps: 15, 16 | Rev 3:1–6 | Act 9:32–end |
| *TUESDAY* | | | **All Saints of England (see p. 64)** | | |
| **8** | W | MP | Ps: 1, 34 | Isa 61:4–9 | ◁ |
| | | | H: 253:1, 3, 7–13 | II Cor 4:5–15 | ◁ |
| | | Mass | *of the saints. Gl; R: Pref of All Saints. (Missal, see National Appendix, November 6)* | | |
| | | | *CW: Ecclus 44:1–15; Ps 15; Rev 19:5–10; Jn 17:18–23* | | |
| | | | *PHG= R: Ecclus 44:1–15; Ps 15; Lk 6:17–23* | | |
| | | EP | | Ecclus 51:1–12 | ◁ |
| | | | Ps: 15 | Rev 19:6–10 | ◁ |
| *WEDNESDAY* | | | **☐ Dedication of the Lateran Basilica** | | |
| **9** | W | MP | [Ps: 65, 147:13–end)] | [Lev 25:1–17] | [Ecclus 21:1–17] |
| | | | | [Mt 19:23–end] | [Acts 11:1–18] |
| | | Mass | *of the Dedication (see p. 64 note 4) (***Margery Kempe***)* | | |
| | | | *(Obit, 2003, of John, First Bishop of Ebbsfleet)* | | |
| | | | *[Wisd 6:1–11; Ps 82; Lk 17:11–19]* | | |
| | | EP | | [Zeph 1:1–9] | [Ecclus 22:6–22] |
| | | | [Ps: 77] | [Rev 3:14–end] | [Acts 11:19–end] |
| *THURSDAY* | | | *S Leo the Great Pp Dr* | | |
| **10** | W | MP | Ps: 145, 148 | Neh 12:27–end | Ecclus 22:27 – 23:15 |
| | | | | Mt 20:1–16 | Acts 12:1–24 |
| | | Mass | *of the Saint* | | |
| | | | *Wisd 7:22 – 8:1; Ps 119:89–96; Lk 17:20–25* | | |
| | | EP | | Zeph 3:8–13 | Ecclus 24:1–22 |
| | | | Ps: 34 | Rev 4 | Acts 12:25 – 13:12 |
| *FRIDAY* | | | *S Martin of Tours B (see p. 64, para 5* | | |
| **11** | W | MP | Ps: 23, 125, 147:1–12 | Neh 13:1–22 | Ecclus 24:23–end |
| | | | | Mt 20:17–28 | Acts 13:13–43 |
| | | Mass | *of the Saint* | | |
| | | | *Wisd 13:1–9; Ps 19:1–4; Lk 17:26–end* | | |
| | | EP | | Zeph 3:14–end | Ecclus 27:30 – 28:9 |
| | | | Ps: 142, 143 | Rev 5 | Acts 13:44 – 14:7 |
| *SATURDAY* | | | *☐ S Josaphat B M* | | |
| **12** | R | MP | Ps: 92, 97, 149 | Ezra 7:1 & 6–end | Ecclus 31:1–11 |
| | | | | Mt 20:29–end | Acts 14:8–end |
| | | Mass | *of the Saint* | | |
| | | | *Wisd 18:14–16 & 19:6–9; Ps 105:1–5 & 35–42; Lk 18:1–8* | | |
| | G | 1 EP of foll | | Zech 1:1–6 | Ecclus 34:9–end |
| | | | Ps: 84 | Rev 7:1–4 & 9–17 | Acts 15:1–21 |

| | | | | | |
|---|---|---|---|---|---|
| ✠ *SUNDAY* | | | **33rd SUNDAY and WEEK of YEAR; CW: 2nd before ADVENT BCP TRINITY 25 (BCP PROPERS FOR EPIPHANY 6)** | | |
| **13** | G | MP | Ps: 98 | Dan 10:19–21<br>Rev 4 | Wisd 9<br>James 4 |
| R: Ps I | | Mass | *Gl; Cr; Sunday Pref (**Remembrance Sunday**)*<br>*CW: Zeph 1:7 & 12–18; Ps 90:1–8 (9–11) 12; I Thess 5:1–11; Mt 25:14–30*<br>*R: Prov 31:10–13 & 19–20 & 30–31; Ps 128; I Thess 5:1–6;*<br>*Mt 25:14–15 (16–18) 19–20 (21–30) (The Profitable Servant)* | | |
| | | 2 EP | Ps: 89:19–37 | I Kgs 1: (1–14) 15–40<br>Rev 1:4–18 | Ecclus 18:1–13<br>Mt 21:33–end |
| *MONDAY* | | | *Feria* | | |
| **14** | G | MP | Ps: 139, 150 | Ezra 8:21–end<br>Mt 26:1–16 | Eccles 1<br>Acts 15:22–35 |
| | | Mass | *of Sunday; no Gl or Cr, Common Pref (**Samuel Seabury B**)*<br>*I Mac 1:10–15 & 41–43 & 54–57 & 62–64; Ps 79:1–5; Lk 18:35–end* | | |
| | | EP | Ps: 15, 16 | Zech 2:1–5<br>Rev 11:15–end | Eccles 2:1–23<br>Acts 15:36 – 16:5 |
| *TUESDAY* | | | *Feria (☐ S Albert the Great B Dr)* | | |
| **15** | G (or W) | MP | Ps: 116, 146 | Ezra 9<br>Mt 26:17–25 | Eccles 3:1–15<br>Acts 16:6–end |
| | | Mass | *of Monday (or of the Saint)*<br>*II Mac 6:18–end; Ps 11; Lk 19:1–10* | | |
| | | EP | Ps: 73 | Zech 4<br>Rev 12:7–12 | Eccles 3:16 – 4:6<br>Acts 17:1–15 |
| *WEDNESDAY* | | | *Feria (S Margaret of Scotland SCOTLAND Festum; ☐ S Gertrude V; S Edmund of Abingdon B)* | | |
| **16** | G (or W) | MP | Ps: 65, 147:13–end | Ezra 10:1–17<br>Mt 26:36–46 | Eccles 4:7–end<br>Acts 17:16–end |
| | | Mass | *as Monday (or of the Saints) (**Our Lady of Divine Providence**)*<br>*II Mac 7–1 & 20–31; Ps 116:10–end; Lk 19:11–28* | | |
| | | EP | Ps: 77 | Zech 8:1–13<br>Rev 14:1–5 & 12–13 | Eccles 5<br>Acts 18:1–23 |
| *THURSDAY* | | | *See p. 64* | | |
| **17** | G (or W) | MP | Ps: 145, 148 | Neh 9<br>Mt 26:47–56 | Eccles 6<br>Acts 18:24 – 19:7 |
| | | Mass | *I Mac 2:15–29; Ps 129; Lk 19:41–44* | | |
| | | EP | Ps: 34 | Zech 9:9–12<br>Rev 14:14–end | Eccles 7:1–14<br>Acts 19:8–20 |
| *FRIDAY* | | | *See p. 64* | | |
| **18** | G (or W) | MP | Ps: 23, 125, 147:1–12 | Obadiah vv 1–16<br>Mt 26:57–end | Eccles 7:15–end<br>Acts 19:21–end |
| | | Mass | *I Mac 4:36–37 & 52–59; Ps 122; Lk 19:45–48* | | |
| | | EP | Ps: 142, 143 | Ezek 1:1 & 4–13 & 22–end<br>Rev 15:1–4 | Eccles 8<br>Acts 20:1–16 |
| *SATURDAY* | | | *See p. 64* | | |
| **19** | W (or G) | MP | Ps: 92, 97, 149 | Isa 65:17–end<br>Mt 27:1–14 | Eccles 9<br>Acts 20:17–end |
| | | Mass | *I Mac 6:1–13; Ps 124; Lk 20:27–40* | | |
| | W | 1 EP of foll | Ps: 99, 100 | Isa 10:33 – 11:9<br>I Tim 6:11–16 | ◁ [Eccles 10:5–18]<br>◁ [Acts 21:–16] |

| Day | Colour | Service | Psalms / Hymns / Propers | Reading | Weekday Lectionary Year 1 |
|---|---|---|---|---|---|
| ✠ *SUNDAY* | | | **SOLEMNITY OF CHRIST THE KING** | | |
| **20** | W | MP | H: 142 (NEH 129) | Isa 4:2 – 5:7 | ◁ |
| | | | Ps: 29, 110 | Lk 19:29–38 | ◁ |
| | | Mass | *Gl; Cr; Proper Pref (CW p. 327 = R:)* | | |
| | | | *CW: Ezek 34:11–16 & 20–24; Ps 95:1–7a; Eph 1:15–23; Mt 25:31–46* | | |
| | | | *R: Ezek 34:11–12 & 15–17; Ps 23; I Cor 15:20–26 & 28; Mt 25:31–46* | | |
| | | 2 EP | H: 419 pt 2 (NEH 386) | I Macc 2:15–29 | ◁ |
| | | | Ps: 93, 97 | Mt 28:16–20 | ◁ |
| *MONDAY* | | | □ *Presentation of the BVM (p. 64)* | | **34th WEEK of YEAR** |
| **21** | W | MP | Ps: 139, 150 | Joel 3:1–17 | Wisd 1 |
| | | | | Mt 27:15–26 | Mt 5:1–16 |
| R: Ps II | | Mass | *of our Lady (Zech 2: 14–end; Ps Mag; Mt 12:46–50* | | |
| | | | *[Dan 1:1–6 & 8–20; Canticle: Bless the Lord; Lk 21:1–4]* | | |
| | | EP | | Ezek 20:39–44 | Wisd 2 |
| | | | Ps: 15, 16 | Rev 19:11–16 | Rev 1 |
| *TUESDAY* | | | *S Cecilia V M* | | |
| **22** | R | MP | Ps: 116, 146 | Nah 1:1–13 | Wisd 3:1–9 |
| | | | | Mt 27:27–37 | Mt 5:17–end |
| | | Mass | *of the Saint* | | |
| | | | *Dan 2:31–45; Canticle: Benedicite vv 1–3; Lk 21:5–11* | | |
| | | EP | | Ezek 33:1–9 | Wisd 4:7–end |
| | | | Ps: 73 | Rev 21:1–8 | Rev 2:1–17 |
| *WEDNESDAY* | | | *Feria (S Clement Pp M; S Columbanus Ab IRELAND Festum)* | | |
| **23** | G (or R or W) | MP | Ps: 65, 147:13–end | Obadiah vv 5–21 | Wisd 5:1–16 |
| | | | H: * | Mt 27:38–56 | Mt 6:1–18 |
| | | Mass | *of Sunday, no Gl or Cr; Common Pref (or of the Saint)* | | |
| | | | *Dan 5:1–6 & 13–14 & 16–17 & 23–28; Canticle: Benedicite vv 4–5; Lk 21:12–19* | | |
| | | EP | H: * | Ezek 34:1–6 | Wisd 6:1–21 |
| | | | Ps: 77 | Rev 21:9–21 | Rev 2:18 – 3:6 |
| *THURSDAY* | | | □ *S Andrew Dung Lac Pr Comp Ms* | | |
| **24** | R | MP | Ps: 145, 148 | Zeph 3:1–13 | Wisd 7:15 – 8:4 |
| | | | | Mt 27:57–end | Mt 6:19–end |
| | | Mass | *of the Saints* | | |
| | | | *Dan 6:12–end; Canticle: Benedicite vv 6–8a; Lk 21:20–28* | | |
| | | EP | | Ezek 36:22–36 | Wisd 8:5–18 |
| | | | Ps: 34 | Rev 21:22 – 22:5 | Rev 3:7–end |
| *FRIDAY* | | | *Feria (S Catherine of Alexandria V M)* | | |
| **25** | G (or R) | MP | Ps: 23, 125, 147:1–12 | Isa 24:14–end | Wisd 8:21–9 end |
| | | | H: * | Mt 28:1–15 | Mt 7:1–14 |
| | | Mass | *as Monday (or of the Saint) (**Isaac Watts**)* | | |
| | | | *Dan 7:2–14; Canticle: Benedicite vv 8b–10a; Lk 21:29–33* | | |
| | | EP | H: * | Ezek 37:1–14 | Wisd 10:15 – 11:10 |
| | | | Ps: 142, 143 | Rev 22:6–15 | Rev 4 |
| *SATURDAY* | | | *Our Lady on Saturday or the Feria* | | |
| **26** | W (or G) | MP | Ps: 92, 97, 149 | Micah 7:11–end | Wisd 11:21 – 12:2 |
| | | | | Mt 28:16–end | Mt 7:15–end |
| | | Mass | *Introduction Paragraph 26(b)* | | |
| | | | *Dan 7:15–27; Canticle: Benedicite vv 10b–end; Lk 21:34–36* | | |
| | P | 1 EP of foll | | Ezek 47:1–12 | Wisd 12:12–21 |
| | | | Ps: 123, 130 | Rev 22:16–end | Rev 5 |

* Optionally, *Dies Irae.* EH 351 (NEH 524) MP vv. 1–8; EP vv. 9–18.

## 2005–6 SUNDAYS B WEEKDAYS 2

| Month | Date | Day | Observance |
|---|---|---|---|
| NOV: | 27 | SUNDAY | Advent 1 |
| | 28 | Monday | Feria |
| | 29 | Tuesday | Feria |
| | 30 | Wednesday | S Andrew |
| DEC: | 1 | Thursday | Feria |
| | 2 | Friday | Feria |
| | 3 | Saturday | S Francis |
| | 4 | SUNDAY | Advent 2 |
| | 5 | Monday | Feria |
| | 6 | Tuesday | (S Nicolas) |
| | 7 | Wednesday | S Ambrose |
| | 8 | Thursday | Immaculate C |
| | 9 | Friday | Feria |
| | 10 | Saturday | Feria |
| | 11 | SUNDAY | Advent 3 |
| | 12 | Monday | Feria |
| | 13 | Tuesday | S Lucy |
| | 14 | Wednesday | S John |
| | 15 | Thursday | Feria |
| | 16 | Friday | Feria |
| | 17 | Saturday | Feria [O Sapientia] |
| | 18 | SUNDAY | Advent 4 |
| | 19 | Monday | Feria |

| Month | Date | Day | Observance |
|---|---|---|---|
| DEC: | 20 | Tuesday | Feria |
| | 21 | Wednesday | Feria |
| | 22 | Thursday | Feria |
| | 23 | Friday | Feria |
| | 24 | Saturday | Feria |
| | 25 | SUNDAY | CHRISTMAS DAY |
| | 26 | Monday | S Stephen |
| | 27 | Tuesday | S John |
| | 28 | Wednesday | Holy Innocents |
| | 29 | Thursday | In the Octave |
| | 30 | Friday | Holy Family |
| | 31 | Saturday | In the Octave |
| JAN: | 1 | SUNDAY | Mary or Name of Jesus or Xmas 1 |
| | 2 | Monday | Ss Basil & Gregory |
| | 3 | Tuesday | (Name of Jesus) |
| | 4 | Wednesday | Feria |
| | 5 | Thursday | Feria |
| | 6 | Friday | Epiphany? |
| | 7 | Saturday | (S Raimund) |
| | 8 | SUNDAY | Baptism |

(or: Epiphany on Sunday 8 January; Baptism on Monday 9 January)

ELEVATIONS. (i) Should the Body and Blood of the Lord still be shown for adoration in the traditional places, after the Words of Institution, when a CW Eu Pr is being used that defers the epiclesis until later? For those determined to use such prayers and who would like an answer out of the older Western Catholic Tradition: Yes! Fortescue (The Mass, 1912) wrote: 'The whole consecration-prayer is one thing, of which the effect is the change of the bread and wine into the body and blood of Christ. During this prayer we ask continually for that grace; although the prayer takes time to say and God grants what we ask at one instant, not necessarily the last instant of the prayer. So in all rites constantly people still ask for what presumably, they have already received. Our baptism and ordination services furnish obvious parallel examples. The Epiklesis is surely also to be explained in this way . . . the Canon is one prayer. Consecration is the answer to that one prayer. It takes place no doubt at the words of institution, but it is the effect of the whole prayer. There is no sequence of time with God. He changes the bread and wine "intuitu totius orationis" [In consideration of the whole prayer].' And in Cardinal Ximenes' edition of the Mozarabic rite, in which some 20 or so of the 200 EuPrs have an epiclesis after the Institution Narrative, the elevations nevertheless always happen at the 'Roman' place. For us, as long as BCP remains doctrinally normative, it is presumably Anglican doctrine that the Institution Narrative consecrates. (ii) The recent Roman revision of the *Institutio Generalis* has taken the opportunity to be more explicit about the Consecration occurring at the Lord's Words; and has restored mentions of the ringing of the handbell, and of the offering of incense, in those traditional places. (Technically, Rome now terms these ceremonies 'Ostensions', showings, rather than 'Elevations', liftings.)

(Is there any truth in the rumour that the CW enthusiasm for 'deferred' epicleses is driven by a desire to rubbish notions of Consecration?)

# 2006

### JANUARY

| | *M* | *B* | *2* | *3* | *4* |
|---|---|---|---|---|---|
| Sun | 1 | 8 | 15 | 22 | 29 |
| Mon | 2 | 9 | 16 | 23 | 30 |
| Tue | 3 | 10 | 17 | 24 | 31 |
| Wed | 4 | 11 | 18 | 25 | |
| Thu | 5 | 12 | 19 | 26 | |
| Fri | **6** | 13 | 20 | 27 | |
| Sat | 7 | 14 | 21 | 28 | |

### FEBRUARY

| | | *5* | *6* | *7* | *8* |
|---|---|---|---|---|---|
| Sun | | 5 | 12 | 19 | 26 |
| Mon | | 6 | 13 | 20 | 27 |
| Tue | | 7 | 14 | 21 | 28 |
| Wed | 1 | 8 | 15 | 22 | |
| Thu | 2 | 9 | 16 | 23 | |
| Fri | 3 | 10 | 17 | 24 | |
| Sat | 4 | 11 | 18 | 25 | |

### MARCH

| | | *1* | *2* | *3* | *4* |
|---|---|---|---|---|---|
| Sun | | 5 | 12 | 19 | 26 |
| Mon | | 6 | 13 | 20 | 27 |
| Tue | | 7 | 14 | 21 | 28 |
| Wed | **1** | 8 | 15 | 22 | 29 |
| Thu | 2 | 9 | 16 | 23 | 30 |
| Fri | 3 | 10 | 17 | 24 | 31 |
| Sat | 4 | 11 | 18 | 25 | |

### APRIL

| | | *5* | *P* | *E* | *2* | *3* |
|---|---|---|---|---|---|---|
| Sun | | 2 | 9 | 16 | 23 | 30 |
| Mon | | 3 | 10 | 17 | 24 | |
| Tue | | 4 | 11 | 18 | 25 | |
| Wed | | 5 | 12 | 19 | 26 | |
| Thu | | 6 | 13 | 20 | 27 | |
| Fri | | 7 | 14 | 21 | 28 | |
| Sat | 1 | 8 | 15 | 22 | 29 | |

### MAY

| | | *4* | *5* | *6* | *7* |
|---|---|---|---|---|---|
| Sun | | 7 | 14 | 21 | 28 |
| Mon | 1 | 8 | 15 | 22 | 29 |
| Tue | 2 | 9 | 16 | 23 | 30 |
| Wed | 3 | 10 | 17 | 24 | 31 |
| Thu | 4 | 11 | 18 | **25** | |
| Fri | 5 | 12 | 19 | 26 | |
| Sat | 6 | 13 | 20 | 27 | |

### JUNE

| | | *P* | *T* | *11* | *12* |
|---|---|---|---|---|---|
| Sun | | 4 | 11 | 18 | 25 |
| Mon | | 5 | 12 | 19 | 26 |
| Tue | | 6 | 13 | 20 | 27 |
| Wed | | 7 | 14 | 21 | 28 |
| Thu | 1 | 8 | **15** | 22 | **29** |
| Fri | 2 | 9 | 16 | 23 | 30 |
| Sat | 3 | 10 | 17 | 24 | |

### JULY

| | | *13* | *14* | *15* | *16* | *17* |
|---|---|---|---|---|---|---|
| Sun | | 2 | 9 | 16 | 23 | 30 |
| Mon | | 3 | 10 | 17 | 24 | 31 |
| Tue | | 4 | 11 | 18 | 25 | |
| Wed | | 5 | 12 | 19 | 26 | |
| Thu | | 6 | 13 | 20 | 27 | |
| Fri | | 7 | 14 | 21 | 28 | |
| Sat | 1 | 8 | 15 | 22 | 29 | |

### AUGUST

| | | *T* | *19* | *20* | *21* |
|---|---|---|---|---|---|
| Sun | | 6 | 13 | 20 | 27 |
| Mon | | 7 | 14 | 21 | 28 |
| Tue | 1 | 8 | **15** | 22 | 29 |
| Wed | 2 | 9 | 16 | 23 | 30 |
| Thu | 3 | 10 | 17 | 24 | 31 |
| Fri | 4 | 11 | 18 | 25 | |
| Sat | 5 | 12 | 19 | 26 | |

### SEPTEMBER

| | | *22* | *23* | *24* | *25* |
|---|---|---|---|---|---|
| Sun | | 3 | 10 | 17 | 24 |
| Mon | | 4 | 11 | 18 | 25 |
| Tue | | 5 | 12 | 19 | 26 |
| Wed | | 6 | 13 | 20 | 27 |
| Thu | | 7 | 14 | 21 | 28 |
| Fri | 1 | 8 | 15 | 22 | 29 |
| Sat | 2 | 9 | 16 | 23 | 30 |

### OCTOBER

| | *26* | *27* | *28* | *29* | *30* |
|---|---|---|---|---|---|
| Sun | 1 | 8 | 15 | 22 | 29 |
| Mon | 2 | 9 | 16 | 23 | 30 |
| Tue | 3 | 10 | 17 | 24 | 31 |
| Wed | 4 | 11 | 18 | 25 | |
| Thu | 5 | 12 | 19 | 26 | |
| Fri | 6 | 13 | 20 | 27 | |
| Sat | 7 | 14 | 21 | 28 | |

### NOVEMBER

| | | *31* | *32* | *33* | *CK* |
|---|---|---|---|---|---|
| Sun | | 5 | 12 | 19 | 26 |
| Mon | | 6 | 13 | 20 | 27 |
| Tue | | 7 | 14 | 21 | 28 |
| Wed | **1** | 8 | 15 | 22 | 29 |
| Thu | 2 | 9 | 16 | 23 | 30 |
| Fri | 3 | 10 | 17 | 24 | |
| Sat | 4 | 11 | 18 | 25 | |

### DECEMBER

| | | *1* | *2* | *3* | *4* | *HF* |
|---|---|---|---|---|---|---|
| Sun | | 3 | 10 | 17 | 24 | 31 |
| Mon | | 4 | 11 | 18 | **25** | |
| Tue | | 5 | 12 | 19 | 26 | |
| Wed | | 6 | 13 | 20 | 27 | |
| Thu | | 7 | 14 | 21 | 28 | |
| Fri | 1 | 8 | 15 | 22 | 29 | |
| Sat | 2 | 9 | 16 | 23 | 30 | |

Clerical Common Sense will indicate whether the italic numbers above the Sunday dates represent Sundays per Annum; or of Lent; or of Easter; or of Advent.